Cardinal Newman's Grave
See Page 87

A
HYMN LOVERS' COMPANION

BY

C. P. HANCOCK

WITH A FOREWORD BY

REV. NORMAN GOLDHAWK

(CHAIRMAN OF THE HYMN SOCIETY
OF GREAT BRITAIN AND IRELAND)

ISBN 0 9509378 0 0

Orphans Press Leominster

FOREWORD

This book owes its origin to the fact that its author made the discovery that many of our hymns take on greater meaning when we know something about the people who wrote them. He found his own interest deepened when he began to search out details of the writers' lives and experiences, and he now introduces these writers to worshippers who may be quite ignorant about them.

He relates his little biographies in a homely style which should make his readers feel at ease with the book and allow the hymn-writers to become more like friends than mere names. Quite apart from its use for personal reading it should help speakers and leaders of fellowship groups to prepare talks on hymns. Experience shows that courses of studies on the hymns can be very rewarding and welcome to many Christians, since they deal with subjects with which many church members are already to a degree familiar. An illuminating part of such studies is information about the authors themselves, and this often causes their words to speak with greater forcefulness and significance.

The material for such talks is not always readily available, and this may prove to be one of the most valuable features of this book, especially in the case of the 19th and 20th century writers.

I wish the book the success its author himself would desire for it, namely, that God, who uses the experiences of men and women for His purposes, may be glorified for many others.

Norman P. Goldhawk.

ACKNOWLEDGEMENTS

I am grateful to many friends without whose encouragement this book could not have been produced, but I owe it to a few who have helped me in special ways to express my sincere gratitude.

Firstly, my wife who helped me with corrections and suggestions (in the first place) - then Rev. Alan O. Barber, Rev. William Whittle and Canon J. S. Leatherbarrow who all made helpful suggestions. Rev. Norman P. Goldhawk has been a good friend in many ways, especially in so kindly contributing a foreword to the book. I feel this is a great honour from so distinguished an author on this subject. Finally my good friend Alec Bryers who not only helped like the others, but willingly typed out the whole for publication and did much of the difficult task of indexing.

Others have supplied material for particular chapters — Mrs. Hettie W. Dormer, Mrs. Marjory Lester, Mr. Ian Liston, Rev. Wilfrid Pile and Mr. Neil Macdonald of C. & J. Clark's archives department, who also gave permission for quotations from Laurence Housman and lastly Lady Mynors for all her help and allowing me to quote from her father's works. For all such help so willingly given I offer my grateful thanks.

Acton Beauchamp
Worcester

December 1983   C. P. Hancock

CONTENTS

A HYMN LOVERS' COMPANION

PREFACE

A friend of mine with the good habit of arriving at Church early and sitting quietly for about ten minutes before the service began would, during that time, read through the hymns shown on the board. One morning he pointed to an author's name and the dates of his birth and death. "Who was he? What was he like? Was he distinguished for anything except writing this hymn? Why was his life so short, while the next lived to a good old age? How were the words of this hymn related to his life and the times he lived in? . . " and so on.

This set me thinking: was this what people wanted to know? So began the monthly articles in the "Link" Magazine on the subject and I found that many people *did* want to know. Later, several friends suggested that the articles should be published in book form: then they would be available for reference, especially by preachers, teachers and speakers; also in a book they might be used as daily readings in conjunction with other devotional books.

The problem of selection then arose, for I had before me a list of over 500 authors whose hymns are in fairly common use. This would have made a book far too large for popular use, so I finally decided that about 100 short biographies would give a fairly good cross-section of the major periods and styles of composition. It would also give room for a few excursions outside our shores to look at great characters of other nations, and could cover the work of all main denominations. There will be regrettable omissions, so don't be surprised if your favourite hymn and author are missing!

While I have included articles on the great giants like Watts and Wesley, I have not attempted to give a full biography, for their lives are fully documented elsewhere; but I have included some minor poets about whom no-one has ever written a book, yet whose lives were of great interest - often very eventful and exciting.

In some instances I have visited places connected with the authors: I have found these 'pilgrimages' a great joy and I hope some readers may do so too. I have also had the privilege of contacting relatives of just a few of the authors, thus getting very personal impressions.

Another problem was the references to the numbers in any of the many hymn books available. The articles were originally written to refer to the 1933 Methodist Hymn Book, but it would be a pity if that restricted the use of this book to Christians of that Church alone. However, I have decided to leave these numbers as they are, for I find that this Hymn Book is owned by members of many other Churches; also, it is not difficult to refer to the index of any other book.

Having said this, I do recommend that this book should be studied with the 1933 book 'at your elbow' - and it may be that with the advent of the new hymn book 'Hymns and Psalms' to replace it, plenty of second-hand copies will be available for reference.

Let me say at this point that I welcome 'Hymns and Psalms' most keenly, discovering in it new riches of hymnody; but that does not alter the fact that the 1933 book will remain a book of reference for a very long time, because of its great size (nearly a thousand hymns) and its wide and varied authorship.

You will find that many of the hymns considered in these pages will be in the new book, and those that will not are included here because of some special intrinsic merit or as illustrating something particularly interesting about the authors or their careers.

The authors are treated mainly in chronological order, so that the development of the art of expressing Christian truth and feeling can be seen as it progressed through the centuries. I hope and pray that this book may be a means of quickening the interest of many, not only in this particular subject, but in the faith of our Lord Jesus Christ, of whom these men and women made their songs.

Chapter 1

THE EARLY YEARS

"HAIL GLADDENING LIGHT"

In writing these stories it is a good thing to start at the beginning. Hymns began with the Psalms, some of which are very ancient in their origin, yet they have continued in use, for they speak of the unchanging aspirations and needs of the human race. Even when Jesus and his disciples 'sang an hymn' on the fateful night of his betrayal, it would have been one of the Psalms.

The New Testament continues with the Benedictus, Magnificat and Nunc Dimittis, as well as fragments of liturgical song quoted in the Epistles, just as naturally as we might use a few lines of a hymn to make a point. All this, however, lies outside the scope of this book.

Probably the earliest example of a hymn in use in the early Church is the lovely Greek evening hymn "Hail gladdening Light" (937 MHB). This is the translation by John Keble, but Robert Bridges has rendered it metrically as "O Gladsome Light, O grace of God the Father's face" (936 MHB), while the beautiful version "O Gladsome Light of the Father Immortal" is from Longfellow's 'The Golden Legend', with music by Sullivan.

The original may well be as early as second century, when there could have been some old people still alive who had heard Peter or Paul preach. It was known as the 'Candlelight Hymn' because it was sung as candles and lamps were lit in the evening in Christian homes in those early days.

It is even thought it may date back to the times when Christians were being savagely persecuted by the Romans and had to worship for safety in the catacombs, those eerie subterranean tunnels where they buried their dead in cavities excavated in the walls.

1

We have no idea who wrote these beautiful, yet simple words of evening worship, or to what music they were sung, but what a picture they conjure up of those oppressed people in their gloomy underground surroundings, lighting their dim lights and singing reverently and softly, so that no-one outside could hear...

"Now we come to the sun's hour of rest,
The lights of evening round us shine,
We hymn the Father, Son, and Holy Spirit divine."

Most hymns pose a challenge to us - this one certainly does - could we be as faithful to our Lord in such circumstances as tried these early Christians?

ST. AMBROSE (340 - 397)

A few ancient hymns have come down to us from the early Church but we have to come to the fourth century to find hymns of whose authorship we can be sure; so we shall look at three writers of this period - St. Ambrose, Prudentius and Synesius. The first two wrote in Latin and Synesius in Greek.

Ambrose was a remarkable man, but the extraordinary way he became a leader of the Church must be unique. He had no intention of going into the Church, in fact he trained in law and after several promotions was appointed at the age of 30 to be supreme judge at Milan. Later, when the bishop of Milan died, it was Ambrose's duty to preside in the Cathedral over the election of his successor. There was some dissension among the delegates as to the best candidate and only by Ambrose using his great tact and diplomacy did he avoid an unseemly row developing. As he was endeavouring to bring the opposing parties together, the crowd was so impressed that someone (some versions say a child) called out "Ambrose is Bishop!" and the crowd took up the cry "Ambrose is Bishop!" When he had quietened them, he objected that he was not even ordained - he was a layman, and in fact, although he was a believer, he had never been baptised. He fled from the city, but was brought back and finally agreed to serve in the post. So he was baptised, ordained and made Bishop - all in a week!

The job was a tough one, but Ambrose was a strong man and matched up to it. Paganism was strong and aggressive; Arianism, one of the many deviations that troubled the early Church, was strong too;

the city fathers were antagonistic; and the threat of invasion by the Goths was always in the background.

All these problems he tackled with great courage and he was evidently a man who knew the joy of the Lord even in difficult times and could express that joy in song, so wrote many hymns - mostly of praise. His style is rugged, with a strong doctrinal content. "O Strength and Stay" is a great hymn which is found in many books (but not in MHB), while the glad morning hymn "O splendour of God's glory bright" (932 MHB) is one that should be sung more.

St. Ambrose is also credited with the authorship of at least part of that noble hymn of praise "Te Deum Laudamus". We know that Ambrose and Monica, mother of St. Augustine, were both deeply concerned about the wild and sinful ways of Augustine after his good upbringing. They had prayed for him for years, then to their joy, through Ambrose's influence he turned to Jesus Christ - as he describes in his "Confessions". He wished to witness to his new faith by being baptised by Ambrose, and tradition says that at the conclusion of the ceremony Ambrose was so overcome with joy that, quite spontaneously, he sang in a loud voice "We praise Thee, O God, we acknowledge Thee to be the Lord", to which Augustine replied "All the earth doth worship Thee, the Father everlasting", and so they continued, replying to one another antiphonally to the end. Some have doubted this story, dismissing it as a piece of pious wishful thinking, but should we limit the Holy Spirit's working to what happens normally? After all, Sankey was known to sing and play impromptu in some of his meetings, and even today we hear of similar happenings in the charismatic movement, in times of great joy. Perhaps Ambrose realised at that moment what a distinguished soldier of the Cross he had just baptised.

The version of this great hymn I have quoted is from the Book of Common Prayer and is noted for its dignity of expression. Possibly it is a translation by Cranmer, the genius behind the Prayer Book. There are other versions, the best being possibly the metrical rendering by Charles Wesley "Infinite God, to Thee we raise our hearts in solemn songs of praise" (33 MHB).

We must also remember that Ambrose introduced so much hymn singing into his Churches at a time when Church leaders were beginning to frown on congregational singing, reserving singing for the priests and trained choirs.

I have mentioned the fight Ambrose had with the Arians; well, no less personages than the Emperor and his domineering mother demanded to take over the greatest Church in Milan for this heretical worship - even sending an army to occupy it and designate it as imperial property. Ambrose, now really roused, rallied the Christians and organised a 'sit-in', filling the Church so that the soldiers could not enter. He boldly declared he would not fight - only pray. He led the huge congregation in singing his own militant hymns to keep up their spirits. He won! Rather than shed blood, the Emperor gave in; and some of the soldiers, impressed by the heroism of Ambrose and his followers, laid down their arms and became Christians.

In days when the Church had to endure hardship to maintain its witness, here was a true soldier of the Cross who used only the weapons of prayer and sacred song.

AURELIUS PRUDENTIUS (348 - 413)

The next author who wrote Christian poetry in the early days of the Church was Aurelius Clemens Prudentius, a Spaniard, who like Ambrose trained for and practised law, but unlike him confessed he led a gay life, spending lavishly and making a good living as a lawyer, "sinning with deceitful pleadings". I wonder if things have changed much over the centuries! In middle life he became a magistrate, then a judge; finally at the age of 57 he retired and devoted himself to writing poetry. He had for some time looked back on his life with some regret and even shame, asking the question "Cui bono?" (which we might render "What's the good?"). Many of his compositions were about Nature - we should now call him an ecologist at heart. His protests about pollution and his advocacy of vegetarianism have a quite modern ring. I quote part of a lengthy grace before meals: "Leave to the barbarous brood the banquet of the slaughtered beast, ours is the homely garden food. . " and he goes on to praise the virtues of milk, butter, cheese, honey and fruit.

All this is a long way still from a Christian standpoint, and we do not know what influences led him on to really spiritual subjects, but that there was a change of heart is certain when we read his later poetry. "Of the Father's love begotten" (83 MHB), that sublime hymn on the Incarnation, is his most popular - the crowning glory of his late-found faith in Christ. I wonder if the lines "Boys and girls together singing with pure heart their song of praise" express a tinge of regret that he did not learn to serve the Lord in *his* youth?

4

SYNESIUS (375 - 430)

The hymn "Lord Jesus, think on me" (239 MHB) has long been a favourite hymn for many people. Again we go back right to the early days of the Church.

Synesius was born in Cyrene in 375 A.D. of a long and aristocratic line, with a family tree going back over 500 years. He had a good education and soon made his name as a philosopher and an expert in the wisdom of the East; also he was a gifted orator. His main task, however, was in the diplomatic service of his country and it was in this role that he became increasingly concerned, like Ambrose, that the whole Middle East was threatened with invasion by the Goths. So anxious was he that he travelled to Constantinople to try to rouse King Arcadius to united action to repel this menace; but in Gibbon's caustic words: "They indulged his zeal, applauded his eloquence and neglected his advice." An old story, indeed!

We know he was married and had a large family, and to his great grief three of his sons died while quite young. We do not know if these sad events, or his diplomatic failure, contributed - but various influences turned his thoughts to Christ at this time and he became a devoted believer. He immediately turned his great gifts of thought and speech to his new Master's service and became noted as a preacher. The Church welcomed this distinguished new convert and soon he was being pressed to be a bishop. He was most reluctant, but the call was so insistent that at last he was consecrated Bishop of Ptolemais.

In spite of his conversion, Synesius retained his interest in Greece and the mysterious East with their religions. As a result he was often suspected of being unorthodox in his beliefs and even of holding the Greek view of immortality in preference to the Christian doctrine of resurrection; but his devotional writings soon dispelled this suspicion. These works included ten 'Odes' from which this little gem was taken. These might have remained an old Greek manuscript in a museum if someone had not realised their beauty and translated them; so now is the time to say something of translators.

This brings us much nearer in time and place, for Allen William Chatfield (translator of the Odes of Synesius), after graduating at Trinity College, Cambridge, served as vicar of Much Marcle (near Ledbury, Herefordshire) for the remarkable period of 49 years. So, to Much Marcle I went, and there in the church (well worth a visit for its many points of interest) was a brass plate commemorating Chatfield's

5

scholastic achievements and his long, faithful ministry. Here he published his 'Songs and Hymns of the Earliest Greek Christian Poets' when he was aged 68.

The year I visited Much Marcle was the year celebrating the centenary of Rev. Francis Kilvert's death and one of the delights of reading his diary is to come across names of eminent Victorians - and even hymn writers. He relates how in 1874 he was best man at a friend's wedding at Much Marcle and how he stayed at the vicarage. Mr. Chatfield, then aged 66, impressed him as a kind-hearted and hospitable man - original and amusing, and he adds, "rather eccentric."

So we are indebted to this brilliant scholar, who was content to serve God in a rather obscure parish almost until his death at the age of 88, for bringing us this devotional treasure from the distant past and clothing it in beautiful, dignified English, so that it speaks to our hearts still, as we pray "LORD JESUS, THINK ON ME".

Chapter 2

THE GERMAN CONTRIBUTION

We have seen how hymns were part of the worship of the Church from the earliest times, but that congregational singing was not always encouraged; in fact as early as 380 A.D. it was decreed that "Beside the canonical singers, shall none sing in church". Similar rules were laid down later. This seems unbelievable now, but there may have been reasons: hymns with unorthodox doctrines and very trivial and unworthy carols were often composed and sung, not meeting with official approval. We shall find that opposition to any composition not in scriptures emerges many times and in many forms - Calvin forbad the singing of anything but the Psalms or paraphrases of them, and this ban still persists in a few places.

So now we take a long jump - a millenium in fact. This is not to say there were no hymn writers during these long years: we still rejoice in the heritage left us by such great men as Patrick, patron saint of Ireland, with his famous "Breastplate" (392 MHB); Fortunatus, "The royal banners forward go" (184 MHB); Stephen the Sabaite in his lonely monastery in the wilds sighs "Art thou weary?" (320 MHB); John of Damascus rejoices in "The day of resurrection" (208 MHB); - to name but a few whose writings found favour with the Church.

In spite of the efforts of such saintly men and many others whose names we do not know, we have to wait until the fifteenth century and go to Germany for a really new and large scale development. This land, more than any other, has contributed significantly to the hymn books of all Christians throughout the world. The solid, stately chorale set a new style of words and music which influenced church music ever since.

MARTIN LUTHER (1483 - 1546)

At the head of this innovation was that towering personality, Martin Luther - and what a many-sided character he was! As an evangelist he did a work for Germany similar to that which Wesley later did for England, and like him - without intending it - founded a Church which has become world-wide. In addition he was both a writer and collector of hymns, an accomplished musician, and a composer and arranger of chorale tunes which have an enduring quality all their own. The fact that many of our great composers, notably Bach and Mendelssohn, have used these melodies testifies to their value.

Luther's aim in all this work was quite clear: "The worship of God must be intelligible to the people". This involved using traditional melodies already popular with the people, writing new ones in their native style, and also producing biblical paraphrases and original poems in German.

This leads us to another achievement of his - the translation of the whole Bible into German - surely a lifetime's work on its own! He was acutely aware that while the Bible was open to him in Latin, it was closed to the less educated until rendered in their mother tongue, so he used his enforced idleness in the Wartburg for this good purpose. It was during this time, chafing at his confinement, that the improbable story tells that the Devil appeared, taunting him at the uselessness of his life, and that he picked up the inkpot and threw it at him! I am assured that guides will still show tourists the stain on the wall! However that may be, we do know that after a period of depression, he 'snapped out of it', took up his pen and began translating, and the tempter didn't bother him again. Incidentally, did you know that when Brahms wrote his great 'Requiem' he used Luther's Bible for the text?

All this activity did not include the time spent in controversy with the authorities of his day over the glaring abuses of the Church.

How did this amazing life begin? Born of peasant stock with rough down-to-earth ways, he began to feel his own sinfulness and his need of God's forgiveness and finally, much to his father's disgust, entered the Monastery at Erfurt. After a temporary feeling of satisfaction, induced by the penances which he gladly undertook, the old unease crept back, so rather like Wesley he countered it with ceaseless work and study. He then moved to Wittenburg, a good monastery for those days, and there he found the opportunity to learn the classics and to read in other languages, especially Latin. So proficient did he become that he was appointed to teach theology in the University close by.

The inner struggle still went on, but his writings reveal that light was dawning gradually; and then one day he was reading Paul's Epistle to the Romans when he came to the words "The just shall live by faith". Light flooded into his mind; this was it! Justification was by faith and faith alone, not by penances of increasing severity or by harder study.

He still did not act in any precipitous manner until he heard that the infamous Tetzel was selling indulgences in a neighbouring town to pay off the Archbishop's debts and help towards the building of St. Peter's in Rome. Saddened and angered by this racket, he was goaded into action by one of Tetzel's gimmicks: "As your money tinkles into the box, your loved ones' souls fly out of Pergatory".

So began his dangerous campaign of protest by writing his "Ninety-five theses upon Indulgences" and nailing them to the door of the great Church at Wittenburg. By this dramatic act he set in motion the whole movement which led to the Reformation in Germany, and with it the constant threat of his martyrdom. Oddly enough he died eventually of natural causes, but his courage in face of the threat of death when he was sure he was doing right was proverbial: "Here I stand - I can do no other - so help me God!"

Two of Luther's hymns, "A safe stronghold our God is still" (494 MHB) and "Out of the depths I cry to Thee" (359 MHB), are worth reading. Both are based on psalms but speak of present, urgent needs, and indeed both were frequently sung by him and his friends in times of crisis.

We have seen Luther as a valiant fighter for truth. There was also a homelier side of this great man who has been described as a Tyndale, an Isaac Watts, a John Wesley, a Charles Wesley and a few other lesser characters all rolled into one.

By the time he was 38 he had been excommunicated for heresy and so was free to marry, and indeed he thought he ought to, to demonstrate his rejection of compulsory celibacy for the priesthood. He felt, however, that it was almost inevitable that he would soon die a martyr's death at the scaffold or the stake, and so he dismissed the idea as being unfair to any woman and certainly to a family.

Four years later the situation had changed so much - he still had plenty of enemies, but support for him was growing and he felt danger had receded - that once again his thoughts turned to marriage. While he was hesitating he had his mind made up for him in an amusing way. Twelve nuns from a nearby convent had renounced their vows as a result of his teaching, and he felt some responsibility for their future, so he set about finding them suitable positions - or husbands! Finally only one was left, Katherine von Bora, aged 26, of aristocratic birth and in a temporary domestic job. He had two attempts to 'marry her off'; to the first the man's parents objected, and to the second, *she* objected - so he married her himself!

She took on a tough job, for she found that his preoccupation with work had made him careless about his appearance and even about ordinary cleanliness; she was horrified when he admitted his bachelor bed hadn't been changed for a year! She went to work on him with a will and prepared the disused Austin Friary, which had been placed at their disposal, to make a comfortable home for him.

He found he had to alter things, but he seemed willing enough - sometimes jokingly referring to her as 'My lord Katie'. Although the marriage had started rather unromantically, he became increasingly fond of her as the years went by, until he confessed "I sometimes wonder if I love my Katie more than Christ, to whom I owe everything, including her!"

What a haven of joy his home was in the midst of all the turmoil and bitterness he had to endure, and what a new world opened to him when the children came along! He especially loved Christmas, for he was always filled with wonder at the thought of God coming to earth as a baby in the stable at Bethlehem, so this seemed the right time to rejoice with his own children. One Christmas, when the tree was decorated and the candles were lit, he suddenly disappeared and all wondered where he had gone. Not long after he came out of his study, beaming at everyone, with a piece of paper in his hand. "I have written a Christmas hymn", he said and began to read "Vom Himmel Hoch" ("From Highest Heaven"), and soon they were singing this new carol round the Christmas tree. There are some verses from it in the hymn No. 126 MHB. Reading this, we sense the tenderness and affection under the tough exterior of the old warrior.

Some think he also wrote "Away in a manger" (860 MHB) but others say this is absurd - quite out of character with the man; but I'm not so sure - are you?

MARTIN RINKART (1586 - 1649)

In considering later German writers, I am 'stepping out of line' chronologically in order to remain in Germany to see further its contribution to hymnody. We advance a century from Luther's time to look at the life of a poor boy, the son of a cooper in Eilenburg - Martin Rinkart.

Martin was a bright boy with a good voice, but his parents could not afford further education; but by singing and giving music lessons he managed to pay his own fees. He won a choral scholarship to St. Thomas's School, Leipzig; and from there he went to University to study theology and became a pastor in the Lutheran Church. Going back to his home town to minister he found some resentment - "Who does he think he is?" attitude - but his able preaching and his caring ministry soon overcame this and he was made Archdeacon at the age of 31. All seemed set for a good and successful career but, alas, the thirty-years war broke out a year later. We know how a five-years war with all its dangers, uncertainties and heartbreaks seemed as if it would never end, but can you imagine the misery of *thirty* years of warfare - and with the worst of the fighting on your doorstep?

Eilenburg was an old walled town, so throughout the war, with every country in Europe except Britain being dragged into the conflict, refugees fled to the town for safety, bringing famine and disease. The town was attacked twice by the Swedes and once by the Austrians and each time only saved from complete destruction by Martin's intervention. On one occasion the Commander demanded a ransom quite beyond the town's ability to pay and Martin pleaded to have it reduced - which it was, although he had to collect the money himself.

On top of all this horror, plague broke out in epidemic proportions. As it raged through the town, Martin found himself the only Pastor left alive and almost daily he was conducting mass funerals of 40 to 50 bodies. It is thought he must have buried a total of nearly 5,000 while at times the death rate was so high that another 3,000 were buried without ceremony. Can we imagine the strain on this good man as he sought to minister spiritual as well as material help in the midst of all this suffering? - and the added strain and grief when his wife caught the plague and died? As if this was not enough, his own townspeople turned against him over agonising decisions he had to make.

When peace came at last, his greatest hymn "Now thank we all our God" (10 MHB) was sung, not only in his own Church but all over Germany. Did he write it for this occasion? We do not know; it would have been a natural reaction to sit down and do this, but it is thought more probable that he had written it years earlier. If so, this is even more remarkable, for what cause for thankfulness was there then? What an example of Christian fortitude this man was!

A year after the war was over, Martin died; tired out - a sick man - worn out by thirty years of bearing others' troubles; but rejoicing that God had spared him so long to serve Him.

PAUL GERHARDT (1607 - 1676)

A few years later than Rinkart we come to Paul Gerhardt. He was only eleven years old when the war began. He too trained for the ministry but because of the disturbed war conditions he suffered during his early life he did not obtain a settled pastorate until he was 44, by which time he also had lost his wife. Things were returning to normal after the war, but damage to property and agriculture was colossal, the people dispirited and the Church lethargic and formal - and very divided. Paul had visions of better things and he worked, wrote and preached to encourage a more spiritual outlook. He was indeed the precursor of the revival that followed after his death, for he stressed that the cure for the Church's ills was for every believer to have a close personal relationship with Jesus Christ: only then would worship become more vital and meaningful; and then the charitable and humanitarian work of the Church would flourish. The next generation brought this new life - the movement known as Pietism, of which Paul lived long enough to lay the foundations.

As a hymn writer, Paul was held to be the greatest since Luther. His hymns do not bear any traces of the scars he bore for his Master: his carol of pure Christmas joy, "All my heart this night rejoices" (121 MHB); his beautiful hymn on Christ's sufferings, "O sacred Head once wounded" (202 MHB); his sublime meditation on the love of Jesus, "Jesu, Thy boundless love to me" (430 MHB); and the delightful evening hymn, "Now all the woods are sleeping" (946 MHB) all illustrate this. Only one, perhaps his greatest hymn, "Commit thou all thy griefs and ways into His hands" (507 MHB), makes any reference to his sufferings and this does so in a very positive way. I commend it to anyone in trouble.

No one could have been in deeper trouble than Dietrich Bonhoeffer in 1943, yet we find him in prison without his beloved books, writing to his parents of the strength and courage which Paul Gerhardt's hymns brought him; he knew many by heart and repeated them to himself when fear gripped him. Later he had a few books, so he learnt more and still loved them when death seemed - and eventually was - near, a death which he faced bravely, as a Christian.

COUNT NICOLAUS LUDWIG VON ZINZENDORF (1700 - 1760)

Finally we move on to Count von Zinzendorf, who, as his title suggests, was a wealthy nobleman, holding high office.

To begin at school: he became a Christian when a boy and was earnest enough to witness to his faith, even when laughed at, and founded "The Order of the Mustard Seed", a little group pledged to make the love of Christ known to others. Later he threw himself into the Pietist movement and, being a rich man, founded the first Moravian Settlement on his estate at Hernhutt. The work he was most famed for was his promotion of Moravian Missions, for it was one of his missionaries, Peter Bohler, who influenced John and Charles Wesley towards their conversion and the launching of their evangelistic career.

Zinzendorf wrote about 2,000 hymns, beginning when he was a boy and continuing until he was an old man. Into them he poured his fervent Pietist spirit - deep personal love of his Lord; in fact many of his hymns are unacceptable because they go too far in expressions of familiarity and endearment to the Deity; but others show an intense and stable love of God.

His best known hymn, "Jesus, still lead on" (624 MHB) is of quite a different type - a devout prayer for guidance from the heart of a lover of Nature (for there is even a tinge of regret that he will have to leave "sweet earth and skies"). Rather less known, but fine hymns are "Jesu, Thy blood and righteousness" (370 MHB) and "O Lord, enlarge our scanty thought" (449 MHB) - both are an inspiration to sing.

— — — — — —

This brief survey of the richness of German hymns should not end without a tribute to the many who, by translating them, have made them available to those of us who are no linguists. Prominent among these are John Wesley and Catherine Winkworth, who both specialized in the German language.

We shall hope to meet them both later.

Chapter 3

ST. FRANCIS XAVIER (1506 - 1552)

Contemporary with Martin Luther, and equally energetic and sincere, though entirely different in outlook, was St. Francis Xavier, born in Pamplona in the Basque region of Spain. Like Luther he experienced a dramatic conversion, but his work was to reform the Catholic Church from within.

Francis was studying at Paris University where he met, first Calvin, then Ignatius Loyola. It was the latter who influenced him most, by gathering a group of young disciples - including Francis - who together founded the 'Society of Jesus', dedicating themselves to a really daunting discipline of life with the aim of evangelising the illiterate and the heathen. Apart from Ignatius, Francis became the most outstanding of this group and it was he who gave us the fine hymn "My God, I love Thee" (446 MHB). Doubts have been expressed about Francis being the author, but these verses so perfectly reflect the spirit of man, that if he did not write them, he certainly loved them and lived them.

The significance of this movement is that it marks the first missionary effort on the part of Western Christianity. In contrast to the Crusades which only sought to exterminate the infidel, these men felt the Christian Gospel was for all men and that the people of the East could be converted and brought to Christ. Loyola trained his men with his stern 'Spiritual Exercises', after which he felt they could face any discouragement, opposition or danger.

After some years working in Europe, Francis did what seemed to his friends an absolutely crazy thing: on his thirty-fifth birthday he sailed from Lisbon on an unwieldy great merchant ship, bound for Goa, a Portuguese colony on the east coast of India. There he found a few priests, who had gone out to minister to the white population. He did not stay there long, but long enough to found a training college for priests and to register a strong protest against the evil lives of the whites, who were terribly exploiting the native population. He then moved on to South India, for he was anxious to do pioneer work. Later he moved on to Ceylon, Malaya, then right on to Japan. Finally he went to Canton, China, intending to open up that great country for Christ, but he was ill when he arrived and died later at the age of 46.

If, like me, you are curious enough to trace these journeys on a map of the world, you must be astonished at the vast distances he travelled in those few years, especially as they had to take the route round the Cape - and he returned to his base at Goa several times. It makes St. Paul's wonderful journeys seem like a local enterprise! The dangers too were incredible; these merchant venturers were prepared to lose half their ships on each expedition and still make a profit! For it was not 50 years since Vasco da Gama had made his daring explorations and the safety and comfort of shipping had not improved much since New Testament times.

What was the motive force that drove this intrepid man round the world? He makes the answer quite clear - look again at this hymn, verse 5 of which says:-

"Not with the hope of gaining aught;
    Not seeking a reward;
But as Thyself hast loved me,
    O ever-loving Lord."

So Francis was glad to wear himself out by middle life for the love of his Master who had first loved him; he must repay Him - even if it cost him his life.

We know quite a lot about Francis's work from his 'progress reports' that he sent to Loyola, so perhaps we can look at more of this exciting man's life, whose ambition is stated in a quotation from one of his letters: "My aim is to increase our holy faith and gain much fruit in souls."

The long periods he spent travelling by sea were not wasted months, for there were often 100 or more passengers - even 300 on some ships. Usually there were few cabins, most passengers having to live and sleep in the open air. Often food was short and medical aid non-existent, so Francis would divide his time between ministering to the physical needs of his companions and preaching to them. He seemed very persuasive and many were baptised.

When he landed he would begin by obtaining permission to evangelise from the local ruler: this saved him a lot of persecution and gave him an official status on which he relied heavily. He would then begin his mission by planning a sort of circuit of towns and villages which he would tour systematically, ringing his bell at each place and reading a few simple items until his congregation could say the words with him. The Creed, the Lord's Prayer and the Commandments with some Catholic prayers were the main items. After several visits he would question the people on the Creed, ask them if they believed all this, and then baptise them - often en masse.

Language was, of course, a big problem, but Francis was a good linguist; he had learned the classical languages at University and was proficient at several European languages, including his native Basque, and he soon mastered the languages of South India. Francis was a restless character, so he tended to move about and encounter more languages than even he could master. In these cases he would get a local interpreter to help him translate the stock items mentioned and to rely on these to obtain assent to the Christian Doctrine; then he would pack his bags and move on, leaving instruction to his most hopeful convert, meanwhile getting a message back to Goa to send a man to build the Church on these hastily laid foundations!

We may think that these methods were not above criticism but he obtained impressive results - later Jesuits claiming that he made 700,000 converts! This is difficult to believe, for if you work it out it comes to 2,000 a week! What we do know is that Churches he founded still exist, while the Church in Japan was subjected to the most awful persecution, large numbers being crucified.

Francis firmly believed in adapting harmless local customs and festivals for the use of the Church, but one wonders if he went too far in this respect, for in later years, after his death, stories of abuses filtered through to Rome and the authorities felt bound to intervene. Unfortunately this was often done tactlessly and without knowledge of local conditions, with the result that local chiefs resented interference in what they regarded as "their saint's" teaching; in extreme cases they sent the Papal emissaries packing and reverted to their old religion. A typical case of disastrous bureaucratic interference!

The more I think of Francis's life, the more I marvel at what he packed into those eleven years after he sailed from Lisbon. The hardships he had to endure and the disappointments that dogged the steps of such a forward looking man, could have broken all but the stoutest heart, but he carried on with the determination embodied in the prayer of his leader Ignatius Loyola:-

"Teach us, good Lord, to serve Thee as Thou deservest, to give and not to count the cost, to fight and not to heed the wounds, to toil and not to seek for rest, to labour and not to ask for any reward save that of knowing that we do Thy will. Through Jesus Christ our Lord. Amen."

Chapter 4

THE ENGLISH PIONEERS

THOMAS STERNHOLD (1500-1549) and JOHN HOPKINS

We are in England at last, and it is a good thing to look right back to the originators of English hymnody. Luther was, of course, the first one to use sacred song in Europe to further the cause he led; and in England, the great translator, Miles Coverdale, an admirer of Luther, translated some of his hymns and published them under the title "Ghoostly Psalmes and Spirituall Songes", but this book, although a historic step forward, did not really 'catch on'.

While he was working on the book, two boys were growing up in Gloucestershire who were to be the pioneers of English psalm singing - their names, Thomas Sternhold and John Hopkins.

Thomas was the real innovator, and oddly enough he had no intention of beginning anything new. He went from his birthplace (still standing) in the village of Blakeney to Oxford to study and then moved to London, where later we find him in a succession of responsible posts at the court of Henry VIII. He found himself among a set with low morals, so he began versifying the Psalms for his own amusement and edification, and - good Christian that he was - singing them to simple well-known tunes. This came to the notice of his friend John Hopkins, who began to help him, but what was more important, the King himself heard of it and began to encourage him to publish his work. So, with royal approval, he compiled his "Certayne Psalmes, chose out of the Psalter of Dauid, and drawe into Englishe metre by Thomas Sternhold, grome of ye Kynge's Maiestie's roobes". A copy of this rare old book is in the British Museum.

Thomas's aims are clearly set out in a later edition: "Very mete to be used by all sort of people privatly for their godlie solace and comfort; laying aparte all ungodlie songes and ballades, which tende only to the nourishment of vice and corruption of youth.'' Obscene songs are evidently no new phenomenon!

When Henry VIII died and Edward succeeded him, Thomas stayed on and continued to write his paraphrases, hoping to complete the whole book of Psalms in time. He did complete a larger edition and dedicated it to the new King, who gave it his approval. The royal patronage ensured the use of the book, not only privately, as originally intended, but in cathedrals and churches in their public worship.

Unfortunately, Thomas died at the age of 49, so it was left to his friend to carry on the good work, but it took him another thirteen years to complete the whole 150 Psalms and the later additions were often rather inferior.

It must be admitted that the quality of the book is very uneven, varying from examples like ''O God, my strength and fortitude'' (24 MHB) to others that were utter doggerel. Many literary men of following generations were inclined to poke fun at the simple rhymes of some of the numbers; Dryden was scathing about them and even Wesley didn't think much of them; but it cannot be denied that this book brought about a revival of sacred song that has never been surpassed in our land. An eyewitness described scenes in Elizabeth's reign when crowds of several thousand would gather at ''Paul's Cross'' to hear famous preachers of the day and to sing these new adaptations of the Psalms in their own language. The effect was so impressive that he declared he would never forget it.

Hopkins's village was Awre, close by Blakeney, and there in the Church records we are informed that Sternhold and Hopkins's version of the Psalms was first used in this Church; but its influence was to spread far and wide, for the book sold more copies in its time than anything except the Bible and the Book of Common Prayer - and *they* were quite novelties in those days!

Read the hymn quoted above, a simple, homely version of part of the 18th Psalm, yet with dramatic touches in it, as it pictures God flying to help the sincere believer who prays to Him in time of trouble.

WILLIAM KETHE (d. 1593?)

There is some mystery about the date and place of William Kethe's birth, but that is not surprising, seeing he grew up in Scotland in the troubled and dangerous times following the Reformation. We know that he was ordained and that in 1555, like many others, he fled to the Continent when Queen Mary was ruthlessly trying to stamp out all traces of Protestantism; and its major leaders - Cranmer, Latimer and Ridley - were martyred in what was surely the most barbarous way, burning at the stake.

After living in Germany, Kethe moved on to Geneva where we find out more about him, for he came to know the great Calvin and his followers, and became involved with their work of versifying the Psalms and setting them to music.

He must have been a scholar of some standing, for he played an important part - along with other refugees from Britain - in the translation of the Bible into English. This was an important work, for when it appeared in 1560 it was known as the Geneva Bible and it remained popular until superseded by the well-known King James's Version, which was closely based on it. (This is the version which was later nicknamed the 'Breeches' Bible, because of the quaint rendering of the difficult Hebrew word in Genesis 3, v.7, rendered 'aprons' or 'loincloths' in other versions.).

It seems that Kethe was so engrossed in his work there that he did not return to England until three years after the death of the dreaded Mary. When he did, he was inducted to the living of Childe Okeford, Dorset, where he seems to have remained for the rest of his life, except for an interval when he acted as Chaplain to the Forces.

Two of William Kethe's hymns are still popular and widely sung. "All people that on earth do dwell" (2 MHB) is by far the most famous; we find references to its being sung on great occasions throughout history and it is still one of the most regularly used hymns in all branches of the Church. It is, of course, a paraphrase of Psalm 100 and invariably (and appropriately) sung to the old Genevan Psalter tune, the 'Old Hundredth'.

"My soul, praise the Lord" (45 MHB) is much less known and is a much shortened form of Kethe's paraphrase of Psalm 104. When Sir Robert Grant (of whom we shall hear more later) wrote his popular hymn "O worship the King", he acknowledged the suggestion of this older hymn - it is interesting to compare the two.

It is also interesting to compare William Kethe's hymn with Psalm 104: I wonder if readers (especially the young ones) can spot which verses of the Biblical Psalm are paraphrased in the hymn?

Chapter 5

POETS, PURITANS and PLATONISTS:
EARLY 17th CENTURY

GEORGE WITHER (1588 - 1667)

Almost 400 years ago, in a Hampshire village, was born a boy who was to lead a most varied and adventurous life, yet his friends thought him a strange lad, composing little poems and having little interest in games or in practical things like most boys. Neighbours were quick to offer advice: "Put him to some mechanic trade, to make a man of him"; but his father had other ideas and sent him to a Grammar School, then to Magdalen College, Oxford. While there, George heard much of Shakespeare's success at the Globe and thought "Why couldn't I make a name for myself like him?"

Now, George all through his life was most unpredictable, full of energy and with no fear of the consequence of hasty decisions, so now to his father's disappointment he left Oxford without graduating and took lodgings in London. For a while he got nowhere, although he made some literary friends; then he was brought to the notice of Royalty. He wrote an elegy on the death of the King's son, which was well received; and a nuptial ode to celebrate Princess Elizabeth's wedding. She was delighted with this and became a firm friend, even after he had fought against the Royalist Army.

But now, young and headstrong, he enlisted in the King's Army, and it was this that changed the course of his life. He saw behind the scenes of court life and was disgusted by the vices he saw: avarice, corruption, gluttony and adultery; and he became a convinced Puritan, willing - in his words - "to forfeit the King's favour to serve the King of Kings". He gave vent to his feelings by publishing his famous satire "Abuses Stript and Whipt". Although this was of a general nature, the 'cap fitted' some officials so well that they did not rest until he was in prison!

Like many other prisoners of conscience, George used his time in prison writing - in fact much of his best work was done at this time, including one of his best known songs:

"Shall I, wasting in despair,
Die, because a woman's fair?"

I wonder if some story of unhappy, unrequited love lies behind those lines? One poem "A Satyre, to the King" got to its destination and helped to get him a royal pardon.

With his freedom, George turned his attention to the need he saw of writing devotional verses to supplement the Psalms sung in Church. How far ahead of his time he was! Another century was to pass before Isaac Watts began to do the same for dissenters and TWO centuries before hymns were officially allowed in the Anglican Church. However, he set about the task with a will, using poems written in prison and adding new ones. He had the great Orlando Gibbons as musical collaborator and all the latter's tunes in our hymnal were written for George's book. Always an opportunist, George sought the King's favour to help the project on its way and was granted a Royal Patent to have the book bound with the Psalms and the Prayer Book. Even this royal backing did not prevent trouble for when at last "Hymnes and Songs of the Church" appeared, George was again in trouble. Church authorities denounced it and the Company of Stationers threatened legal action - yet this was a historic book, the first of its kind, and although banned for use in Church it remained a valuable book of devotion.

Years later, George revised and enlarged it under the title "Hallelujah: Britain's Second Remembrancer". This was a quaint book in which he added headings to each hymn, suggesting its suitability, e.g. "When slandered" or "When we cannot sleep"; then there are hymns "For Lovers", "For a Physician" and most intriguing of all "For a widow delivered from a troublesome yoke-fellow"!

When the Civil War broke out, George, with characteristic rashness, sold up his estates and raised a troop for the Parliamentary Army, rendering distinguished service, first as a major and then as major-general. Finally he was taken prisoner by the Royalists under Sir John Denham and condemned to be hanged. Denham, however, was a merciful man with a saving sense of humour; he fancied himself as a poet and petitioned the King: "His Majesty must not hang Wither, for so long as he lived no one would account *me* the worst poet in England!"

By the time the monarchy was restored George was over 70 years old and again in deep trouble. With his record of fighting against the King's army the threat of execution again hung over him, but his life was spared at the cost of imprisonment in the Tower and the sequestration of all his property. When finally released, after terrible suffering, he was a tired, broken, bankrupt old man, saddened to see the lofty moral standards for which he had fought, carelessly thrown away in the reign of Charles II; yet he still retained some of the old fire to witness to God's truth when his strength allowed.

George Wither was, even after his death at the age of 80, a controversial figure; some hated him and despised his poetry - indeed it was almost forgotten until Charles Lamb and some of his friends revived interest in it in the nineteenth century.

His hymns are worth reading, though most are 'dated' by their language and are hardly suitable for a modern congregation to sing; but a few still retain their charm. There is only one in the M.H.B. - No. 20 "Come, O come in pious lays", a good hymn of praise, based on the Psalms, which should be sung more. Unfortunately it has been shortened by the omission of verses speaking of all Nature praising God, for in spite of his military record, George was also a poet who loved birds, animals, trees, flowers and all God's creatures, for in them he saw His wisdom and skill. This hymn is a good memorial to a man who combined the unlikely qualities of a sensitive poet and a valiant soldier for Jesus Christ.

GEORGE HERBERT (1593 - 1632)

If you ever go to the little town of Montgomery, give yourself time to look over the remains of the Castle, for in addition to having much historical interest, it was the birthplace of George Herbert, writer of Hymn No. 5 MHB "Let all the world in every corner sing", No. 23 "King of glory, King of peace", and other hymns. Then, if you still have time, go into the Parish Church on the other side of the town, for there is the tomb of Sir Richard Herbert, father of George and his elder brother, Edward, Lord Herbert of Cherbury.

Both these men were poets, but there the resemblance ended, for Edward was soldier, politician (siding with the Parliamentarians during the Civil War) and 'man about town' - he was once beaten up by a jealous husband for flirting with his wife! - while George seems to have been shy and retiring, though academically brilliant.

George was eventually ordained and became Rector of Bemerton, near Salisbury, at the age of thirty-seven. He married about the same time and with the help of his wife did a marvellous work, not only as pastor, but as doctor, lawyer and general peacemaker in that small community. So devoted to the people was he that he is still looked upon as an example of what an English clergyman should be.

Sadly this ministry lasted only three years, for he died of consumption when only forty years of age. Before he died he handed a bundle of manuscripts to his friend Nicholas Ferrar, telling him to burn them unless he thought they might cheer "any poor dejected soul". Ferrar was entranced by the poems in these papers and marvelled that he had never shown them to anyone before. He saw to it that they were soon published. Perhaps today his phraseology seems quaint, but can you imagine that anyone could express the transience of life more beautifully than this?:-

> "Sweet daie, so cool, so calm, so bright,
> The bridall of the earth and skie,
> The dew shall weep thy fall tonight,
> For thou shalt die."

Partly Welsh himself, Herbert had the gift of expressing Welsh poetic thought in the English language. Someone has said that Dylan Thomas was the latest master of this Anglo-Welsh style. Personally I should hate to compare him with this saintly poet of three and a half centuries ago! Can anything compare with the combination of poetic beauty and Christian piety in his poem "Love"?

> 'Love bade me welcome,
>   Yet my soul drew back,
>   Guilty of dust and sin'.

Finally, I draw your attention to the poem included in the supplement to the Methodist Hymn Book ('Hymns and Songs' No. 12). I must admit I am doubtful of its suitability for congregational singing, especially when trying to learn a new tune, but read it carefully, many times, until you see the depth of its meaning:

"Come, my Way, my Truth, my Life:
　　Such a Way, as gives us breath;
　　Such a Truth, as ends all strife;
　　Such a Life, as killeth death.

This verse begins with three titles for Jesus Christ and the rest of the verse expands the meaning of these words. For instance, the first title 'My Way' is not a hard way that makes one out of breath but 'such a way as giveth breath', so as we tread it Christ gives us the strength to carry on. Every line is packed with meaning like this, and this is why I question the value of singing these words without the opportunity of pausing to reflect in this way. George Herbert's style seems to need this treatment.

JOHN MILTON (1608 - 1674)

The career of John Milton takes us right back to the time of the Commonwealth with its political and religious upheavals, in which he was deeply involved; but first let us go back to his youth.

John was a precocious child and even while he was at St. Paul's School he was writing poetry which began to attract widespread attention. The story is told that a master one day set the class to write up the miracle of Cana in Galilee in their own words. Silence prevailed, broken only by the scratching of pens and an occasional sigh; but young John Milton seemed to be doing nothing, spending most of his time in a dream. The master made up his mind to chasten him when the period was over. When it was, and the essays were collected, he looked to see what John had written and his anger began to rise when he saw only one line on his paper - just eight words; but as he read those words, tears formed in his eyes, for he read: "The conscious water saw its Lord - and blushed". What wonderful words! Still able to bring tears to the eyes! (I know some have disputed the story, attributing it to John's contemporary, Richard Crashaw, but I like to think it was John who wrote it).

What we do know is that at the age of 15 he had paraphrased many of the Psalms - although they were not published until he was a man. As might be expected, he was unmercifully 'ragged' by the other boys because of his youthful piety, but he didn't seem to let this worry him, but showed the courage of his convictions, as he had to do many times in later life.

We are fortunate in having parts of two of these renderings of Psalms in "Let us with a gladsome mind" (18 MHB) and "The Lord will come, and not be slow" (813 MHB). I found it quite fun searching out the verses of the Psalms that John had used as the basis of his verses. If I give you the clue that No. 18 is from Psalm 136, while No. 813 is composed of verses from Psalms 82, 85 and 86, can you spot which particular verses he used?

May I also suggest that you compare "Let us with a gladsome mind" with "Praise, O praise, our God and King" (19 MHB) - the latter being by the Rev. Sir Henry Williams Baker, and an obvious imitation of Milton's words. If we had his full poem we should see how Baker has adapted Milton's lines, making them less quaint '17th century' into rather dull 'Victorian'; for example, verse 3 of Baker's hymn "And the silver moon by night, Shining with her gentle light" originally ran like this:

"The hornèd moon to shine by night
Mid her spangled sisters bright"

Much more picturesque!!

After his promising start at school, young John went to Cambridge and soon graduated M.A., intending to prepare for ordination. But he found himself to be in disagreement with Archbishop Laud, renounced the idea and turned to Puritanism. He was now able to support himself by his writing, supplementing it with private teaching.

When the agitation against Charles I developed, there was no doubt where his sympathies lay; in fact, he was suspected - quite wrongly - of complicity in the King's execution.

When Cromwell came to power he recognised John's value and offered him the important post of 'Secretary of Foreign Tongues'. The duties included translating foreign diplomatic documents and letters, many of which were in Latin, and acting as interpreter when diplomats from abroad conferred with ministers of state.

Not surprisingly, pressure of business pushed poetry into the background, but he had already written many long poems, including 'Comus, a Mask' with music by Henry Lawes for performance at Ludlow Castle. (Perhaps you remember this being repeated there to celebrate the tercentenary of its first performance).

Then the great blow fell - he became blind, from incessant study and writing: but he was indispensable to the State, for few had his linguistic talents, so assistants were employed to write from his dictation.

John's first marriage was not ideally happy, for his wife was the daughter of Royalist parents, and at this critical time she decided to leave him and return home. She came back to him later and they were happier; then at the birth of their third child she died. Troubles seldom come singly. Helpless and unable to see and care for his young children, he married again, but 15 months later his second wife died. Can we imagine his grief? Holding on to his faith, he prayed earnestly for a helpmeet and especially a good mother to his children. His prayer was answered by Elizabeth Minshull coming into his life, seeing his plight and, moved by compassion, agreeing to marry him. What a wonderful wife and mother she turned out to be! - and how he was to need her loyalty in the trying days still to come.

At the Restoration came the collapse of his job, and worse, the threat of punishment - even of death. He escaped this extreme penalty, for although he was deeply involved in the controversies of his time, he was highly respected, even by his enemies. He was tried for treason, and although he escaped execution, he was so heavily fined that he had to leave his beloved home at Chalfont St. Giles (now happily a Milton Museum) for cheap lodgings, destitute and bankrupt. He seems to have been financially better later on, for he returned to Chalfont during the Plague.

The rest of his life he devoted to poetry, 'Paradise Lost' and 'Paradise Regained' being his most important works. He would rise early, between four and five o'clock, and compose poetry 'in his head' while the house was quiet, then after breakfast he would dictate his poems to his beloved Elizabeth or, if she was too busy, to his daughter.

Thus he lived quietly and worked happily, but he was still suspect and his output was checked for any subversive material. Books had to be 'licensed' or censored. Dryden's dirty plays were passed - probably because the Censor didn't bother to read them through - while Milton's works were carefully scrutinised. When 'Paradise Lost' was submitted, the 'Licenser of Books' was one Dr. Thomas Tompkins (not to be confused with his famous namesake - his uncle - composer and organist of Worcester Cathedral for 57 years, both of whom have memorials in Martin Hussingtree Church). Well, Tompkins hesitated long over the lines:

> " . . . . the sun's eclipse
> Disastrous twylight sheds, with fear of change,
> Perplexes monarchs . . . . "

As an ardent Royalist, he had grave doubts about this: was Milton doubting the omniscience of Kings? - was it treason? After all, we must uphold the divine right of Kings, especially the Stuarts! We can smile now, but it wasn't considered a joke then!

Happily wiser counsels prevailed and this immortal epic was allowed to be published.

HENRY MORE (1614 - 1687)

It is often illuminating to note the date when authors of our hymns were active. In the case of Henry More it is certainly significant. There had been a long history of bitterness and persecution between the Church of England and both Catholics and Dissenters; this had bred hatred in return and, perhaps even more serious, a general disillusionment with religion of any sort on the part of many thoughtful people.

More was born in Grantham, his father being several times Mayor of that town; he was educated at Eton, graduated at Cambridge, and was ordained priest soon after. He became a Fellow of Christ's College when only 25, and his intellectual gifts soon brought him offers of preferment - including two bishoprics; but he refused them all, preferring to devote his life mainly to teaching. (He did, however, accept the prebend of Gloucester at the age of 61).

While at the University he became a leader of the group of scholarly men known as the 'Cambridge Platonists'. They were drawn together by a common concern about two things: the legacy of bitterness, and the rising tide of unbelief, mentioned above. They deplored the fanaticism of rival groups in their own cause and came to the conclusion that there was a 'golden middle way' which would avoid all party spirit and commend the Christian faith to those who had become estranged. They were also convinced that faith and reason would go hand in hand.

The Platonists, being either professors, writers, clergy or teachers, quietly inculcated their doctrines of moderation, and the marriage of faith and reason, in their respective spheres of influence, and succeeded in cooling down the atmosphere and then proclaiming the gospel in a more acceptable form. The benefits were gradually felt in the Church which, released from party strife, now found time to minister to the spiritual needs of the people.

It is unfortunate that a good movement like this could have had any bad after-effects, but it was so. The next generation, benefiting from this progress, became complacent; moderation was carried to such lengths that enthusiasm was a 'dirty word'. This was the atmosphere in which the Wesleys grew up and even approved, until the new zeal following their conversion shattered the slumber into which Christians had fallen, and the gospel spread like wildfire.

John Wesley greatly admired More and his hymns, and included some of them in his own collection of hymns, altering most of them to suit his purpose. Three of them are "God is ascended up on high" (220 MHB), a hymn on the Ascension of Christ, "Father, if justly still we claim" (284 MHB) and "On all the earth Thy Spirit shower" (301 MHB), these two dealing with different aspects of the work of the Holy Spirit. How about reading these hymns? - they illustrate the truth "there are diversities of gifts, but the same Spirit".

It seems to me that Henry More was in a way a predecessor of John Wesley: they both believed in the Holy Spirit as the driving force of their lives - but how differently He worked in the two men! Quietly dispelling doubt and bringing harmony in More's day, and then about a century later bringing revival to the land under Wesley in ways with which we are more familiar, in answer to the special needs of his age.

Who knows how the Holy Spirit may work in our age if only we, the Church, are obedient to His guidance?

RICHARD BAXTER (1615 - 1691)

I suppose Richard Baxter is something of a local hero for those who live in Hereford and Worcester, for although born at Rowton in Shropshire, he spent most of his influential life in Worcestershire. The fine black and white house where he spent much of his boyhood is worth seeing, at Eaton Constantine, on the lower slopes of the Wrekin. Unfortunately the prosperity which this house seems to signify was squandered by his father's gambling. Richard, however, was determined to rise above his family's poverty and responded well to his education locally and later at Ludlow.

He trained as a schoolmaster but soon forsook teaching because he was sure God was calling him to be ordained. His first curacy was at St. Leonard's at Bridgnorth, and the picturesque house he lived in, close to the Church, is now clearly signed. He stayed only two years, for he had a disappointing start, as the people did not respond to his sincere and burning enthusiasm. Then came the call to Kidderminster, where his fame as a preacher was established.

The story of his move is curious, for the vicar of Kidderminster was an unworthy, drunken man who was in trouble with the Long Parliament, at that time trying to weed out such scandalous characters from their livings. He seems to have thought he could save his skin by inviting this rising young clergyman with strong Puritan views as his assistant.

Richard's success was immediate. Today you can see in St. Mary's Church the marks where a pulpit was fixed for him to a pillar half-way down the long nave, and galleries were erected - all to accommodate the vast crowds that flocked to hear him preach. Nor did he confine his activities to the pulpit, for he acted as pastor, doctor and legal adviser to his large flock. He is credited by many disinterested observers with having completely reformed the town. There were often as many as 600 communicants at St. Mary's, and so closely did Richard keep in touch with them that he declared there were few whose sincerity and piety he had cause to doubt. This remarkable ministry is commemorated in many ways in the Church, while outside stands his statue - vested in his robes, with his hand raised as if preaching.

He suffered several periods of ill-health - no doubt brought on by his self-sacrificing life - and one serious illness, when he found the love and care he needed at the home of good Sir Thomas Rous - Rous Lench Court (another place worth a visit). Here, frustrated by enforced leisure and, as he thought, near to death, he wrote the most famous of his many books 'The Saints' Everlasting Rest'. The words written on the title page are eloquent: "Written by the author for his own use in the time of his languishing, when God took him off from his public employment".

After many years came the Restoration and, being the man of strong convictions that he was, he found himself in conflict with the authorities over the Act of Uniformity and was finally ejected from his living at the age of 45. Persecution became worse and soon this saintly man was brought before the infamous Judge Jeffreys who threatened to have him tied to the back of a cart and whipped through the streets of the town. This was never done - perhaps even this arrogant man realised the outcry that would ensue. Macaulay called Jeffreys "this foul monster on the bench, unfit to clean Baxter's shoes". In spite of all the accusations Richard bore himself with a dignity and humility reminiscent of his Lord and Master at His trial, but he could not resist one retort, for when Jeffreys raved "You are a dog, a knave, a villain; I even see the rogue in your face", he replied quietly: "I had not known before that my face was a mirror!"

He was finally fined an enormous sum, quite beyond his means to pay, so all his goods were seized and he was thrown into prison where he remained nearly two years. He came out broken in health through the harassment and sufferings he had endured. Was it to ease a guilty conscience that Charles II then offered him the bishopric of Hereford? Whatever the reason, Richard refused, preferring to use his little remaining strength in humbler ways.

There are several of his hymns in the Methodist Hymn Book. Two of them - "Lord, it belongs not to my care" (647 MHB) and "He wants not friends who hath Thy love" (714 MHB) - date from the time of his persecution. What a revelation they are of the faith that kept him going! Read them, and I am sure you will appreciate the background against which they were written. Do we not feel rebuked for singing such words thoughtlessly when they were wrung out of such bitter experiences? Read also Nos. 26 MHB and 639 MHB.

The fact is that Richard Baxter was three centuries ahead of his time. We can hardly visualise the intolerance of his day: the religious upheavals and the civil war. Yet he took as his motto 'In things essential, unity; in things doubtful, liberty; in all things, charity.' It is significant that he was in turn chaplain to Cromwell and to Charles II. Yet he was no 'Vicar of Bray' - simply opposed to extremists of both sides because he believed so implicitly in the unifying love of Christ.

HENRY VAUGHAN (1621 - 1695)

I am a compulsive reader of book reviews. It saves a lot of time reading books you're not going to enjoy - and it saves a lot of money too! The other day I saw the review of a book about literary shrines, which referred to 'Henry Vaughan of Breconshire, whose lonely grave is one of the 'sights' of English literature'.

Curiously, only a few days before, I had, after some difficulties (including a bite from a savage dog!), made this very pilgrimage to Llansantffraid, about halfway between Abergavenny and Brecon. It seems as though the local authority realises the beauty and interest in the spot, for there is a nicely arranged picnic area not far from the church where you can get the benefit of the lovely views over the River Usk. (One of the joys of compiling a book like this is that, when distance permits, it helps to go to the place connected with the writer, for example, we hope to go to Rednal to find out about Cardinal Newman, and to Llanleonfel to re-live Charles Wesley's wedding.).

Having admired Henry Vaughan's poems, the opportunity came to go to Llansantffraid on a fresh, bright Spring day when the Usk valley was at its loveliest. It was easy to imagine how scenery could influence art; as Malvern's beautiful district inspired the music of Elgar, so the vale of Usk affected the man who was called 'the Swan of Usk' but who styled himself 'the Silurist' after the ancient name for Breconshire.

Initially, it was a disappointment to find that the church in which Henry worshipped and his brother Thomas ministered had been demolished, to be replaced by a new one built in 1884 by the munificence of the family whose pompous and ostentatious tomb almost blocks the view from the church door. It was also sad to read on the notice board that the church has to be locked for security reasons; but it is not inside where the main interest lies, but at the top of the steep churchyard, where the ground around Henry's grave has been cleared and the memorial stones re-set against the hillside. This is so that the congregation can gather round to pay homage to this quiet country doctor who was also a poet and visionary, after the annual service in his memory, held in the church on the Sunday nearest the anniversary of his death, 23rd April.

Pondering the view from the churchyard, with the mighty Brecon Beacons in the background (still with some snow on them), I wondered if Henry once stood there one frosty night and if, the conditions being right for a spectacular halo round the moon and his thoughts turning - as they often did - to eternal things, the vision had come to him which he expressed in his poem 'The World':

> "I saw Eternity the other night
> Like a great ring of pure and endless light,
> All calm - as it was bright"

What a staggering and unforgettable vision: William Blake must have envied him! However, such apocalyptic insights do not always make good hymns.

If you explore the Welsh Marches you will come across branches of the Vaughan family in various places, some of them fearsome warriors in the turbulent past, and at least one formidable woman, Ellen Vaughan of Kington (but that's another story!).

We are thinking of gentler members of this ancient family, the twin boys Henry and Thomas. Both were serious and studious lads and their father had them educated by the Rector of Llangattock, with whom they progressed so well that they went on to University, Thomas to be ordained, and Henry to read law. We don't know why, but Henry changed course during his time there and studied medicine.

Unfortunately, these were troubled times and the Civil War interrupted the boys' studies; but eventually Henry qualified and began to practise in Brecon. Meanwhile Thomas was inducted to the living at Llansantffriad, but being a Royalist he was ejected from the living for a while. Later on, Henry left the town of Brecon to come and settle in his brother's parish to spend his life as a country doctor.

Henry was an admirer of George Herbert, who died when Henry was a boy of twelve. He read his poems during his student days and was impressed by Herbert's godly life, declaring afterwards that these influences led to his conversion and the formation of his style as a poet. I have written about George Herbert earlier in this chapter: he too was a border Welshman, and both poets combined the Welsh subtlety of image and metaphor with English form and language.

Henry was a great lover of Nature, watching the land awake in the spring, progress into summer and bear fruit in the autumn. He watched the habits of the woodland animals, the birds and insects, and marvelled how they regulated their lives by unchanging instinct. Here all seemed orderly, while men were fighting for power; so he writes, after describing the ordered habits of wild creatures:

> "I would, said I, my God would give
> the staidness of these things to men"

The only one of Henry Vaughan's hymns in the Methodist Hymn Book, "My soul, there is a country" (466 MHB), is not often sung. It has many choice thoughts, but its language is rather 'dated' for use today - though to be fair to Henry, he did not intend it for a hymn. He could not have visualised his poems being sung, yet several of them are found in other hymnals and a few modern composers have found his lines inspiring, setting them to fine music.

I feel the compilers of the Methodist Hymn Book were right to include the above hymn which, even if seldom used, is there as a memorial to a good, quiet Christian doctor, a poet and a true SEER.

33

JOHN BUNYAN (1628 - 1688)

We began this chapter with a stormy character and we shall end it with another, John Bunyan, the famous tinker of Bedford. I do not propose to give a full biography of this extraordinary man - these already exist; but perhaps I can whet your appetite to read one - and a thrilling story it is.

I think you need to visit Elstow to see the cottage where he was born; to see the church (even the actual font) where he was baptised, worshipped and rang the bells; to see too the old Moot Hall around which the fairs were held which gave him the idea for Vanity Fair later on; the village green where he played tip-cat with the local lads, when a vision came to him as stunning as St. Paul's on the Damascus road, completely altering the course of his life. You need to go, too, to Bedford to see the statue erected to his memory, to look round the Bunyan Meeting House where are preserved such precious relics as the prison doors brought here when the prison was pulled down, the grill through which his intrepid wife passed jugs of soup to help keep him alive during his total of twelve years of confinement for preaching the Gospel - even a jug she used to do this. Imagine him teaching her, and she teaching their children, to make boot laces which they would stand and sell in the streets of Bedford to eke out a precarious existence; while her breadwinner was in prison writing his immortal books of which 'Pilgrim's Progress' was the most successful, catching the imagination of all generations since.

I wonder what John Bunyan would have thought of his poems being sung, even in highly respectable churches? He never boasted about his poetry - he admitted it was a bit rough and ready. Also, in his day Independents and Baptists were still refusing to allow singing in their meeting houses. Services consisted of the spoken word only - scripture, prayer and exhortation. In his later life he may have heard of Benjamin Keach and his pioneering efforts to introduce music, but it was not until after Bunyan's death that he had much success.

He would be surprised, therefore, if he could hear us sing the ragged shepherd boy's song of contentment in the Valley of Humiliation: "He that is down needs fear no fall" (514 MHB). He would have been even more astonished to know that Mr. Greatheart's song, wounded and weary after his victory over temptation: "Who would true valour see" (620 MHB) had 'caught on' as few hymns have in the twentieth century. He would smile, too, if he knew that the well-meaning Percy Dearmer had produced a tidier version ("He who would valiant be") and that most hymnbooks have now gone back to his original "hobgoblins, foul fiends" and all!

Some scholars have thought that the suggestion of this song was the chorus of Amiens' song in the Forest of Arden in Shakespeare's play "As you like it":

> " . . . Come hither - Here shall we see
>   No enemy,
>   But winter and rough weather"

If this is so, the interesting point arises, was John Bunyan the ignorant, uneducated man some suppose him to have been?

Chapter 6

THE LATE 17th CENTURY

BISHOP THOMAS KEN (1637 - 1711)

The Civil War is now over, but we are still in troubled times in the seventeenth century for our next hymn writer - and what a character he was! Left an orphan as a child, Thomas Ken was brought up by the famous Isaak Walton. He grew up to be a small but very determined man with a swarthy complexion and black hair. He trained for the Church and was ordained when he was twenty-six, when his clerical garb gave him an even darker look! He was also elected Fellow of Winchester and New College, Oxford, and, when thirty-two, became Prebendary of Winchester.

Ken was also appointed in turn Chaplain to Princess Mary and King Charles II, and from the many stories that gathered round him it seems that he could be very outspoken, Royalty or not! A curious relationship existed between him and the King, he disapproving of Charles's amorous adventures, and Charles sometimes tolerating him, sometimes sneering or being good-humourdly amused, yet underneath deeply respecting him for standing up so consistently for his principles. "I must go and hear little Ken tell me of my faults!" he would say laughingly on his way to chapel.

Perhaps the most famous story is of Charles in his travels being stranded in Winchester with Nell Gwynn 'in tow' and having the audacity to go to Ken's house for lodgings. Ken would have nothing to do with the royal scandal. "Not for your kingdom would I allow such an insult on the house of a Royal Chaplain," he declared. How would the King react to such a snub? Would he be angry and make him suffer for it? Even extreme reprisals like beheading were a real danger - or did Ken know his man better than this? To his great credit the King did not even bear a grudge; in fact, soon after, the bishopric of Bath and Wells became vacant and Charles appointed him to it. "Odds fish," he said in his playful way, "who shall have Bath and Wells, but the little black fellow who would not give poor Nelly a lodging!"

One day Charles complimented him on a sermon on an obscure text, and Ken rashly remarked that every verse of the Bible should furnish the text for a sermon for any preacher worth his salt. The King, always ready for a leg-pull, opened a Bible and read out the verse "Roll yourselves in the dust" (Micah 1, v.10). "There, preach on that," said the King. Ken obliged and Charles had to admit "It was very learned, but I found the application comical."

It was his duty to attend at the King's death-bed; his sincerity as he sought to awaken his conscience made a deep impression on all present and had the joyful result of reconciling him to his queen.

Ken left various writings, but he is chiefly remembered by his hymns for morning and evening: "Awake, my soul, and with the sun" (931 MHB) and "Glory to Thee, my God, this night" (943 MHB). These, with a third hymn entitled 'Midnight', were in an appendix to his 'Manual of prayers for the use of Scholars of Winchester College'. The Doxology with which each hymn ends is the most famous of these verses and many instances of its being sung with fervour at times of crisis are recorded.

The life of this great man reminds us that sticking up for principles (as opposed to being just obstinate or awkward) may bring persecution, but by no means always so; and usually earns the respect of all - even those who do not agree with us. It all depends how we go about it, and the good bishop did all by seeking God's guidance. His prayer is contained in the morning hymn mentioned above:

> "Direct, control, suggest this day
>   All I design, or do, or say,
> That all my powers, with all their might,
>   In Thy sole glory may unite"

He used to rise early every morning to pray, and he would sing this hymn, accompanying himself on his lute (on which he was very accomplished), and furthermore encouraged his scholars to do the same!

Now we shall see how the good bishop was plunged into conflict with the new King, James II, and how he continued to fight for the right, come what may.

After Charles's death, his brother James, Duke of York, came to the throne and soon made himself unpopular by his high-handed actions. Hatred was most intense in the south-west, where rebellion broke out, led by the Duke of Monmouth. The King reacted by sending a huge army, mercilessly crushing the insurrection and taking Monmouth prisoner at the battle of Sedgemoor. Ken was sent for to minister to the prisoner and kept in touch with him until he was beheaded. When he returned to his diocese he was horrified to find the cruel Judge Jeffreys there, in his fury condemning all who had had the slightest part in the rebellion to be hanged. In addition, 800 more suspects were later transported to slavery in the West Indies.

Bishop Ken did what he could, comforting the relatives of those executed, even sheltering terrified suspects in his own home. In desperation he appealed to the King to have this barbarity stopped, but far from stopping it he honoured Jeffreys "for his services to the State"!

With all this horror in his mind, Ken had to travel to London to consider another rash action of the King's. He was insisting that all bishops and clergy should sign his 'Declaration of Indulgence' which, under the cloak of tolerance, many felt was designed to undermine the Church of England. This was indeed a test: had they the courage to defy this headstrong King? The Archbishop of Canterbury and six bishops (including Ken) refused to sign. Hundreds of clergy followed their brave example, including Samuel Wesley (father of John and Charles) who preached from the text "Be it known to thee, O King, we will not serve thy gods".

James was furious, locking these seven ringleaders in the Tower. Among them was Bishop Lloyd, later Bishop of Worcester, whose memorial is in Fladbury Church. Another was the famous Trelawney, and the stirring chorus of the 'Song of the Western Men' shows that their execution was planned:-

"And shall Trelawney die?
Then twenty thousand Cornish men
Will know the reason why!"

The story of what followed is too long to tell, but the reaction was so strong that James had to 'climb down', the seven were acquitted and returned to their sees, James was deposed and the Stuart line came to an end, its death-knell sounded by the action of seven brave men.

In the reign of William, Ken found himself in trouble again and was eventually deprived of his see as a 'non-juror'. By this time he was worn out by controversy, and being offered a home at Longleat by his old friend, Lord Weymouth, he retired to spend his remaining years there and was buried in nearby Frome churchyard, while inside the Church we see him in stained glass giving food to the hungry.

Ken has been called the greatest of all Anglican Bishops, a man who always strove to live up to his own words:-

> "Let all thy converse be sincere,
> Thy conscience as the noonday clear,
> For God's all-seeing eye surveys
> Thy secret thoughts, thy words and ways".

JOHN MASON (1645 - 1694)

The hymn "How shall I sing that majesty which angels do admire" (78 MHB) has become popular during recent years; its dignity, reverence and humility of approach ensure that it remains so. Yet it is 300 years since John Mason wrote it. What kind of a man was he?

We know his father was a Nonconformist minister who struggled to give his son the best possible education and that John went to Cambridge, graduated and trained for the Church of England ministry. We must remember that at this time many Church livings were filled by Puritans and it seems that John saw more scope and opportunity in the established Church, while still holding his father's views. He may have been influenced by the great Richard Baxter, who thought highly of him. Later he declared John to be "a light in the pulpit, a pattern out of it - the glory of the Church of England".

John's life does not seem to have been very eventful, at least until the end. After a short curacy he became Vicar of Stantonbury, then moved to Water Stratford, Bucks, where he remained for the rest of his life. If you go to this pretty village on the River Ouse, with its Norman church, you would hardly credit what happened there 300 years ago, for the last month of John's life was quite sensational. Whether the death of his wife or the disease that was soon to kill him unhinged his mind we do not know, but one Sunday he announced that he had seen a vision of the Lord Jesus Christ with a glorious crown on His head and a look of unutterable majesty on His face. Preaching from the parable of the wise and foolish virgins, his subject was 'The

Midnight Cry'. He declared that Christ's coming was nigh and called on Christians to trim their lamps and the whole nation to tremble and repent. The congregation was deeply moved, no doubt to John's satisfaction, but he could not have foreseen the consequences.

The excitement escalated, wild reports spread, until crowds came expecting to see the Second Advent there - at Water Stratford! All the available lodgings were taken and people camped in the fields. Many even sold their possessions, so convinced were they that this was the end. The most amazing scenes followed, thousands singing, dancing, praying, even leaping and shouting in frenzy. At the height of the excitement the vicar, who was by now thought of as the prophet of the last things, was taken ill and died within a few days, blissfully unaware of the strange goings-on around him. Some went away disillusioned; others denied that he had died and refused to move. A new vicar moved in, finding a problem on his hands, and is said to have had the body exhumed to convince everyone that John was really dead. Most went away, many having to seek new jobs, homes and possessions, for everything had been sold or given away. A small, hard core of fanatics still would not go, believing that the old vicar would rise again. Finally the fields were cleared by force.

It is sad to think that such a devoted life should end in such a bizarre way, so it is best to think of what he achieved before this strange episode. He wrote many hymns and compiled several books of them. Their quality was so good that men as unlike as Pope, Wesley and Watts acknowledged their debt to him.

John Mason was by no means the first man to write hymns (as distinct from metrical Psalms) but it does seem that he was the first to have had his hymns sung in the Church of England.

Happily, he died peacefully as if nothing unusual had happened; his reason had returned and his old calm faith asserted itself. As his loved ones watched by his bedside they heard him say, a few moments before he breathed his last, "I am full of the loving kindness of the Lord".

NAHUM TATE (1652 - 1715) and NICHOLAS BRADY (1639 - 1726)

We have seen, in chapter 4, how Sternhold and Hopkins brought out their metrical Psalms at the time when the English Bible and Prayer Book were very new. With all its faults this book was a great success and served the Anglican services for over a century and a half. Other versions proliferated but in spite of many imitators their Psalter, now known as 'The Old Version', held sway; but the language was changing and the need for a better, official version was felt. This was supplied by that oddly assorted pair, Tate and Brady.

Nahum Tate was the son of an Irish clergyman who had written some poetry, and the young Nahum soon discovered that he too had a gift in the same direction. He graduated at Trinity College, Dublin, and came to England in search of experience and, he hoped, work.

He became friendly with Dryden, already an established playwright, who had recently published his controversial poem 'Absalom and Ahithophel' Part 1, and was being pressed to hurry on with Part 2, while at the same time trying to finish a play; so he gave Nahum the outline of the plot and left him to get on with it - just revising it here and there before sending it off to the printers. This was rather humiliating for the aspiring young poet, but it was a good apprenticeship and he went on to write poems and plays on his own. Perhaps his best known works were the libretto of Purcell's opera 'Dido and Aeneas' and his Psalter, which became known as 'The New Version'.

It is worth noting that some original hymns had been produced during the long period since 'The Old Version' had come out; George Herbert and Henry Vaughan hardly expected their poems to be sung in church; Baxter and Milton were Puritans, so their hymns were taboo; and poor George Wither really tried to introduce hymns into the services of the Established Church, but in so doing landed himself in a lot of trouble. Hymns would still be 'out' for another 150 years, but an improved version of the Psalms would be welcomed.

Nahum Tate was honoured by being appointed Poet Laureate and later 'Historiographer Royal', but unfortunately he became addicted to drink, a good-natured and fuddling fellow someone called him. It was his downfall, for he got into debt and spent his declining years in a 'refuge for debtors' where he eventually died - a sad object lesson on the evils of drink.

Nicholas Brady was also an Irishman and also graduated at the same college, but he was a more stable, if less talented, character. He was awarded a Doctorate of Divinity for his services to the Church. He is said to have saved his native town of Bandon from being burnt down by rebel mobs three times, and when he eventually came to London it was to petition the King on its behalf. The King was sufficiently impressed by this earnest young clergyman to offer him the post of

Royal Chaplain and thus the collaborator of Tate. It is interesting to note that in later life he was Rector of Stratford upon Avon.

Many unkind things have been said about these two men, but both were fluent, could rhyme well and had typical Irish charm, their work often rising above the commonplace. Some people clung to The Old Version, condemning the new one as being too "fashionable and modish" - like the opposition to The New English Bible encountered when it came out!

Looking at their hymns which have survived, I think the best is probably "Through all the changing scenes of life" (427 MHB) - their version of Psalm 24. How appealing is their expansion of verse 8 "O taste and see that the Lord is good", which they render:-

> "O make but trial of His love;
>   Experience will decide
> How blest they are, and only they,
>   Who in His truth confide."

But the touch of imagination which illustrates that verse sometimes runs away with itself, as for instance in "As pants the hart for cooling streams, when heated in the chase" (455 MHB), those last words seeming to interpolate a purely English hunting scene instead of the animal simply seeking the water-brooks in the intense heat of an Eastern noontide.

One other famous hymn, thought to be Tate's own work, is the carol "While shepherds watched their flocks by night" (129 MHB) which appears in the supplement to The New Version, a fine paraphrase of Luke 2, verses 8-13.

Chapter 7

PREPARING FOR REVIVAL

JOSEPH ADDISON (1672 - 1719)

I suppose this period did not produce a more distinguished man of letters than Joseph Addison. The great Dr. Johnson held him up as an example to all who would aspire to the best English style; Macauley praised his skill as a satirist who "without inflicting a wound, effected a great social reform"; while John Wesley declared "God raised up Mr. Addison to lash the prevailing vices and profane customs and show the excellence of Christianity", evidently having in mind the licentiousness of the Restoration period, when a restatement of moral standards was sorely needed.

Joseph was the son of Rev. Lancelot Addison, of Milston, Wilts, who had risen from a poor family by hard work to obtain this living; his dearest wish was that his son should follow in his footsteps, so he would struggle to give him a good education. Joseph did splendidly and graduated from Oxford, but then changed course and studied law. Later, impelled by the injustices he saw, he entered politics and was elected as a Whig. With his legal knowledge he was soon in positions of increasing importance, and had the satisfaction of seeing some reforms become law. Finally he became secretary to the Lord Lieutenant of Ireland - as tricky a job as it would be now! He earned the reputation of being one of the few Englishmen who attained popularity with the Irish.

About this time he resumed an old college friendship, with Richard Steele, the famous journalist who founded The Tatler and The Spectator, and began to write his famous social articles for these periodicals. During this period the Whig government fell from power, resulting - as the uncertainties of politics dictate - in Joseph losing his position. Naturally he regretted this, but it did leave him more time for his writing which had developed into more than a spare time job. Within two years, however, the Whig government was back in power and Joseph back in his old job, but he felt the need of a newspaper to be the mouthpiece of his party, so he started one 'The Freeholder'.

After two years he had another promotion, to be Secretary of State, thus reaching the top of the tree. He had seemed a confirmed bachelor, but then at the age of 44 he decided to marry. Unfortunately he made an unwise choice - the rich widow, the Countess of Warwick. Although her wealth enabled him to retire a few years later - with a pension of £1,500 a year, an incredible sum in those days - the money did not bring happiness. His stepson was a dissolute fellow, causing him much anxiety; he was subjected to bitter attacks for his political views, even from old friends; and finally his health broke down. Realising he was dying, he sent for his wayward stepson and without any reproach just said: 'See in what peace a Christian can die''. He also sent for the poet Gay to beg forgiveness for some slight wrong he thought he had done him, so that he could die in peace.

Joseph Addison left us a great heritage - the incomparable character studies of Sir Roger de Coverley, ''a gentleman of Worcestershire'' (inventor of the dance of that name) at home and in Church where ''he sometimes stands up when everyone else is on their knees, to count the congregation and see if any of his tenants are missing, and to see that all are behaving with due reverence!''

All this appeared in The Spectator, as also did his few hymns, which we see were thus intended to be read, not sung. Many sacred poems were published in this way and a good deal of research has gone into which are Addison's and which may have been by other contributors. We will stick to those that are certainly his, of which the majestic ''The spacious firmament on high'' (44 MHB) is perhaps the best known. Based on Psalm 19, it has impressed great men of all generations since. Even the militant atheist Tom Paine admired it and confessed it almost made him believe in a Creator. The hymn of praise for God's providence ''When all Thy mercies, O my God, my rising soul surveys'' (413 MHB) is unsurpassed in its class, being typical of the faith of this man. A lesser known hymn in sombre vein is ''When rising from the bed of death'', an honest facing of the Last Judgment; it has a solemn and impressive beauty when sung to Tallis's fine music, as in the English Hymnal (No. 92). I mention this hymn also because it expresses the basis of belief which was the driving force of this great man's life, in its closing words:

"For never shall my soul despair her pardon to procure,
Who knows Thine only Son has died to make her pardon sure."

ISAAC WATTS (1674 - 1748)

I do not intend to write more than a brief note about Isaac Watts, despite being one of our greatest hymn writers, because his life is so well documented; yet he must have a tribute as a true innovator at a time when even the Nonconformist Churches were still opposed to 'man-made' hymns. His work marks the transition from metrical Psalms, which although Biblical have no Christian content, to hymns which had. The title of one of his books shows his aim: 'The Psalms of David imitated in the language of the New Testament'.

This all began by the young Isaac criticising the poor quality of the Psalm paraphrases used at the Independent Chapel in Southampton which he attended and where his father was a deacon. He was told rather sharply that if the old book was not good enough for him he should write something better. To father's surprise, the boy produced his first hymn "Behold the glories of the Lamb" in time for it to be sung the following Sunday. The congregation liked it and asked for more, so he wrote another - and so on for two years. If there was ever any prejudice against hymns, it was broken down by a boy's efforts; therefore he is not unjustly called "the father of the modern British hymn", paving the way for Charles Wesley's hymns which were to set England ablaze forty years later.

Isaac Watts has been criticised as well as praised; certainly not all his hymns are of a high level and have fallen out of use, but enough are so good as to ensure that a large number are found in all books. His style is always 'tidy'; you feel he must have revised them carefully to eliminate bad rhymes that make any sensitive person 'curl up'. We know he always tried to compose lines which were not too broken up by punctuation marks and to make pauses in the most natural places, at the end of couplets. This makes his hymns pleasant to sing, avoiding awkward long sentences which carry on over pauses in the music. I think if you look through any of his hymns you will find how strictly he keeps to these rules; there was never anything slovenly about Watts' writing. How many later writers and poets would have done well to imitate him!

His best known hymns are: "O God, our help in ages past" (878 MHB); "Sweet is the work" (665 MHB); "Jesus shall reign" (272 MHB); and "When I survey the wondrous Cross" (182 MHB). The last is thought by many to be the most perfect hymn ever written - and with good reason. It is one of those hymns which can be sung repeatedly, and is worth reading again and again and pondered on until our natural reaction is "Love so amazing, so divine, demands my soul, my life, my all".

Dr. JOHN BYROM (1692 - 1763)

Another contributor to The Spectator was Dr. John Byrom, who wrote the famous words "Christians, awake, salute the happy morn" (120 MHB). He was such a weakly baby that his parents had him baptised the day he was born, but he gained strength as he grew older and when he went to school he was always the bright boy of the class. He went to Trinity College, Cambridge, where he graduated M.A. and was elected to a Fellowship.

During his time at University, John became a very independent thinker; he even resigned his Fellowship because it was expected that he should be ordained; instead he went abroad to study medicine and obtained his diploma.

Returning to his home at Kersall, Lancs, he did not practise as a doctor but began to take pupils for private tuition. One of his successful accomplishments was to invent a system of shorthand, with the result that many more pupils came to him to learn it. He taught the system to the Wesleys, and Charles used it to jot down his hymns when pressed for time.

He began to read the works of William Law (whose teaching influenced John Wesley deeply) and became an evangelical Christian. He became very friendly with the Wesleys and, although an older man, often met them to take coffee and talk theology.

When John was 49 years old his elder brother died and he inherited the family property, so he retired from teaching and devoted his time to writing. Among other things he contributed to the famous 'Spectator' under the nom-de-plume of 'John Shadow'.

Dr. Byrom was quite a character, very tall and striking in appearance, and dressing in unusual and rather eccentric styles, but he was loved by many and respected by all.

There was another and more homely side to his character: he was especially fond of his daughter Dorothy, and one Christmas morning she found an envelope on the breakfast table marked "Christmas Day for Dolly". Opening it, she found, not an ordinary Christmas greeting, but written especially for her the carol "Christians awake".

Dr. Byrom wrote many other poems, some not very interesting but others very witty, and also some devotional gems like "My spirit longs for Thee" (467 MHB). Do read this - and re-read it - noting the repetition of each last line as the first line of the following verse, not simply to emphasise the thought but to lead on to a new one.

It would be a pity simply to admire the skilful construction of this little poem; let us make it our prayer. Although not a Christmas hymn, it is a sincere confession: "Unworthy though I be of so divine a Guest" is the first step to receiving the lowly Guest who was born in a poor stable and laid in a manger.

PHILIP DODDRIDGE (1702 - 1751)

"Ye humble souls that seek the Lord" (217 MHB), an Easter hymn that bids us ponder on Christ's empty tomb and so rejoice in our own resurrection from sin and death, is by Philip Doddridge - a weak man who got a lot done. He wrote about 400 hymns - not a large number compared with some authors - but of these perhaps more have survived than those of more prolific writers. There are only seven in the Methodist Hymn Book, but it is significant that three more have been rescued from oblivion in the supplement 'Hymns and Songs'.

Yet we nearly did not have Doddridge or his hymns, for, his mother's twentieth child, he was such a weak little thing that when he was born he was thought to be dead. The nurse was concentrating on the exhausted mother when she noticed a slight movement of the little 'body' and turned her attention to him. Although he lived and gained strength, he was never a tough boy, but at school he was a brilliant scholar. The Duchess of Bedford, seeing his remarkable progress, offered to send him to University to study for holy orders.

Philip was by now a sincere Christian, but regretfully felt bound to decline this golden opportunity, for one of the disadvantages, even sufferings, inflicted on 'dissenters' at that time was exclusion from Oxford and Cambridge. He was proud that his grandfather was ejected from his living in 1662 for conscience's sake and that his mother was a

Protestant refugee; and he determined to be loyal to their principles, so at the age of 17 he went to train at a 'Dissenters' Academy' at Kibworth. After four happy years there he was ordained and took charge of the local Independent Chapel, combining with the pastorate a teaching post at the school.

Six years later he moved to Castle Hill Chapel in Northampton, where he stayed for the rest of his life. Soon he gained a Doctorate in Divinity and was anxious to use his talents for teaching again, so he opened his own 'Theological Academy for Young Gentlemen' where he worked happily for over twenty years, training a total of 200 men for the ministry. John Wesley records a visit to him thus: "Dr. Doddridge desired me to take his place expounding the Scripture to the young men". John must have been very impressed, for he later wrote to Philip requesting "a list of books suitable for young readers". I wonder if he recommended his own most influential book - "The Rise and Progress of Religion in the Soul"?

How often in the past the dread disease tuberculosis has shortened useful lives. Philip preached for the last time when he was 49; he was *very* ill and the doctors ordered the only cure they knew, a cruise to the South; but it was too late - he died three months later in Lisbon.

So here we have a man dogged by ill-health, yet using all his strength in his Master's service, at a time when religious life was in the doldrums - for the great surge of the Methodist Revival did not get under way until after his death.

Do look up his hymns: "Hark the glad sound" (82 MHB), a grand Advent hymn; "O God of Bethel" (607 MHB), the song of pilgrimage; "O happy day that fixed my choice" (without the refrain) (744 MHB), his joyous hymn of personal consecration; and many others. But I would particularly like to draw your attention to the three I have mentioned in 'Hymns and Songs': "The Saviour, when to heaven he rose" (69 H. & S.) is typical of the man and his work, for it is about training men for the ministry; "My God, and is thy table spread?" (46 H. & S.) is a beautiful hymn of the Lord's Supper; and "Jesus, my Lord, how rich thy grace" (36 H. & S.) is a strong appeal to have Christian compassion on the needy and to engage in social service. It is based on our Lord's words of judgment: "Inasmuch as you did it to one of the least of these My brothers, you did it to Me." I quote one verse:-

"In *them* (the needy) *Thou* may'st be clothed and fed,
And visited and cheered,
And in *their* accents of distress
My Saviour's voice is heard."

The spirit of this hymn illustrates another of Philip Doddridge's great achievements, his part in the founding and running of Northampton General Hospital.

A young doctor named Stonhouse came to the town; it was known that he was an atheist, even writing pamphlets arguing that Christianity was a load of rubbish and attacking the Churches, but Philip met him in a friendly manner and soon discovered that they had some common ground - they both had a sincere desire to alleviate the lot of sufferers in the town and believed the best way to do this was to build and equip a hospital. They called meetings, under Philip's Chairmanship, raised money, and finally got the job done. So these two men, so deeply divided spiritually, co-operated in a great scheme of healing.

In all their dealings religion was never mentioned, but gradually John Stonhouse began to admire this new Christian friend, yet still refusing to go to any church. Then one Sunday, a little while after Philip had commenced his service, the door opened quietly and to his joy, in crept John who found a seat out of sight. During the singing of the last hymn he went out, observed only by Philip. He did this several times until he realised he must do it openly, for he was now a convinced Christian. It may well be that many of us find ourselves in a situation rather like this; if so, this episode could teach us a lesson.

You see how apt is the hymn I have quoted to be written by a man who helped to found a hospital. I will conclude with another verse:-

"Thy face with reverence and with love
I in Thy poor would see;
O let me rather beg my bread
Than hold it back from thee."

Chapter 8

THE PERIOD OF THE METHODIST REVIVAL

We have seen something of the worthy Anglican, Independent and Baptist authors who preceded the Methodist Revival, each in his way preparing for it. Now we come to that revolutionary time, with the Wesley brothers, who were the prime movers, some of their faithful helpers, and some rebels who branched off on their own. Joseph Hart, Newton and Cowper must also be included, for they represent a parallel revival in the Independents and the Church of England, while William Williams was the hymn writer for the Welsh Calvinistic Methodist Church.

So first to the more famous of the Wesley brothers . . .

JOHN WESLEY (1703 - 1791)

As with his brother Charles, I shall not attempt a full biographical sketch of John Wesley, for like Bunyan and Isaac Watts, good and full biographies are easily available. Suffice it to say that, while Charles numbered his hymns by the thousand, John numbered the miles he travelled on horseback by many thousands, but his output of hymns was comparatively small.

If you look at the index of authors in the Methodist Hymn Book, you will see that John has twenty-five hymns, whereas his brother Charles has about ten times that number. Also you will find that only two of these are original hymns of his, and some doubt is cast on these by the experts. Then there are three written by others, which John altered for inclusion in one of his collections of hymns for the early Methodists. When he did this he usually improved the hymns; he abhorred what he called 'fondling expressions' for the Deity, 'dear' 'sweet' and such adjectives were always cut out, repetitious lines or verses were omitted and the language generally made more dignified and tasteful.

This leaves us with twenty numbers, all of which have asterisks by them, indicating that they are translations. Here we come to one of John's most remarkable accomplishments, that of linguist. At University he learned the classical languages, Latin, Hebrew and Greek, yet he does not seem to have translated any of the vast store of ancient hymns in these languages into English: I wonder why?

Later he learned German in order to converse with Peter Böhler and other Moravians who, as we know, had such a profound influence on his spiritual development. The fellowship he had with these men led him to explore the riches of their hymnody, to translate them and so be the first to bring them to the British public. Read, for example, the following: "Jesu, Thy blood and righteousness" (370 MHB), "Now I have found the ground" (375 MHB), "Jesu, Thy boundless love to me" (430 MHB), "Thou hidden love of God" (433 MHB), "O Lord, enlarge our scanty thought" (449 MHB), "Commit thou all thy griefs" (507 MHB), "Lo, God is here! let us adore" (683 MHB), and "What shall we offer our good Lord" (784 MHB). This will do you more good than what I have written! and you will see something of the value of John Wesley's work in pioneering the opening up of these German treasures.

Then in 1737 he writes of having parishioners who were immigrant Jews from Spain, so he promptly learned their language to communicate with them. He says he found them "nearer to the mind that was in Christ than many who call him 'Lord'". These contacts led him to come across an anonymous Spanish poem based on Psalm 63, which he rendered as the hymn "O God, my God, my all Thou art" (471 MHB).

Again he showed himself master of another language, French, for the hymn "Come, Saviour, Jesus, from above" (546 MHB) is an admirable version of Antoinette Bourignon's 'Renouncing all for Christ'. I wonder if he knew yet more languages?

What is remarkable is that John Wesley did not merely love learning for learning's sake, but as a means of imparting the love of his Lord, which meant everything to him, to others; as he says in two lines of one of the hymns (784 MHB) mentioned above:-

> "Throughout the world Thy gospel spread,
>   Thy everlasting truth declare."

CHARLES WESLEY (1707 - 1788)

A ROMANTIC INTERLUDE

I intended, when starting this book, to avoid the two 'giants' of hymn writing, Charles Wesley and Isaac Watts, because they are so well covered by biographies; but I was intrigued by a reference to Charles Wesley's courtship which set me on to a new line of enquiry —

Charles Wesley refers to his wife occasionally in quite endearing terms such as "my faithful Sally" - but who was she and what was her background? It was to find answers to such questions that we set off on a bright spring morning for Builth Wells and then, a few miles further on, the village of Garth. Slowing down, we looked out for Garth House, a little way beyond, up on the hill to the right, and Llanlleonfel Church on a slope on the left - with the little river Dulas between them, close to the road. This was the setting for Charles's courting - and what a beautiful and peaceful scene it was!

But why did he come to this remote spot to find his lady love, the girl who would gladly ride behind him on his horse and lead the singing at his evangelistic meetings?

The story begins when John and Charles were on a preaching tour in these parts and a young clergyman named Phillips was accompanying them and acting as interpreter when they were in wholly Welsh speaking areas. (I am surprised John, at any rate, needed an interpreter; he seemed to master any language quickly - surely he didn't let Welsh beat him!) But to continue the story - Mr. Phillips introduced the brothers to Marmaduke Gwynne, a wealthy landowner, Squire of Garth, a magistrate and a zealous churchman, who had been influenced by the evangelist Howell Harris. He welcomed the famous pair to make his home their base while they were working there.

They found great comfort in this large country house with its twenty servants and its warm hospitality - and two charming daughters for good measure. It was one of these, Sarah, with whom Charles fell instantly and hopelessly in love. Unfortunately the course of true love never did run smooth. First it transpired that young Mr. Phillips had designs on Sarah himself, which rather soured the friendship between him and the Wesleys; also, Mrs. Gwynne was of a rather more worldly turn of mind than her husband.

Mrs. Gwynne's first reactions were good, it is true, and she professed that "she would rather Sarah marry Mr. Wesley than any man in England", *but* she obviously would have preferred a wealthy suitor for her daughter. She does not seem to have raised any objection to the difference in their ages, Charles being a mature 42 and Sarah only 22. Poor Charles sensed the atmosphere and hesitated to ask Mrs. Gwynne for her daughter's hand; but urged on by her sister, he finally plucked up courage and got what he expected - no objection but "want of fortune".

Charles mentioned he had just had a legacy of £50 and that he was publishing the first volume of his hymns soon, for which he had high hopes of a large sale, but she was *not* impressed by these assets. Mr. Gwynne seems to have washed his hands of these negotiations and left the whole thing to his wife's discretion! So Charles went back to London with doubts and fears in his heart to finalise the publication of his hymns.

As soon as the first volume was off the press he sent Sarah a copy. All excited, she showed it to her mother, whose response was a bomb-shell - her attitude had hardened, for to her, hymns were a doubtful asset, broad acres and a large income being the things that mattered!

The couple seemed to have had their fondest hopes shattered, but they continued to correspond. Some of their love letters have been preserved, and how affectionate they are! "I know not how to finish," he writes, "my heart so overflows with love for you." Having suffered this major hitch in his plans to marry Sarah, Charles resorted to constant prayer on his problems: "The door of prayer is always open," he wrote in his diary.

At this point one of his old and trusted friends took a hand in the affair. The Rev. Vincent Perronet, Vicar of Shoreham, (father of Edward, who wrote "All hail the power of Jesu's name") wrote a long letter to Mrs. Gwynne. He pointed out that Wesley's hymns were a real asset - in one publisher's opinion worth £2,500, but in his opinion far more than that; also that he (Perronet) had a similar problem, for his own daughter was betrothed to a very poor man but with such qualities that he "Would not exchange him for a 'Star and Garter'".

It seems that the letter had the desired effect and Mrs. Gwynne relented and wrote indicating that the marriage had their full consent.

With a heart overflowing with joy Charles travelled to Garth in April 1749 for his wedding, only to be met with another rebuff. Even as he embraced his beloved Sally she burst into tears, saying that her brother had come and was violently opposing the marriage. However, this latest snag was overcome, for having given her consent, mother remained firm. "What I have written I have written" seems to have been her attitude!

So the great day arrived, Saturday, 8th April. It had been a cold night, but the sun rose in a clear, cloudless sky, inspiring Charles to quote George Herbert's lines:

> "Sweet daie, so cool, so calm, so bright,
>   The bridall of the earth and skie"

But Charles had been up before sunrise, to prepare himself for this important step by prayer, meditation and thanksgiving to God, who had guided him past all the obstacles to this happiness. He was joined later by his brother John, Sally and her sister, and together they "prayed and sang praises to God".

Then at eight o'clock he led his bride down the slope, across the stream and up the hill to the church, where John pronounced them man and wife.

The day we visited the church was an April morning, just as Charles described two and a quarter centuries earlier. Unfortunately the present church bears little resemblance to the one in which Charles was married, for the Gwynnes were to leave Garth; and the church was in such a poor state when Kilvert visited it that no doors, windows or seats were left, and when he entered, several white owls glided silently out to roost in the ancient yew in the churchyard... So it had to be rebuilt in 1876, retaining little but the Gwynne memorial tablets on the wall to connect it with this happy event. But as we went out and stood under the same old yew, we looked across the little valley to Garth House on the far slope and could picture the little procession coming up the hill in the sunshine long ago, and John Wesley saying "it is a solemn day - such as befits a Christian marriage".

To Charles, however, it was a day of crowning joy, for he and his beloved Sally were to enjoy forty years of perfect happiness. After Charles died, Sally lived almost another thirty years, dwelling on her happy days with the greatest hymn writer of all time.

Would she remember the day when, before their marriage, Charles was staying at Garth and a violent thunderstorm broke out? Charles rushed to the window to close it when a robin flew in out of the storm. Charles was silent and in his mind were forming lines which were to become part of his most famous hymn "Jesu, lover of my soul" (110 MHB):-

> "Hide me, O my Saviour, hide,
> Till the storm of life be past".

JOSEPH HART (1712 - 1768)

Following close on the Wesleys we come to Joseph Hart - John was a boy of nine when he was born - a boy well brought up by parents who, though not wealthy, could afford to give their son a good education. He studied well and became a teacher of languages in a London school, but he rebelled against the Christian atmosphere of his childhood and drifted into a rather debased life-style and seemed quite satisfied with it until he was about forty years old.

We do not know the forces that influenced him, but Joseph began to feel the emptiness and aimlessness of his life. This feeling deepened into real distress and in despair he began to attend worship again. Now a man of forty-five, he went to the Moravian Chapel in Fetter Street. The preacher spoke from the words in Revelation, Chapter 3: "I will keep thee from the hour of temptation which will come upon the world". He went home in a very thoughtful mood, knelt down to pray, and eventually felt as if a great burden was lifted from his shoulders. In his own words, "I ran to dangerous lengths of both carnal and spiritual wickedness, but now felt myself melting away with a strange softness of expression; tears ran in streams from my eyes, I was so swallowed up in joy and thankfulness that I hardly knew where I was."

So by means of the Moravians was born yet another apostle of the revival, for this experience was the turning-point in his life. Within two years, after a brief training, he was accepted as minister of an Independent Church.

Hymn writing and preaching went hand in hand. He had only another nine years to live, but he packed them with zealous service for his new-found Master. It is said that, in spite of such a short ministry, 20,000 people crowded to his funeral at the famous cemetery at Bunhill Fields, so great was the respect he had engendered.

Whether it was a premonition of the brevity of his life, or the regret for his best years wasted, it is hard to say, but he seems to have done everything in a hurry. Consequently, many of his hymns were soon discarded for their poor quality, some were revised by other people, but a few have lived on because of their feeling of spontaneous inspiration.

His famous contemporary, Dr. Johnson, had a poor opinion of his work, as you can judge by reading between the lines of this entry in his diary: "I went to Church, and seeing a poor girl at the sacrament in a bed-gown, I gave her privately half a crown - though I saw Hart's hymns in her hand."

I will end by quoting two of his hymns that have lived because they deserve to. The one is the well known two-versed hymn, "This, this is the God we adore" (69 MHB); the other, not so well known, is a great 'Gospel Call' type of hymn, "Come, ye sinners, poor and wretched" (324 MHB). Perhaps it is rather unfashionable to think of ourselves in these terms, but Joseph Hart had felt exactly like that in the years before his late conversion, and there are few hymns which compress so much truth in so few lines. Jesus, he says, is " . . . Full of *pity,* joined with *power*;" then reversing the thought he adds: "He is *able,* He is *willing;* doubt no more." Finally, lest we have any further doubts or excuses to delay a decision to come to Christ:-

> "If you tarry till you're better,
> You will never come at all:"

> "Let not conscience make you linger
> Nor of fitness fondly dream;
> All the fitness He requireth
> Is to feel your need of Him."

If Joseph Hart preached like that, no wonder he drew the crowds!

THOMAS OLIVERS (1725 - 1799) - Wesley's faithful helper

We know that Charles and John Wesley wrote or translated so many hymns that they tended to overshadow all others, but there was a group of younger men, all Wesley's preachers, burning with zeal, who made notable contributions to all hymn books.

One of these was Thomas Olivers, whose only surviving hymn "The God of Abraham praise" (21 MHB) has found its way into most hymn books.

Thomas had a bad start with few advantages and almost all drawbacks, yet he became one of John Wesley's most loyal and trusted assistants - so how did it all begin and what led up to his becoming such a committed Christian?

Born at Tregynon, a few miles from Newtown, Powys, both of his parents died before he was five, and the little boy was cared for by anybody he could find to take pity on him. Unfortunately he got into bad company and soon the little orphan became known as the worst boy in the village. A kindly shoemaker tried to teach him his trade, but he disgraced himself again and again and finally had to leave the district. He became a restless wanderer and worked (or robbed!) his way from place to place, arriving eventually in Bristol. Here he found a great crowd gathering one day and enquired what was going on - was it a fight or something like that? - and could he join in? Imagine his disgust when he was told it was a great preacher, the Rev. George Whitefield, going to speak in the open air! However, he went to listen, curious to see why this man could draw such numbers. Whitefield with his stentorian voice and earnest manner preached on 'A brand plucked from the fire' - and the wild young Tom was stopped in his tracks.

Obviously, to such a man conversion was likely to be a major upheaval; he felt himself so sinful, so hopeless, that he fasted until he grew faint, and prayed until he couldn't straighten his knees, but he finally found Christ as his Saviour - even from *his* sin. He joined the Methodists at Bradford on Avon, where he had settled now, and his new-found union with his Lord led him to do two important things: first he returned to his birthplace to try to repay the trail of debts he had left; and then he became a local preacher, to commend the Saviour to others.

At the age of 28, still restless, he set out to walk to Cornwall to join Wesley, who was working there, and to offer himself as a regular itinerant preacher. On the way he bought a colt for £5 and on this faithful companion he rode 100,000 miles on his Gospel errands.

While in London, Thomas formed one of those odd friendships - often very rewarding - with someone with whom he disagreed over his deepest beliefs, a Jew named Leoni. He was a concert singer of note and was cantor at a local synagogue. Thomas even went to some Sabbath services and was so impressed by part of a creed sung to a fine minor tune, that he skilfully adapted the words for Christian use, still using the same tune. This is still wedded to this fine hymn 'The God of Abraham Praise' and is named LEONI after Thomas's friend.

So an orthodox Jew and a fiery early Methodist combined to give us a great hymn.

JOHN CENNICK (1718 - 1755)

When John Wesley's evangelistic work was expanding, he needed to recruit a large band of preachers to travel where he - in spite of his ceaseless activity - could not go. He found many gifted and zealous converts, but it was inevitable that a few strong-willed young men found themselves unable to submit to his strict discipline. John Cennick was just such a man.

Born of Quaker parents, he turned to the Church of England in boyhood, then attended Methodist meetings where, at the age of 19, he found Christ as his Saviour. He was training to be a land surveyor, but Wesley was so impressed with this bright youth that he offered to train him to teach in his Kingswood School and accepted him as a lay preacher. He found great happiness in this work and made time to write a good number of hymns, publishing them when he was only 24 under the lengthy title 'Sacred Hymns for the Children of God in the Days of their Pilgrimage'. This included some antiphonal hymns - men singing two lines as a question, then women replying with the answer. None of these have survived, but all his hymns in use today come from this youthful book.

"Thou great Redeemer" (104 MHB) is a great hymn which he headed 'The Priesthood of Christ'. Unfortunately the key verse 'Thou Great Melchizedek' has been omitted (Did the compilers think we didn't know our Bibles well enough to digest this?); then there is "Children of the Heavenly King" (696 MHB), typical of his simple, direct style - often used as a children's hymn; while "Ere I sleep" (947 MHB) is one of our loveliest evening hymns. It is a pity we have not its companion hymn "Rise my soul", which fits the same tune.

Perhaps it is not so well known that the grace before and the thanks after meals - "Be present at our table, Lord" and "We thank Thee, Lord, for this our food" - were also written by Cennick.

58

He later became Pastor of a Dublin Church, where in spite of opposition, his eloquence drew large crowds. It was here that he once preached about 'The Babe in Swaddling Clouts'. A hostile priest heard of this and coined the derogatory name 'Swaddlers' for Methodists, and the name seemed to stick - to Cennick's surprise. Wesley's dry comment was "He probably did not know the expression was from the Bible - a book he was not much acquainted with".

Cennick's thinking then swung towards Calvinism, but Wesley hated this narrow, forbidding creed, so they parted. He joined up with Whitefield and the Welsh evangelist Howell Harris. It seems that he later moderated his views and joined the Moravian Church, remaining in their ministry for the rest of his life, which only lasted 37 years; in fact, it seems difficult for him to have fitted all he did into this short time.

He was a wealthy man, and at his own expense he founded a Moravian Settlement at Tytherton, in Wiltshire, after the pattern he had seen elsewhere, with farm and domestic buildings and a Church, based on the ideal of a 'Christian Communism'.

A century later, the diarist Kilvert was curate in the adjoining parish of Langley Burrell, and the community was still flourishing, and some old people had heard of Cennick's exploits in the district.

He was preaching at Lyneham one day in the open air on the 'Blood of Christ' when some men fetched a syringe filled with animal's blood and sprayed it on him. Shocked as he was by the blasphemy of this 'joke' and bespattered, he went on to denounce the act, emphasising that Christ's blood was the symbol of the outpouring of his love for mankind.

It is interesting to note that Lewis West, composer of the tune set to hymn 385 MHB, appropriately named Tytherton, was minister to the Tytherton Community after Cennick, and is buried by the Church there.

In his later years, Cennick twice travelled to Germany to minister to Moravian congregations there, with notable success.

It is a good thing to know that the man who was so much an individualist that he could not 'fit in' with Wesley, found a true spiritual home elsewhere and did yeoman service for the Lord he loved with all his heart. It would be a dull world without such characters - whose dynamic preaching might be ridiculed but never ignored.

EDWARD PERRONET (1726 - 1792) and JOHN RIPPON (1751 - 1836)

At Ascensiontide, the climax of our celebrations of the closing events of our Lord's earthly life, the hymns are triumphant, like the Easter ones; no sorrow because He leaves us, but joy for His return to His home as King. The Ascension has been called the Coronation of Christ. Read these hymns and see how often the words 'King', 'reign' and 'rule' occur. One such hymn is "All hail the power of Jesu's name" (91 MHB), written by Edward Perronet and finished by John Rippon. Who were these men and what were they like?

As the dates show, Dr. Rippon was 25 years younger than Perronet and he was an outstanding and influential Baptist minister who spent the whole of his working life as minister of a large London Church. He published 'A Selection of Hymns' in 1787 and included this hymn, adding the last verse himself.

Edward Perronet was, perhaps, a more colourful character. His grandfather, a Huguenot, came over from France to escape the great persecution of 1685, and his son Vincent, who was vicar of Shoreham, Kent, for 57 years, was deeply influenced by John Wesley, giving him loyal support and useful advice. Charles playfully used to call him the 'Archbishop of Methodism'.

Vincent's sons, Charles and Edward, became two of the first Methodist 'Preachers' (i.e. Ministers), but their youthful enthusiasm was often too much for John Wesley who said "I have to hold the reins firmly"; but they and others rebelled against the reins and among other things played a leading part in giving preachers the right to administer the Lord's Supper.

As the years passed these tensions became more acute and to the Wesleys' grief Edward published, in 1757, a long poem entitled 'The Mitre' - a bitter satire on the Church of England. They pleaded with him to withdraw it, which he agreed to do, but continued to give copies to preachers. This precipitated his break with Methodism, but a man of his talents was welcomed by the Countess of Huntingdon's Connexion as Minister of their Chapel in Canterbury.

As Edward grew older he became more individualistic and difficult; he finally offended the Countess (presumably because she too had tried to hold the reins firmly!), so he left to be minister of the Independent chapel in the city. Here he seemed to be a law unto himself and continued a fruitful ministry until his old age. He died as he had lived, full of spirit, giving 'glory to God'.

This was, as far as we know, the only hymn Edward wrote. Each verse was headed with a title: 'Angels', 'Martyrs', etc. Some verses are omitted from modern hymnbooks, but all include Dr. Rippon's magnificent last verse, which gathers up the thoughts of the rest of the hymn by calling on us, who sing the hymn, to "Crown Him Lord of all".

If the greatness of a hymn is measured by the number of composers who set it to music, then this is a great hymn. 'Miles Lane' was by Edward's chorister friend at Canterbury Cathedral; a century later J. Ellor composed 'Diadem'; and in our time W. H. Ferguson has given us the fine tune 'Ladywell', to be found in many modern hymn books.

ANNE STEELE (1716 - 1778) - First Woman Hymn Writer

We now turn from the Wesleys and those who worked with them to people who worked quite independently, yet were influenced by the Revival.

I read once that "Anne Steele was a very minor poet who led an uneventful life". I forgot who wrote those contemptuous words, but when I came to look at the life of this shy country girl, I had to disagree.

Anne's father was a timber merchant by trade, who early became a sincere Christian and soon felt called to preach at the Baptist chapel in their village - Broughton, Hants. So acceptable was he that they appointed him pastor (unpaid!) - and so he continued for sixty years.

The vicar there complained to his Bishop that his congregation was drifting to Mr. Steele's chapel; he replied, "Go home and preach better than Mr. Steele and they will soon return." The chapel is still there - one of the oldest Baptist chapels in England. Does any reader know it?

But to return to Anne. As a child she had an accident which left her crippled and slightly deformed, but her faith and character grew, and at the age of 14 her father had the joy of baptising her publicly. In spite of her disabilities, her disposition was a lovely one and she and a young man named Elscourt were attracted to one another. Fondness deepened to love and finally the date of the wedding was fixed.

The great day dawned warm and bright, and her lover, rejoicing in his strength, went off for an early morning swim in the nearby river Test. Whether he had cramp or became entangled in weed, we do not know, but while the Steele household was in a state of joyous anticipation and excitement, someone brought the tragic news that the bridegroom's body had been found in the river. One does not need much imagination to understand the shock to everybody, and especially to Anne. The pretty dresses, the feast, the lovingly prepared home - all seemed a mockery now. It was a blow which left a pain for years, but her faith won the battle over despair. She began to employ the time which she had hoped to devote to being a wife and possibly a mother, to writing her poems. Her response to this trial is enshrined in one of her verses:-

> "Lord, teach me to hold fast Thy hand,
>   and when my griefs increase
> To see beyond this lower land
>   the hills of heavenly peace."

Not until she was forty could she be persuaded to publish her work. Her father wrote in his diary: "This day 'Nanny' sent part of her compositions to London to be printed . . . I pray God to bless it for the good of many - and to keep her humble." He need not have worried. A few years later she had her larger work published - 'Poems on Subjects chiefly Devotional', hiding her identity under the nom-de-plume 'Theodosia'.

When Anne was 53 a new Baptist Hymn Book was published and she was honoured by the inclusion of sixty-two of her hymns in it.

She grew to love the old home, the village and the scenery around, and lived a serene, unostentatious life, dying at the age of 62 in the house where she was born - yet, in her quiet way, a pioneer.

In her day hymns were a novelty, and mostly the most dreadful doggerel anyway; but a *woman* author was quite unheard of, and not very respectable! Yet Anne had the urge to write - and write such polished verse as Hymn 302 MHB, "Father of Mercies", her only hymn in our book.

JOHN NEWTON (1725 - 1807) and WILLIAM COWPER (1731 - 1800)

Not every author of hymns began life as a scholar or had a brilliant university career. We were thinking of Thomas Olivers earlier, and he is a case in point, for he had a wild and adventurous youth, but *his* life was tame compared with John Newton's!

His mother, a pious dissenter, unfortunately died when he was seven and his father, a seaman, had to spend long periods abroad, so the boy was left very much to his own devices and soon threw off his mother's influence, professing himself an unbeliever. When he was only eleven, his father, concerned at his attitude and behaviour, decided he must accompany him on his voyages. Being now master of a ship, he thought he could keep his eye on the lad, but all that seemed to happen was that he fell in with the bad ways of the worst of the sailors, disgracing himself and his father repeatedly.

Later, while ashore, the press-gang seized him and he was forced to serve on a man-of-war, but he soon rebelled against the harsh discipline of the Navy. Then came a chance to desert while the ship was in an African port and he joined a slave dealer in those parts, but he was treated even more brutally, so escaped at the first chance and returned to England.

It was at this point that he met a boyhood friend, Mary Catlett, a sweet girl who was to have the most profound influence on his life. They became engaged, and although he loved her sincerely, the call of the sea was too strong and he began his wanderings again. It would take too long to tell of his adventures, his near escapes from death and the scrapes he got into, but he declared that dear Mary was never far from his thoughts and saved him from doing many evil deeds and even from suicide - lest she should be disappointed in him.

At this time he began to read the Bible and books like Thomas à Kempis's 'Of the Imitation of Christ'; he also resumed his study of other subjects, including mathematics.

Then happened what he loved to call 'The Great Deliverance'. He had been shipwrecked and just managed to climb on to a waterlogged raft, and it was after passing a terrifying night on the heaving ocean, when death seemed certain, that he made a deep renunciation of evil and begged God to save him and make him a new man.

In spite of his good resolves, he was blind to the evils of slave trading, for, on his return to England, he accepted the job as master of a slave ship. It was at this time, between voyages, that he married his faithful Mary; before long he felt uneasy about his job and finally decided he must have no more to do with it, and in fact became a keen abolitionist.

John therefore settled in Liverpool, becoming tide surveyor, and here came under the influence of Wesley and Whitefield. So at the age of thirty, he became a fully committed Christian and soon after felt the call to offer himself for the ministry in the Church of England; but the Anglican authorities were reluctant at first to accept a man with such a record! Wesley protested at this delay, so convinced was he of Newton's fitness, and when nearly forty, after years of careful study, he was ordained and was appointed curate (to an absentee vicar) of Olney, Bucks. So began the second part of this amazing man's life - how different from the first part! - but I think no less interesting because he was now devoted to Christ.

So Newton was installed at Olney after thirty years of dissolute life and nearly ten as a Christian. He threw himself into Church work with great zeal, full of a sense of indebtedness to God for saving him from sin and eager to lead others to the faith he had found. In his beliefs he was a Calvinist, for he was convinced that he had been so evil that he couldn't have been saved unless God had chosen him before he was born; however, he jokingly referred to himself as a "sort of speckled bird among Calvinists", which meant that he was moderate, compassionate and understanding towards Christians of other persuasions. How far he was ahead of his time is revealed in one of his letters where he says "Party walls - stronger than the walls of Babylon - must come down".

A few years after settling at Olney, the poet Cowper came there to live and immediately the two became friends. What a strange pair! Newton extrovert and joyful in his comparatively new-found faith; Cowper fearful, doubting, suffering occasional attacks of insanity followed by feelings of guilt because of suicidal tendencies during these attacks, yet finding in Newton someone on whom he could lean.

Newton acknowledged that his strange friend had poetic gifts much greater than his own, and he proposed the compiling of the 'Olney Hymns' for prayer meetings and other weeknight devotional gatherings. The intention was that they should contribute equally to this work, but Cowper's attacks were frequent enough to delay it for several years and when it was at last published Cowper's contribution was only about a quarter of the total.

It is interesting to compare the hymns of these two collaborators. Most of Newton's have a note of triumph - or at least of calm assurance. "How sweet the name of Jesus sounds" (99 MHB) shows the latter, while "Glorious things of Thee are spoken" (706 MHB) is a grand expression of joy born of a firm faith. "Begone, unbelief" (511 MHB) is more introspective, based on his shipwreck experience as if even the ebullient John had times when his trials got him down a bit! - but we must remember what a trial it must have been for him to have to cope with the problems of his pathetic friend William Cowper.

His style was always clear and forthright. He didn't profess to be a poet, aiming to be a mere 'versifier' - for he thought much poetry too involved and profound to be of much help to the simple worshipper he had in mind. (See also Nos. 100 and 540 MHB).

Cowper, on the other hand, was a poet of the first rank, but he was also a fine and sensitive hymn writer. "Ere God had built the mountains" (60 MHB) is a dignified hymn on the glory and grace of God. "Hark, my soul, it is the Lord" (432 MHB) is a unique hymn in that the first three lines are a preparation to listen to the voice of Jesus; then there could be inverted commas to indicate Jesus's words to us - words full of divine love, ending at the fifth verse with the appeal, "Say, poor sinner, lov'st thou me?" The last verse is our response to His love.

There are two well-known hymns which reveal something of the mental torture William suffered from time to time - "O for a closer walk with God" (461 MHB) and "God moves in a mysterious way" (503 MHB). Both are said to have been written during severe mental depression which seemed to precede a period of insanity, and if we read them carefully we can feel for his state. The third verses of each of these hymns are particularly revealing. (See also Nos. 155, 307, 527 and 675 MHB).

The 'Olney Hymns' had a deep and abiding influence during the long period before there was an official Anglican hymn book, because of its variety of approach and expression from these contrasting characters.

The parting of the ways came when Newton was presented with the living of St. Mary Woolnoth in London. Cowper lived with the Rev. and Mrs. Unwin happily until Mr. Unwin's death, when Mary Unwin alone cared for him, nursing him through his periods of depression and insanity so tenderly that he fell deeply in love with her, and in spite of the obstacles they became engaged to be married. The marriage never took place, for further attacks made it impossible. Eventually the strain told on Mary and she became ill and died. During her illness, poor William had to do his best to nurse her, and in his lucid moments reproached himself for having burdened her with the strain of his afflictions. During this time he wrote some verses which Tennyson thought were too moving to be read aloud; were ever such words of pathos wrung from a sensitive soul? . . .

> 'Thy spirits have a fainter flow,
> I see thee daily weaker grow,
> 'Twas my distress that brought thee low,
> — — My Mary!'

He did not survive long without her, yet we are told that his sadness lifted before he died, and smiling he passed to the Lord he loved, yet Who had been so often obscured from him.

As for John Newton, he went from strength to strength, preaching in his London Church until he was over eighty. When someone hinted that he should give up, he replied, "What! shall the old African blasphemer stop while he can still speak?"

He was buried in his Church (although his body was later moved to Olney), with his own epitaph:

> "John Newton, clerk. Once an infidel and libertine:
> A servant of slaves in Africa;
> Was, by the rich mercy of our Lord and Saviour Jesus Christ preserved, restored and pardoned; and appointed to preach the Faith he had long laboured to destroy.
> Near sixteen years at Olney, Bucks.
> And twenty-seven years in this Church."

A good summary of an astonishing life!

WILLIAM WILLIAMS (1717 - 1791)

We have seen how the Wesleys did some preaching tours in Wales, but they did not seem to keep it up, for by this time Howell Harris, the great Welsh preacher, and his helpers were evangelising Wales quite thoroughly and effectively.

It may be that Wesley considered that Harris, being a Welshman, could 'spread the word' more effectively than he could - or he may have found himself disagreeing with Harris over his Calvinist views.

Howell Harris was in his way as remarkable a man as Wesley: banned from preaching in Parish Churches, he still attended his Church at Talgarth and four times offered himself for the priesthood, each time being turned down. The Anglican Church in Wales at that time could not hold a fiery apostle like him! Most men would have given up at such a series of snubs - not Harris! Like Wesley, he took to the open air. He would attend Church as usual, then after the service would mount a table-tomb in the churchyard and preach the Gospel. Most of the congregation would stay to listen and those hanging about in the town would go up to listen too.

One Sunday a young medical student was passing through Talgarth from his home at Pantecelyn, near Llandovery, on his way back to college after a break. He heard a stentorian voice, joined the crowd in the churchyard and listened to Harris's forthright preaching. The message was so dynamic that it 'went right home' and completely changed that young man's life's direction. He decided he must give up his medical studies and prepare himself to preach the love of Christ which had entered his heart in such a dramatic way that Sunday. His name - William Williams.

He went to theological college, studied and was ordained deacon when he was 23 - something Howell Harris was denied. Soon however, he was in trouble with his bishop for the tone of his preaching, for working with nonconformists, and for preaching outside his parish, - all of which were severely frowned on in those days - so he was denied ordination to the priesthood.

Meanwhile Harris, cold-shouldered by the Church, was forming his converts into the Calvanistic Methodist Church, so Williams did the only thing open to him and became one of their ministers.

The Methodist Revival in Wales, under Harris, was a parallel movement to that in England, under Wesley, but as yet it had no one to give it that contribution of sacred song that Charles Wesley had given England. William Williams filled this gap and gave his nation hymns which sang themselves to their hearts. Later he saw that his hymns would have a wider influence if they were translated into English, so he and other helpers did this with some of the most suitable.

His dramatic hymn "O'er the gloomy hills of darkness" is in some books and deserves to be more widely known, but the one which has become the most famous is "Guide me, O Thou great Jehovah" (615 MHB), which finds a place in all books. The first line - a prayer for guidance - is typical of its author, whose youthful ambition was to cure bodies, but God had given him exceptional gifts to cure souls and guided him in that direction. So, too, the lines "I am weak but Thou art mighty; hold me with Thy powerful hand" speaks of the humble dependence on God's strength, which enabled him to labour so success-fully to spread the Gospel.

THE ORPHANAGES OF THE EIGHTEENTH CENTURY

It is surprising what a lot of hymns, and tunes, had their origin directly or indirectly from the impetus of the evangelical movement usually associated with Methodism - but in fact flowing through other Churches as well. The upsurge of evangelistic effort was felt also in the Church of England and this was the seed from which a great social work grew. If anyone tries to say that the Methodist Revival cared only for people's souls and ignored their bodies, they must think again of the number of philanthropic institutions that sprang up in the wake of the spiritual revival. For the moment we shall look at just two, the Foundling and the Lock Hospitals.

A hymn which has become most popular, finding its way into all hymn books, is the anonymous "Praise the Lord, ye heavens adore Him" (13 MHB). You will see it is from the Foundling Collection, 1796, but this is not strictly correct. The hymn was printed as a leaflet and stuck in the back cover of that edition and was not included until the book was re-issued in 1801.

Another author, whose name we know, was James Edmeston, a self-employed architect and surveyor who often had to visit the Foundling Hospital, and so admired the Christian work done there that he continued to visit when business did not demand it. In his spare time he wrote a great number of hymns and wrote his best known for the children, whose singing he loved to hear. It was "Lead us, Heavenly Father, lead us" (611 MHB). He had a pupil, Gilbert Scott, whose grandson, Sir Giles Gilbert Scott, was the architect of Liverpool Cathedral.

The Foundling Hospital was begun by a retired Captain of the Merchant Navy, Thomas Coram. He was going to service at St. Andrew's, Holborn, when he found an abandoned baby left on the steps. He and his wife had no children, so they took the child home and cared for it. His Christian compassion was stirred when he found that this was only one of many illegitimate babies left to die. He took some more children in, but realised the need for a much more ambitious enterprise. He petitioned the King for financial aid and was eventually granted a charter to found a Home. All this took time, so he appealed for immediate voluntary funds, and found a wonderful response. In this way the 'Hospital' was built which saved thousands of young lives. Only in this century this institution moved from London to fine premises at Berkhamstead, where under the name of the Thomas Coram Foundation for Children it still receives these pathetic cases of child neglect.

But back to the eighteenth century: it may be surprising to find such enlightened attitudes, for the children were well trained. The boys were sent to sea, like Captain Coram, or apprenticed to trades; the girls were taught domestic duties; and *all* were given training in singing. We have seen that hymns were written for them. Haydn was most impressed by their performances, writing in his diary for 1792, "I was more touched by their innocent and reverent music than by anything I had ever heard". Handel, too, encouraged them and gave them an organ on which he had played - still carefully preserved, and he left them a manuscript copy of 'The Messiah' from which he had often conducted the children, in his will. The list of musicians, literary men and artists who helped is a long one, even Hogarth, who satirised almost everything, having good words to say for them and donating paintings to help the funds.

There were huge united services at St. Paul's Cathedral, when contemporary accounts speak of the thrill of hearing four or five thousand young voices singing heartily. They also tackled difficult music as well as straightforward hymn tunes - the florid, fugal type of tunes were composed and sung, setting the style for the so-called 'Methodist' tunes of the next century, like 'Diadem'. Cantatas and Oratorios were composed for great occasions.

The next most famous of these 'hospitals' was the Lock Hospital, founded in 1746. Here again much was specially written for them. John Wesley took a great interest here and once records hearing an oratorio performed at the Hospital Chapel and comments on the high standard. The chaplain at the 'Lock' was that gifted but strange man, Martin Madan. He compiled several hymn books and had a flair for altering other people's hymns, presumably to adapt them for juveniles. Watts's "He dies! the Friend of Sinners dies' (195 MHB) is a case in point, vastly improved on the original. He also altered Wesley's "Hark how all the welkin rings, Glory to the King of Kings" to the more familiar: "Hark the herald-angels sing Glory to the new-born King" (117 MHB).

I called Martin Madan a strange man: eager to be ordained in the Church of England, he found his attachment to Wesley a barrier, but finally reached his goal and was appointed chaplain to the 'Lock', a position of some responsibility for the whole running of the place, where he served for twenty years; then he got some strange ideas which he expressed in a pamphlet which seemed to advocate polygamy! His term of office came to an abrupt end! He did not take another job and died ten years later, almost forgotten. One of the few sad stories in hymnody.

You may wonder who were the wonderful choir trainers who got such amazing results from these children. Charles Wesley, Junior (son of the great Charles), was one; Charles Lockhart, composer of the fine tune "Carlisle", was another; also William Horsley, whose tune 'Horsley' is inseparably wedded to "There is a green hill" (180 MHB). François Barthélémon, the French violinist and conductor, was trainer for a while and permitted his 'Morning Hymn' (set to Bishop Ken's "Awake, my soul, and with the sun", 931 MHB) to be included in their hymn book.

All these held the position of organist, some for long periods, and contributed to the high musical standard; and all wrote their famous tunes for the orphans to sing, thus giving these Foundations a reputation not only for real Christian concern for the underprivileged, but also as the main centres of culture outside Cathedral choirs.

Chapter 9

THE QUIET YEARS

This is a chapter of change: the outburst of hymn production associated with early Methodism had spent itself and the enormous output of new hymns in connection with the publication of 'Hymns Ancient and Modern' was still in the future. This does not mean that nothing was happening: for Methodism it was a time of consolidation and steady progress; while for the Church of England it was a time of preparation for the future new hymn book.

First we look at Benjamin Rhodes as an example of the generation after Wesley (he was 40 years younger); then, after another 30 years, we come to James Montgomery who, though he moved about somewhat, was mainly a Methodist. He could be classed as one of our major authors, giving us a large number of hymns, so much up to date that they still sound modern in style.

Turning to the Anglican Church, we have Thomas Cotterill, who struck an important blow for the freedom to sing hymns in his Church, allowing Bishop Heber to follow discreetly in his steps; and finally, with hymns now respectable and accepted, there emerges the first *lady* to write hymns for use in Morning and Evening Prayer - Charlotte Elliott.

Here we must include Sir Robert Grant, as an instance of Scottish piety at this stage: hymns, as distinct from paraphrases of Psalms, had hardly begun to develop, and Grant's one famous hymn is still only a paraphrase of an older paraphrase.

Yet another contributor from this time with an impressive record of service was Sir John Bowring, whose Unitarian hymns have found favour with Christians of all persuasions.

BENJAMIN RHODES (1743 - 1815) - Wesley's faithful helper.

We have seen that several talented preachers who joined up with Wesley in the early days of Methodist expansion left him and went their own way for various reasons. These disappointments were in the minority, most converts being life-long, faithful servants. Benjamin Rhodes was one of these.

Born in Mexborough, Benjamin's father was a schoolmaster who, seeing his son's potential, gave him the best possible education.

When he was eleven, he heard Whitefield preach and that sermon awakened the desire to know more of Jesus and His love, so he attended Methodist meetings and several years later accepted Him as his Lord and Saviour. Keen to serve his new Master, he soon accepted the call to preach and at the age of 23 Wesley ordained him as a full-time preacher (or minister, as we should call him).

He soon became one of Wesley's most trusted helpers, his effectiveness as a preacher being enhanced by his having a fine singing voice; so it became his habit to sing a solo, reinforcing the message of his sermon - to the delight of his congregations.

As he grew older, he did it gracefully and his gentleness, dignity and depth of thinking endeared him to all.

He wrote a long poem 'The Messiah', from which verses have been taken to form the hymn "My heart and voice I raise" (115 MHB), and what a fine hymn it is, in praise of the suffering, yet triumphant Christ. This is a fitting memorial to a long and devoted life to the Lord; he began to serve so young and lived to the age of 72 - to make a span of service of fifty years. He wrote many other hymns, a lot of them for young people. It is strange that no others have survived, yet this one has the merit to be included in many books and be widely used.

When John Wesley was near to death he handed on to Benjamin Rhodes the responsibility of a fund which he had started - and which still functions today - for providing pensions for retired ministers.

Not an outstanding man, perhaps, but typical of a great army of God's faithful servants who have not even the memorial of one great hymn.

JAMES MONTGOMERY (1771 - 1854)

I hope I have not given the impression that most of our hymns were written in the quiet and seclusion of some rural vicarage, in a more leisurely age. It is true that many of our great hymns had their beginnings in such favourable circumstances, but many were born in difficulty and conflict. James Montgomery's hymns were among the latter, for they were written during all too brief spells of relaxation from the hectic and often harassed life of the editor of a newspaper - a controversial one, too!

James had a hard upbringing, his parents being earnest Moravian missionaries, who had felt the call to minister to slaves in the West Indies, moved to pity by the stories of their sufferings under the barbarous traders. Tragically, they only lived a few years after this decision, and the little orphan was left in the care of the Moravian school at Fulneck, later working at a baker's shop at Mirfield. Here he began writing poems, but he was so unhappy that he ran away to London, in the hope of finding a publisher for his work.

Nobody wanted to know about this raw, north country lad and his poetry, but when he was almost at the end of his tether he got a job with a kindly bookseller, who gave him valuable experience of the publishing trade. Here he stayed until he saw an advertisement for a clerk at the office of a paper called the 'Sheffield Register'; he was accepted and so travelled back to the north.

He found the editor, Mr. Gales, was a Liberal with very radical views similar to his own, so he threw himself into his work with zest. He had not been there long before Mr. Gales met such opposition from the vested interests he was fighting that he felt it judicious to leave England for a while! James was promoted to editor, and almost at once he was faced with a financial crisis, but he found a wealthy backer named Naylor and the paper carried on with slightly modified policies and a new name, the 'Sheffield Iris'.

Even so, James was imprisoned twice, once for an over-enthusiastic poem about the release of innocent prisoners when the Bastille was stormed (for this was during the French Revolution), and once for his account of a riot in Sheffield. The authorities watched this 'dangerous' paper closely! - all the more so because he was friendly with another great reformer, Ebenezer Elliott, author of "When wilt Thou save the people?" (909 MHB).

When he was free, James championed the cause of any who were wronged or oppressed - slaves, political prisoners, and especially the 'climbing boys' used by chimney sweeps. In his old age he had the satisfaction of seeing Lord Shaftesbury get his Bill on child labour through Parliament, forbidding sweeps to send these boys up flues and compelling them to use rods and brushes - as they still do.

Wilberforce was also making headway in his fight for the abolition of the slave trade and James was commissioned to write a condemnation of slavery, the result being his long poem 'The West Indies'. If all these activities were not enough, he found time to advocate Overseas Missions and the Bible Society - both in their very early days.

Here, then, we have a good, courageous man; but I've said nothing about the faith which was his driving force, or about the hymns he wrote; we will see about that now!

Having commented on his character and work, I need hardly say that the stand taken by James Montgomery over the social and political evils of his time sprang from a living faith in Jesus Christ. We know he had earnest and godly parents and his father had been strongly influenced by John Cennick, one of Wesley's first local preachers. (He was also the writer of some well-known hymns, as we have already seen.).

Although left an orphan while quite young, James had a volume of Cennick's sermons - probably from his father's library - and he traced his own conversion to the reading of this remarkable man's works. Understandably he joined the Moravian Church, but after some years he became increasingly associated with the social work of the Wesleyan Church, of which he finally became a member.

Some years later his church life was to take yet another turn, for a notable vicar, Rev. Thomas Cotterill, came to St. Paul's Church, Sheffield, and James collaborated with him over writing and publishing hymns (the next interesting character to look at!) This friendship resulted in his finally becoming a member of the Church of England, which he remained until his death at the age of 83.

When asked by a friend which of his works would live, James replied with a smile, "None, sir, nothing but a few of my hymns". How right he was! Many consider him to be the greatest of all *lay* hymn writers.

His carol "Angels from the realms of glory" (119 MHB) was published in the 'Sheffield Iris' on Christmas Eve, 1816, and is still one of the most popular of our Christmas hymns; "Stand up and bless the Lord" (685 MHB) was written for the Sunday School Anniversary at the Wesleyan Church in Sheffield; and "Hail to the Lord's Anointed" (245 MHB) he wrote and recited for a Wesleyan Missionary Meeting at Liverpool.

The hymn "Sow in the morn thy seed" (599 MHB) was inspired and written in country familiar to readers living in Gloucestershire and Worcestershire. James was travelling (by stage coach) from Gloucester to Bromsgrove, through Tewkesbury and Worcester, when he became interested in groups of women working in the fields. Being a real townsman, he had no idea what they were doing and was told they were 'dibbling' seeds, that is, making holes with a pointed stick and dropping one or two seeds in each hole - this, it was explained, resulted in great economy, for seed was expensive. Being a newspaper man and a skilful propagandist, his remark was typical: "Give me broadcast sowing - in liberal handfuls!" This set him thinking, as they journeyed, of sowing the seed of the Gospel - the free Gospel that we can afford to scatter freely. On arrival at Bromsgrove, where they were to stay the night, he quickly wrote out this hymn which he entitled "The field of the world". It was first sung at the Sheffield Sunday School Union Whitsuntide Festival, 1832.

Many other hymns by Montgomery are to be found by looking up the index of authors in your hymn book.

How did he find time to write all his hymns, totalling nearly five hundred? The answer is that (a) he wrote many in his youth, when he was in uncongenial employment; (b) when he had become a journalist he found writing on spiritual themes a relaxation; and (c) we must remember his terms of imprisonment, for conscience's sake, for in this way he could escape from the miseries of his enforced idleness.

He is buried in Sheffield, where he laboured so long. Inscribed on his statue, over the grave, is the last verse of Hymn No. 533 (MHB):

"O Thou by whom we come to God,
　The Life, the Truth, the Way!
The path of prayer Thyself hast trod:
　Lord! teach us how to pray."

THOMAS COTTERILL (1779 - 1823)

We are looking now at a strangely neglected author and collector of hymns: there is only one of his hymns in the Methodist Hymn Book, No. 762 "In memory of the Saviour's love", a simple sacramental hymn which is occasionally used. Yet Thomas Cotterill was a courageous innovator, playing an important part in breaking down stubborn prejudices and creating a demand for hymnody in the Anglican Church. His work culminated in the publication of 'Hymns Ancient and Modern' half a century later.

Thomas was born in Cannock, educated in Birmingham, and graduated at St. John's College, Cambridge, evidently brilliantly, for he was later elected to a fellowship. After his ordination he served as curate at Uttoxeter, where he soon showed his hand as a go ahead evangelical preacher who used that new - and rather suspect - aid to drive home his themes, the congregational hymn. The results were distinctly encouraging and no trouble was caused.

Then he moved to become vicar at St. Paul's, Sheffield, a largely working-class parish, where he looked forward to introducing his newly compiled hymn book with even more success. He did not count on a group of hard-line anti-evangelicals who raised a storm of protest, objecting that hymns were illegal, as they were no part of any set service in the Book of Common Prayer. They even took their case to the 'top of the tree' - to the Archbishop of York, Dr. Vernon Harcourt, to be tried at the Consistory Court.

This was a time of great disappointment and anxiety for Thomas, but it was a relief for him to discover that Dr. Harcourt had a great respect for him, seeing him as a young man with a great future. We must admire the way he handled this thorny case, for by now Thomas's enemies were 'baying for his blood'. He had a quiet word with Thomas, advising him to be willing to withdraw the controversial book and to compile a new one, submitting it to him for approval, and agreeing to cut out any hymns he did not sanction. Then he said "Dedicate the new book to me". The court proceedings went without a hitch.

Overjoyed by this good man's qualified backing, Thomas set about the work, enlisting the help of the redoubtable James Montgomery - who, you will remember, was a great admirer of Cotterill's and had joined his Church. So in less than two years the new book appeared and the opponents of hymnody dared not object, for it was official!

76

It is interesting to note that this break-through was achieved at about the same time as Reginald Heber was trying out the Olney Hymns at Hodnet - in fact, the tide of hymn singing was advancing irresistibly in the Church of England in many places at this time, to come into full flood by the next generation.

How these men would have marvelled if they could have foreseen that today the B.B.C. would estimate that a world audience of 60 million listen each week to 'Sunday Half Hour' as well as several million more to the popular TV 'Songs of Praise' and other similar programmes!

REGINALD HEBER (1783 - 1826)

When the season of Epiphany comes round, it is good to think of the man who wrote what is perhaps the most popular carol for that season "Brightest and Best" (122 MHB) - Bishop Reginald Heber. The hymn reminds us that, compared with the wealth offered by the Magi, "richer by far is the heart's adoration . . ."

Richard and Reginald Heber were born at Malpas in Cheshire and both had brilliant careers at Oxford; Richard made his name in literary circles because of his wonderful library of rare books, but Reginald was the saint and hymn writer. Both are commemorated in Hodnet Church, where Reginald was Rector - I remember seeing their memorials when I visited the church some years ago.

Reginald began writing poetry early and won the coveted Newdigate prize while at Oxford, but soon realised that he was called to 'care for souls'. Although his father was lord of the manor, he was no formal incumbent - someone describes him "counselling his people in their troubles, comforting them in distress, kneeling at sick-beds at the hazard of his own life, exhorting and encouraging: where there was strife, a peace-maker; where there was want, a free giver; weeping and praying for the bereaved - never have I seen such Christian love!"

Heber was also deeply concerned about the state of singing in church, but confessed he had "High Church scruples against hymns in worship". It is difficult for us to imagine what Anglican worship was like then, before any official hymn book existed, and when authorities frowned severely on any attempt to include hymns in the services. Nevertheless he wrote to a friend "My psalm-singing continues bad - can you tell me where I can purchase Cowper's 'Olney Hymns' with music and smaller size without music to put in the seats? I admire many and they may draw more people to join in the singing". He felt, like others at that time, that hymns were a powerful influence with dissenters and that the Church had better regulate them instead of suppressing them. Thus he began to write verses worthy of Christian worship. He was his own severest critic; he said, "I avoided all fulsome, indecorous or erotic language to HIM whom no unclean lips dare approach". The result has been that his hymns have seldom been tampered with by succeeding generations.

"Holy, holy, holy" (36 MHB) is considered his greatest hymn - a dignified and devotionally perfect treatment of an abstract subject; "Bread of the world" (756 MHB) is on Holy Communion; and "The Son of God goes forth to war" (816 MHB) was intended to be sung on St. Stephen's Day (26th Dec.) in honour of the first Christian martyr; - each of these is a gem in its own class. "From Greenland's icy mountains" (801 MHB) is perhaps the exception; written in a hurry for a missionary service at Wrexham, it is usually abbreviated, the verse "The heathen in his blindness bows down to wood and stone" being felt too disparaging to non-Christian religions!

Heber was one of the few poets who were also good hymn writers; Tennyson praised him, Southey composed the verse on his memorial at Hodnet, and R. H. Barham (that master of impudent rhyme) wrote:

> "A poet of no mean calibre
> I once knew and loved - dear Reginald Heber."

I have left his greatest work to the end. Always enthusiastic for Overseas Missions, he was twice offered the bishopric of Calcutta, but declined because of his work at his beloved Hodnet, but when pressed a third time, he felt that this was God's call and for three years spent himself in the service of Indian Christianity. He had the joy of ordaining the first native priest and of baptising and confirming many converts. He found the climate very trying and after a big confirmation service he took a cold bath as was his custom and died from a stroke, at the early age of 43.

Heber never found time to publish his hymns, but they were in print soon after his death - so "He being dead yet speaketh" . . .

> "Vainly we offer each ample oblation,
> Dearer to God are the prayers of the poor"

CHARLOTTE ELLIOTT (1789 - 1871)

Miss Elliott was born into a devout Anglican family, two of her brothers becoming clergymen, but Charlotte loved music, poetry and art, and found that the religious life of the family did not fulfil a deep need in her, as it seemed to do for others. She was a gifted pianist, could draw and paint well, and wrote poems, including humorous verse - so what else could she need?

When she was 32 years old she had a serious illness which, in the state of medical knowledge at that time, left her an invalid for life. She seemed to adapt herself fairly well to this misfortune, using her time in the home with her varied skills, but she still was very frustrated at times with her restrictions.

A year after this, the remarkable Swiss preacher and theologian, Dr. Malan, was a guest in the home and one day, seeing Charlotte rather sad, wondered if she had a deeper need and quietly asked her if she was a Christian. She was angry, thinking that, as a guest, he was rather tactless. Wisely he dropped the subject but promised to pray for her, adding that she could be a valuable servant of Christ. The seed was sown and later she asked him how one could find Christ. "Come to Him, just as you are," was his reply. She soon found peace and an abiding fellowship with her Lord.

One might think that such a refined, talented lady would not need 'conversion', but the change in Charlotte's outlook was so marked that she accepted her disabilities and began to use her gifts for her new Master in ways unthought of before; and to the end of her life she celebrated the day as her 'spiritual birthday'.

Hymns began to flow from her pen and she developed a style which stamps most of her hymns - that is, a four-lined verse with the last line shorter than the others, making a short, crisp refrain which can hardly fail to impress itself on the memory. "Christian, seek not yet repose" (491 MHB) is a good example, with its repeated "Watch and pray" emphasising the message of each verse. What a strange hymn for an enforced recluse to write! Yet it warns of the danger of temptation from within, like a still better known line "Fighting and fears within, without" - a quotation from her best-known hymn "Just as I am", in which she repeats these opening words many times with telling effect. These words recall Dr. Malan's advice, "Come to Him - just as you are", and one might think this hymn was written when her conversion was fresh in her mind - but this was not so, it was written twelve years later, so we can see what an indelible impression this little phrase had made on her mind.

The hymn just mentioned (353 MHB) was written as the result of a rather trivial incident: Charlotte's brother had organised a charity bazaar and on the big day all was activity in the house; then when they had all gone she was left alone and there was a strange silence. As she thought of all the others busy at the hall, she felt so helpless and frustrated that she was terribly depressed. Then, to quote Bishop Moule, "She felt her troubles must be met and conquered in the grace of God". Having resolved this, she snapped out of the cloud and immediately took pen and paper and wrote these great words.

Later her sister-in-law came in, full of the news of a successful event, and there on the table was the finished hymn. Her brother often remarked towards the end of his life that, though he had been permitted to see some fruit of his long ministry, even more had been done by this single hymn of his sister's. He was yet more sure of this when, years later, after Charlotte's death, a locked box was opened and in it over a thousand letters were found from grateful people who had found help or even experienced conversion because of this one hymn. He would have been more astonished if he had known that it would be translated into many languages and its words still have the same force 160 years later.

When Charlotte was an old lady, her faith was brighter still, and as the days passed peacefully in her seaside home at Brighton she would use an appropriate figure to express her faith: "I cling to Christ as a limpet clings to a rock".

SIR ROBERT GRANT (1779 - 1838)

In Chapter 4 we looked at the disturbed life of William Kethe. Now we turn to the successful career of the man who based his most famous hymn "O Worship the King" (8 MHB) on one of Kethe's paraphrases. What a contrast! After the refugee, we come to Sir Robert Grant, with his brilliant career, proud of his descent from a soldier killed at Culloden; proud, too, to be the son of an adventurous East India merchant.

Having graduated at Cambridge, Robert was called to the Bar and continued in this profession until he was aged 46. It was then that he became concerned about the abuses and social evils of the time and felt that he might bring Christian principles to bear on them by entering politics. He contested Inverness and was elected as their M.P. the following year. His interest in India became known, so it was not long before he was appointed Secretary for the Board of Trade for India.

After some years in this post he was made a Privy Councillor, then rose to be Judge Advocate General. During this period he became aware of the plight of Jews and fought hard for their rights. He had the satisfaction of promoting a successful Bill for their emancipation. After only two years in this responsible position he was made Governor of Bombay.

It was here that he was honoured with a knighthood, but this distinguished life ended with a stroke, at the comparatively early age of 59, after a record of service in which Christian principles were constantly applied to everything he tackled.

The level of admiration for this life of philanthropic activity is shown by the fact that a medical college was founded in his honour in Bombay.

It is not surprising that a busy man like this never found time to publish his hymns, but his brother collected twelve of the best and published them a year after his death under the title of "Sacred Poems".

We have one other of his hymns "Saviour, when in dust to Thee" (726 MHB), a solemn litany, seldom used; but as with many other great men, Sir Robert Grant's name is perpetuated by just the one great hymn.

SIR JOHN BOWRING (1792 - 1872)

Not many of our hymn writers came from wealthy families - in fact it often seems that adversity 'triggers off' really great hymns. However, there are notable exceptions and John Bowring was one.

His ancestors were pious Puritans who founded a woollen goods factory several generations earlier, and by the time John was born the family business was very prosperous. It seemed quite natural for him to enter the business when he was 14. His father, realising his talents, put him to help in the quite considerable export department and soon discovered his ability as a linguist. Every language he had to learn was mastered at an amazing speed, so he was soon promoted because of this gift - not because he was the boss's son! Eventually he could speak 100 languages fluently and had a good knowledge of a hundred more!

When he was 32, John became interested in politics and joined a small group of distinguished radicals which included Jeremy Bentham and James Mill. The 'Westminster Review' (now defunct) was founded to spread their views, but it was another ten years before John entered politics and became an M.P. One of the surprising things he advocated was the use of the florin, which he hoped would lead to a decimal coinage - over 100 years ago!

After some years in the Commons he was appointed consul in Canton and then in Hong Kong, where he was made Governor and knighted for his services. Here again his skill as a linguist had full play. In addition to all these accomplishments, he wrote many books on an astonishing variety of subjects.

A brilliant career, one might think; yet he met criticism and opposition all his life because of his radical political views, which he held to the end.

But what of Sir John's religious convictions? He was a Unitarian - that is he believed in God, but his views about Jesus and probably the Holy Spirit were ambiguous. The Unitarian Church is the most liberal and fluid form of Christianity; perhaps we think of it as weak doctrinally, but its strong point was its tradition of social responsibility and service. Sir John Bowring certainly came into this category, but we shall meet this 'Social Gospel' again in the American Unitarians.

He has two hymns in our book. "God is love" (53 MHB) has a typical Unitarian tone; if you read it you will see no mention of Jesus Christ, and yet it speaks of God as only Jesus could reveal him.

The other hymn "In the Cross of Christ I glory" (183 MHB) is more surprising from a man with his views, although it is not very profound compared with other hymns on the Cross (perhaps you don't agree!). The story of the writing of this hymn is most enlightening. While consul in Canton he was called to investigate a serious riot at Macao. He found that Christian missionaries had suffered badly in the violence and their church had been burnt down by the rioters. Such was the destruction that only the west wall was left standing and on its gable, blackened but otherwise unharmed, was the cross "towering o'er the wrecks of time".

What a lesson for us and what an encouragement when we meditate on the Cross of Christ, which still "towers o'er the wrecks of time". Thanks be to God!

Chapter 10

THE NINETEENTH CENTURY

We have seen how the eighteenth century, dominated by the great names of Watts and Wesley, was a high point in the art of hymn writing, and how the end of that century saw a decline, only broken by those collaborators, Montgomery and Cotterill, who broke down the opposition to hymns in the Church of England. This left the way open for a new type of hymn, so the following years were marked by the composition of a large body of hymns, not by a few outstanding figures, but by a host of authors whose work was brought together later in the 'modern' part of 'Hymns Ancient and Modern'. The sheer number of hymns and authors means that several chapters are needed to deal with the different streams of hymnody that flowed so freely at that time.

The majority of these authors were Anglican clergy, some writing to supply a specific need - to contribute to the proposed new hymn book. It is understandable that some of this 'writing to order' was rather second-rate and was soon discarded in later editions, but much was good enough to become established in most hymn books. There is a tendency to whittle away still more 'Victoriana' in hymns, which I personally think is a pity, especially when one sees the ephemeral stuff which is replacing it.

At this point I think I should give some account of the controversies of this time, for it was against this background that the authors of hymns did their work.

When the century opened there were many abuses in the Church of England. There was much plurality - that is, a rector might hold several livings, drawing the money and employing low-paid curates to do the work; many who did their duties seemed to have their priorities elsewhere. The famous Parson Woodforde was typical of many to whom 'living it up' like country gentlemen, with good food and drink, and mixing well with the fox-hunting fraternity were the main things.

This was accepted fairly well in country parishes, where about half the people were illiterate and the educated parson was a man apart, someone to whom you looked up. In the towns the situation was different: large numbers of workers inhabited poor housing, and while education was not much better, dissatisfaction and unrest were widespread. Feelings ran high against clergy whose incomes were many times greater than those of the workers, while bishops with their astronomically large incomes (as high as £50,000 a year - a fortune in those days) were targets for special anti-clerical wrath. Parsons were mobbed and stoned, windows broken and bishops' palaces vandalised; it seemed as if the country was heading for anarchy.

Most of the clergy, except a few in remote, comfortable livings, agreed that something must be done - but what? Reform of the whole financial system of the Church was urgent - but this did not touch the spiritual problems. It is true that there were evangelical parishes where good work was still being done - like the famous Clapham sect, with their emphasis on philanthropy - but these movements were few and localised. Most clergy had opposed Wesley or were asleep and urgently needed awakening.

Proposals for injecting new life into the Church varied between the return to Catholic practices - as urged by the Oxford Movement - and the Christian Socialist movement, with its aim to remake contact with the working classes. In between were faithful, moderate men, who saw prayer, visiting and reverent ordering of the services as the supreme necessity.

There was a good deal of acrimony between the parties, but at least things were being done - the Church was waking from its slumbers.

This was the period when Philip Pusey, layman brother of the Anglo-Catholic leader E. B. Pusey, took an old German hymn by Lowenstern, with echoes of the Thirty Years War, and freely translated it to express both his misgivings and his faith:-

"See round Thine ark the hungry billows curling;
See how Thy foes their banners are unfurling;
Lord, while their darts envenomed they are hurling,
    Thou canst preserve us."   (729 MHB)
This was how desperate the situation seemed.

S. J. Stone was also on the Catholic side and he expressed a similar cry from the heart for the Church:-

> "Though with a scornful wonder
> Men see her sore oppressed,
> By schisms rent asunder,
> By heresies distressed . . ."   (701 MHB)

So in succeeding chapters we shall look at the hymns of the Tractarian, or Oxford Movement; then those that were written by men who did not think this was the best way to bring new life into their Church (including some who really disagreed with it); also we shall consider the large number of devout Anglican women whose work has made such a distinctive impact on our hymn singing. With the exception of Miss Elliott (in the previous chapter), this was a new and very important factor in the history of hymn writing.

JOHN KEBLE (1792 - 1866)

We have inherited a rich treasury of hymns from the Tractarians. These were clergymen of the Church of England who were concerned with the low level of spiritual life in their church in the first half of the nineteenth century and sought to raise it by a return to Catholic doctrine and practice. They made their views known by their preaching, and also by issuing a series of booklets entitled 'Tracts for the times' - hence the name by which they become known. Keble is credited with preaching the sermon which started the movement.

Understandably, with aims like these they were involved in a good deal of controversy and even suffered persecution. They were accused of being unfaithful to the rubrics of the Prayer Book or of being obsessed with external observances. They did indeed emphasize ritual, but also a real personal devotion to the Lord Jesus Christ through that ritual. It is this devotion that colours all their hymns that have gained popularity.

Not all these men thought exactly alike, naturally, so we find some remained zealous priests in the Anglican Church, while others with more extreme views joined the Roman Catholic Church.

The most important of the first group was John Keble - certainly the most poetic. He was born at Fairford, where his father was vicar; in fact, it seems that members of the Keble family, including John, have ministered here and in nearby Cotswold village churches right up to the present day. (A round trip of less than thirty miles would take in Fairford, with its beautiful church and the extraordinary fifteenth century stained glass - still miraculously intact, the Eastleaches, Southrop and a few other interesting places, from a suitable centre like Cirencester).

John had a brilliant academic career at Oxford, being elected Fellow of Oriel College at the incredibly early age of nineteen! He returned to Fairford when he was thirty-one, and his name is remembered in several churches in that area. At the twin Eastleach villages the crude old footbridge over the River Leach is known as 'Keble's Bridge', while at Southrop the old font was discovered and restored by him after it had been built into a wall and forgotten for centuries.

During this time he published his famous book of devotional poems 'The Christian Year', and preached the Assize Sermon which his friend, J. H. Newman, regarded as the start of the Tractarian (or Oxford) Movement. Later he moved to Hursley, Hants, where he remained until his death and where he is buried.

Keble did not write many hymns as such, but the selections from 'The Christian Year' are many and beautiful. "There is a book who runs may read" (43 MHB) and "Sun of my soul" (942 MHB) are perhaps the best known, but "When God of old came down from heaven" (276 MHB), "O timely happy, timely wise" (927 MHB), and "Blest are the pure in heart" (950 MHB) all show his poetic skill. We also have his wedding hymn "The voice that breathed o'er Eden" (775 MHB) and one translation from the Greek (already mentioned in Chapter 1) "Hail gladdening Light" (937 MHB).

JOHN MASON NEALE (1818 - 1866)

Another of the Tractarian group and a friend of John Keble, was Dr. John Mason Neale - a similar character in many ways.

He had a great flair for translating and he loved the great store of ancient Greek and Latin hymns. Feeling that they should be more widely known, he began to translate them. Others have tackled the same task, but all admit that he had the gift of rendering not only the literal meaning, but the spirit and 'feel' of the original. He did indeed unlock a world of old riches in a new way as we realise that his work includes "All glory, laud and honour" (84 MHB), "O come, O come, Immanuel" (257 MHB) and "Jerusalem the golden" (652 MHB).

We also owe to Dr. Neale the Christmas hymn "Good Christian men, rejoice" (143 MHB) and other well known translations such as "The day of resurrection" (208 MHB), "Art thou weary, art thou languid"? (320 MHB), "O happy band of pilgrims" (618 MHB) and "The day is past and over" (951 MHB). Others are: "Of the Father's love begotten" (83 MHB), "To the Name of our salvation" (93 MHB), "Jesu! the very thought is sweet" (106 MHB), "The royal banners forward go" (184 MHB), "The foe behind, the deep before" (218 MHB) and "Safe home, safe home in port" (977 MHB).

What sort of man was this, with this unusual skill? He was a humble, quiet man, unfortunately restricted by ill-health from an early age, so was never able to be vicar of a parish. He might have been pardoned if he had sunk into depression and self-pity, feeling so useless after gaining his qualifications; but he took a light job, that of warden of a college at East Grinstead, where he was able to devote time to writing; and in this obscure post he remained to the end of his life "content to fill a little space if God be glorified".

JOHN HENRY NEWMAN (1801 - 1890)

We turn now to those Tractarian hymn writers whose Catholic views were extreme enough to make the honest step of leaving the Anglican Church and joining the Roman Catholics imperative. John Henry Newman was the most famous.

His life's work was the founding and running of the Birmingham Oratory, a house where up to twelve priests lived and worshipped together and, although bound by monastic vows, devoted their time to serving the Catholic churches and schools in the city, as well as visiting hospitals, prisons and homes in Birmingham's slums.

In reading Newman's life I kept coming across references to a house at Rednal, but they were not very informative, except for the fact that Newman and many of his friends were buried there; so eventually, on a free day, we decided to go there and explore. We found a pleasant village among woods on the slopes of the Lickey Hills, 'Birmingham's Play-ground'. A few enquiries soon led us to a long drive through a wood, and a sign pointing to Cardinal Newman's grave. We came in sight of a large house with a curious extension which turned out to be the chapel. Here we found the burial ground and the names of Newman and his friends.

Three things were particularly interesting: (a) that Newman was buried in the same grave as Ambrose St. John, his most intimate friend and supporter in the work of the Oratory, who he hoped would succeed him as Superior, but whose rather early death prevented this - much to Newman's grief; (b) that another hymn writer, Edward Caswall - also a close friend and admirer of Newman - was buried, according to his wish, next to him; and (c) the most surprising - the presence (at a discreet distance!) of a *woman's* grave. This was Mrs. Wooton, who was the matron for many years at the boarding school for boys attached to the Oratory and also founded by Newman.

The house is still used as it always has been as a retreat for the fathers when exhausted by the demands of city mission work - either individually or in groups.

One of the biographies of Newman that I had just read was by Father Stephen Dessain and it was a shock to read of his sudden death. He was Superior of the Oratory for some years, and the present Superior paid tribute to his work of collecting and publishing nineteen volumes on the Cardinal's work and writings and said he had provided the groundwork for 'the cause' to have Newman canonised. So no doubt in due time he will be 'Saint John Henry Newman' - which is ironical after the bitter opposition he suffered from many within the Church of his choice, until his belated recognition by being made a Cardinal in extreme old age!

John Henry Newman was a thoughtful youth, who attended an evangelical Anglican church where he experienced a radical conversion, and was later trained and ordained, holding quite Calvinistic views. These gradually changed and he seemed to feel the need of an authoritarian Church, which he finally found by joining the Roman Church. He never married, so there was no barrier to his becoming a priest in that Church.

Although undoubtedly the greatest of the Tractarians and their most original thinker, he was not outstanding as a hymn writer. His hymns "Praise to the holiest" (74 MHB) and "Firmly I believe" (17 'Hymns and Songs' - MHB Supplement) are both selections from his famous poem 'The Dream of Gerontius', and the only other hymn that has lived is "Lead, kindly light" (612 MHB). This was written during a period of doubt as to what he should do next, the answer to this prayer being his determination to start what was later to be known as the Oxford Movement.

Newman was a complex character, appearing - as we have seen - to long for the authority embodied in Catholicism, yet having an independence of mind which did not fit in with the rigid traditionalism of most Catholics when he eventually joined them. The result was that, although attacked by Protestants for being a turncoat, he was bitterly persecuted by some leading Roman Catholics who thought he was still 'half-protestant'.

The fact was he had the inconvenient ability of being able to see both sides of any question; thus rigid Catholics like Manning thought him devious and dishonest, even unfaithful to his vows. Actually he was the most honest thinker of them all, facing up to problems which would harass the Church in the future - in fact the same problems which have had to be faced by Pope John in our time.

Not until he was nearly eighty years old did the opposition die down and a group of laymen (!) campaigned successfully for him to be made a cardinal. The advent of a new and more sympathetic Pope (Leo XIII) paved the way for this belated honour. In his own mild, forgiving words this "put an end to that which has been so great a trial for so long."

He then turned his attention to the serious problem of growing materialism, forecasting darkly that "the atheistic, scientific philosophy held by the few might in succeeding years spread to the many - this is the old pagan idea of Fate in a different form". How up-to-date these words seem! and how timeless his advice. Preaching in St. Chad's Cathedral, Birmingham, nearly a century ago, he declared that "prayer was the only valid weapon Christians could use, prayer against which the science of this day sets itself with bitterness, prayer which can bear witness to the fact that God is true and faithful, powerful and merciful".

I should like to end with two characteristic quotations from this saintly man's sermons:-

> "The thought of God, and nothing short of it, is the happiness of man - God alone is the happiness of our souls."
> "A true Christian may be described as one who has a ruling sense of God's presence with him."

FREDERICK FABER (1814 - 1863)

In thinking of F. W. Faber we are still with the group of men who became Catholics during the Tractarian Movement. Like Newman, he had an evangelical upbringing. It is interesting to note his motive for writing hymns. He was greatly influenced in his youth by the 'Olney Hymns' of Newton and Cowper, and when he became a Catholic he missed them and felt that his fellow-Catholics were deprived of a similar treasury of devotion, so he set himself to supply this need. He wrote a whole volume of hymns, but many of them were too 'Roman' in tone to be widely acceptable and those we have have been drastically pruned and altered for non-Catholic books.

Many critics have found his writings too emotional and sentimental. "Souls of men, why will ye scatter" (318 MHB) is a case in point. Warm and appealing, yet one can understand purists 'curling up' at "Was there ever kindest Shepherd, half so gentle, half so sweet". (This is what Wesley would have called "fondling expressions!")

Other hymns have a wonderful manliness, such as "Workman of God! O lose not heart" (489 MHB) and "Faith of our fathers" (402 MHB) - a strange title for a man with evangelical parents! Perhaps his greatest hymn is "My God, how wonderful Thou art" (73 MHB), a beautifully mystical contemplation of the Glory of God.

It is interesting that Faber, like Newman, found his early religious experiences leading him away from thoughts of marriage, so that when he felt the call to the priesthood he was able to accept it at once. He was a persuasive and eloquent preacher, and he also wrote many devotional books which had a great influence in his day.

He became Superior of the London (later Brompton) Oratory and it was in this capacity that the rivalry between himself and Newman began. It would be out of place and take too long to trace the causes of the ensuing quarrels between these two great personalities, except to say that Faber never really understood Newman or his efforts to prepare the Church for the crises he could foresee; and of the two, Newman emerged as the more understanding and forgiving.

Turning again to Faber's good points, his gift of persuasive words is reflected in his hymns, and Cardinal Newman, though having differed with him for so long, found his hymns a great source of comfort, their value increasing in his old age. I can understand this, for if you will forgive a personal word, I find "My God, how wonderful Thou art" a wonderful corrective if one is tempted to rush thoughtlessly into prayer or worship. Read these words slowly, thoughtfully and repeatedly and I think you will realise with Faber something of the wonder and the greatness of God, yet his amazing, forgiving Fatherhood.

REV. FREDERICK OAKELEY (1802 - 1880) and EDWARD CASWALL (1814 - 1878)

Finally, we shall think about two more of the group of men who began as Anglican clergy and 'went over' to Rome as a result of the Tractarian Movement, for this group included many writers of hymns which have gained great popularity.

If a vote were taken to decide the most popular Christmas hymn, I think "O come, all ye faithful" (118 MHB), might come top. This is a translation of an anonymous Latin hymn, by Rev. Frederick Oakeley who was incumbent at All Saints, Margaret Street, London, at the time. It seems almost the only attempt he made in this line and he wrote it for his choir to sing in the church for Christmas 1841, where it was noticed and permission sought to include it in the 'People's Hymnal'. Soon it had wider success and today no hymn book is without it, being a joyous paean of praise as well as a fine statement of the mystery of the Incarnation.

The other author, Edward Caswall, was notable as a translator but also wrote a few original hymns, one of which is "See, amid the winter's snow" (124 MHB), perhaps not the most popular carol yet, I should think, in the top ten! It bids us think on the sacrifice Jesus made when He came to earth and prays "Teach us to resemble Thee in Thy sweet humility", a *very* hard prayer. What impresses me is that Caswall was as humble as he prayed to be. He was a disciple of J. H. Newman, but unlike him was no leader of men, joining him at the Birmingham Oratory and devoting his intellectual gifts to the literary side of that establishment. Newman declared at his death that "God alone could repay his loyalty and love". As we have seen, he was buried at his wish at Rednal Oratory Home, next to his hero Newman.

Caswall's fame does not rest on one hymn alone: the tender Passiontide hymn "I met the good Shepherd" (174 MHB) shows his ability as a poet. But it is as a translator that he excelled. What a fine start to a morning service is the joyful "When morning gilds the skies" (113 MHB) - a translation from the German. He had a great admiration for St. Bernard's great poem "Jesu, dulcis memoria" and his renderings of parts of this as "Jesu, the very thought of Thee" (108 MHB) and "O Jesus, King most wonderful" (107 MHB) are the best memorial to this scholarly man who so humbly laid his gifts at his Master's feet.

REV. SABINE BARING-GOULD (1834 - 1924)

The Rev. S. Baring-Gould, author of "Onward Christian Soldiers" (822 MHB) and "Now the day is over" (944 MHB), was no ordinary man. With a formidable name like his, it is not surprising! Born into an old landowning family, he inherited his names from its various branches. His father was an odd, self-opinionated man who, after an Indian Army career, retired to the family manor of Lew Trenchard in Devon, but soon found it unbearably boring, so set off with his wife, family, servants and belongings, on a tour of Europe, staying in a hotel suite for a month or two before moving on to a new city. This lasted fourteen years with only a few brief intervals in England.

No doubt this extraordinary childhood, with no settled home and coming into touch with all aspects of European culture in his formative years, helped to make Sabine the man he became. Eventually he went to Cambridge to study for a degree and during the vacations stayed at Lew Manor, which he came to love as 'home'.

At University he became influenced by the Tractarian Movement which, with the Catholic memories of the Continent, soon made him what he was to remain, a rigid High Churchman. With a few like-minded friends, he formed a kind of 'Holy Club', vowing themselves to acts of devotion and self-denial. As might be expected, these young men were unmercifully ragged and even persecuted; but whatever they had to endure, they knew Gould would meet it with a complete indifference to criticism which was to be a strong trait in his make-up to the end of his life. He was already emerging as an individualist, even an eccentric. He constantly came into conflict with bishops and others in authority throughout his long life, and they usually had to give up in the end and let him have his own way! It is said he only attended one Rurideaconal Conference and considered it such complete waste of time that he never went again, in spite of threatenings from above!

After Cambridge he taught in grammar schools for some years before deciding to be ordained; in both these decisions he defied his autocratic father, who practically disowned him.

His first curacy was at Horbury Bridge in Yorkshire, where he built a strong Mission Church and School from scratch. It was here that he wrote "Onward Christian Soldiers" for a Whit Sunday children's procession. It is thought it was then sung to an arrangement of the Haydn tune 'Foundation' set to 133 MHB, but it was Sullivan's setting that made it famous later. It is difficult to realise in these days of tolerance (or indifference) the turmoil that was aroused by the words "With the Cross of Jesus going on before". He probably actually meant the processional cross carried before the children, but his opponents declared he was showing his Catholic colours - a quite unfounded charge.

His marriage was characteristic. At the age of thirty, a tall commanding vicar, he fell hopelessly in love with Grace Taylor, a poor but pretty and charming mill girl of sixteen. Almost illiterate and with a thick Yorkshire accent, he educated her and taught her standard English, and married her with only two witnesses present, because the marriage was bitterly opposed by his family and by the Taylors. However, his intuition was right, for the marriage was happy and successful in every way.

Finally he inherited the Devon family estate and returned there at the age of 47 to become both squire and rector - that peculiarity of his day, the 'Squarson' - and remained in the living until his death at the age of ninety. In addition to Church and estate work, he published about fifty novels and other books, studied and recorded the antiquities of nearby Dartmoor, and made a collection of West Country Folk Songs - all testifying to the wide interests and tireless energy of the man.

Here we meet someone with great gifts although many peculiarities, with whom we might easily disagree, but whose whole energetic nature was dedicated to God and was undoubtedly used by Him for His glory.

CHARLES KINGSLEY (1819 - 1875)

Did you have a copy of 'The Water Babies' when you were very young? Did you enjoy reading it? And what did you make of it? I still treasure a copy given to me by a kind aunt on my seventh birthday. Yes, I read and enjoyed it, although I could not imagine how Tom didn't drown before he had all those underwater adventures! I suppose I had a horror of water in large quantities, having fallen into the sea when I was two! Also the real meaning of the book quite eluded me.

It was not until I grew up that I knew the author, the Rev. Charles Kingsley, had been prompted to write this fairy tale by his horror at the cruelty of making little boys climb up inside chimneys. Imagine the acrid, choking soot filling eyes, nose and mouth; the grazed knees, hands and elbows as the poor lad scrambled up, cleaning the flue as he went. Add to this the fact that many sweeps were cruel men who beat their boy if he did not work well and would not hesitate to light some straw or paper under him if he would not go up as quickly as he thought he should. Good men preached from their pulpits, spoke from platforms, or wrote in their newspapers against this scandal, but Kingsley simply wrote a children's story that helped to awaken people's conscience. This became illegal - chimneys have been built smaller ever since and brushes made with detachable rods, so that never again should boys be imposed on in this way.*

Charles spent his boyhood in Devon, where his father was rector of several villages, including Clovelly. There he was a popular man, for he regularly went down to the famous little harbour to pray with the fishermen for the success and safe return of the boats, before they set off on their fishing trips. He had three clever boys, Charles being the most precocious, writing poetry at the age of four. Father thought that he should move to London so that his sons could attend more advanced schools. He obtained a Church so convenient that Charles could walk to King's College daily. He went on to Cambridge and, following in his father's footsteps, was ordained.

He went as curate to Eversley, Hampshire, where he found the rather ugly eighteenth century Church in a deplorable condition, materially and spiritually. It was a situation which challenged the resources of this young parson, who threw himself into it with a will. This was the time when the Oxford Movement was seeking to remedy parishes as bad as this all over the country, but Kingsley thought their methods were misguided. He was more impressed by the teaching of that great thinker, F. D. Maurice. Like him, he questioned the doctrine of eternal punishment (at least as it was taught then) as being incompatible with the love of God, that Divine Love which he felt filling his own heart. This love expressed itself in a genuine care and concern for his parishioners, and in his wider concern for all who were oppressed. This, coupled with a natural charm, endeared him to all, with the result that the Church was built up, in both senses.

---

* See Montgomery: p. 73-4

Kingsley and Maurice, with others, were often at the centre of controversy, being dubbed 'Broad Churchmen' and 'Christian Socialists' - both terms of abuse that they came to glory in. Yet at the time neither Christianity nor Socialism had much influence and many thought them diametrically opposed to one another; but Kingsley cared for the downtrodden at a time when the rich usually closed their eyes to the privations of the poor. He had many disappointments, both from apathy in the Church and from suspicion among the working classes, yet he laid the foundations on which later Trade Unionists were to build.

Sermons, pamphlets and novels were all directed to the same end, for he passionately believed that the Christian Faith, properly applied, could solve all social as well as personal problems. When he was young he was regarded as a dangerous man, but as time went on, people were impressed by his sincerity and he was finally honoured by being made honorary Canon of Westminster Abbey. Here he had the chance to preach the all-embracing Love of God to vast congregations. His reputation as a novelist had grown, too; 'Westward Ho' still remains popular, while 'Alton Locke' contains his most explicit Christian social teaching.

I have said nothing yet about Charles Kingsley's interest in science. As a boy, he and his brothers carried out experiments in the out-buildings of the Rectory, sometimes with frightening results! He grew up to believe that science should be used to alleviate human suffering; he held that scientific inquiry was a God-given art which should be used to His glory by researching, not means of destruction, but healing. His best-known hymn summarises this conviction: "From Thee all skill and science flow, all pity, care and love" (921 MHB). This was written, typically, for the stonelaying of a new wing of Queen's Hospital, Birmingham. It began on that occasion with the verse:-

> "Accept this building, gracious Lord,
>   No temple though it be;
> We raised it for our suffering kin
>   And so, good Lord, for Thee."

When he was only 55 he became ill, and the healing science he had advocated had not yet found a cure for his disease. He became weaker, lapsing into periods of unconsciousness, but in lucid intervals he softly repeated precious Bible texts; several times he was heard to whisper the prayer he had so often used for others at their burial: "Thou knowest,

O Lord, the secrets of our hearts; Thou most worthy Judge Eternal, suffer us not at our last hour to fall from Thee.'' When his daughter was watching to see if life was still there, he opened his eyes and said quite clearly, "How beautiful God is".

So ended a life in which this beauty was shown to all. If you look in Eversley Churchyard you can see his unpretentious grave among those he treated as his equals, with the three words which are the focal point of St. John's Gospel and of Kingsley's life: "GOD IS LOVE".

We are told that when he was laid here, the crowds that came demonstrated that he was loved equally by rich and poor, high and low Churchmen, and nonconformists, at a time when it was difficult to cross these man-made barriers.

Am I saying that Charles Kingsley was faultless? Perhaps in some of these chapters I have forgotten or glossed over human failings. Well, here is a man who in spite of his virtues had no time for the Oxford Movement, and he most despised those men who left his Church to join the Church of Rome, regarding them as traitors. This led him into the famous controversy with Newman, arising from an ill-considered attack on him - a controversy from which Newman emerged as the more charitable of the two great thinkers. This seems the one lapse in an otherwise unselfish and compassionate life.

Chapter 11

MORE NINETEENTH CENTURY SAINTS

REV. HENRY FRANCIS LYTE (1793 - 1847)

Henry Francis Lyte, son of Captain Thomas Lyte, received a good education, graduating at Trinity College, Dublin, with the intention of training to be a doctor. We do not know what influenced him, but he gave up that ambition and was ordained. He served his first curacy in Ireland and then moved to Marazion, Cornwall.

He seems, like the Wesleys, to have had every good intention, but found little satisfaction in his faith or his work until he visited another young priest who was very ill and feared he might die, confessing he had no peace of mind. The two began to study Scripture afresh and together found the joy of peace through full trust in Christ. The young friend died, but not before he had testified that although he had sinned "there was One whose suffering and death would atone for all his delinquencies". Henry Lyte declared that these events led him to preach as never before.

At the age of thirty he moved to Lower Brixham to take charge of the new church of All Saints. Here he built up an amazing Sunday School of 800 scholars, training seventy teachers to staff it. A high spot in his ministry was when William IV decided to visit the town. Coming by sea, he stepped ashore on the very stone that William III had landed on a century and a half earlier. Mr. Lyte welcomed him with his robed choir and the King was so delighted with his reception that he presented him with a new home - Berry House - on the headland near the town.

Henry Lyte found time to publish several collections of poems and hymns, eight of which are included in the Methodist Hymn Book. He loved to paraphrase Psalms: one of his best loved hymns "Praise my soul, the King of Heaven" (12 MHB) is based on Psalm 103, but his really famous hymn "Abide with me" (948 MHB) was his swan song - not included in any of his own books. At the comparatively early age of 54 he was taken ill with tuberculosis - what a dread killer that used to be! He was advised to move to the South - the only known way to help - so it was arranged for him to go to Nice for the winter. August was nearly over and as he lay in bed he loved to watch a robin that perched on his window sill "sweetly warning me that Autumnal hours are at hand".

On Sunday, 4th September, he astonished everyone by saying he was going to Church to preach that morning; this he did, also assisting at the Communion. He returned exhausted by the emotional as well as the physical strain, for he had a strong presentiment that this was his last sermon. As he rested in the afternoon the words of the disciples to Jesus at Emmaus kept running through his mind: "Abide with us, for it is toward evening and the day is far spent" - but he was thinking of the day of his own life. Quite suddenly these words fell into metrical form and he finished the hymn that evening, even sketching a melody to fit it.

Next day he left for Nice, but it was too late; he died within three months.

When H. W. Baker (qv) was compiling 'Hymns Ancient and Modern' he wanted to include this impressive new hymn but felt the tune was not equal to the words, so he discussed the point with his musical colleague, Dr. Monk. After thinking about it, Dr. Monk suddenly got an idea and wrote the tune 'Eventide' which has become part of the hymn, within a mere ten minutes - and to this day his tune rings out on the Brixham bells each evening.

Originally the hymn was much longer but today all books give only the five well-known verses; nevertheless many of us regret not having verses like this:-

> "Not a brief glance I beg, a passing word,
> But as Thou dwell'st with Thy disciples, Lord,
> Familiar, patient, condescending, free,
> Come - not to sojourn - but abide with me."

Many stories could be told of the helpfulness of this hymn in times of need, but none so dramatic as that of Edith Cavell's last hours. The shameful story of her trial and execution is well known, but not __

98

everyone knows that before the guards came to hustle her out, the British Chaplain went to her cell to pray with her, then together they repeated this hymn. As he left, she smiled and said, "We shall meet again - heaven's morning breaks and earth's vain shadows flee . . ."

JOSEPH ANSTICE (1808 - 1836)

When the great William Ewart Gladstone went up to University at Oxford, he quickly became friendly with an undergraduate a year older than himself, named Joseph Anstice, from Madeley in Shropshire. Gladstone soon recognised that his young friend was far more than a clever boy who had managed to get to Oxford from humble beginnings, as he put it in his own words, "not only a clever man but one of excellent principle, self-command and great industry". He noted his disciplined life and realised this was the way to real success, so he began to imitate his good habits. In their leisure time they took long walks together and Joseph led the conversation into deeper matters than wordly success - those of the spiritual life. Gladstone declared later that these talks not only knitted them closer in friendship but gave him "the light from on high to discern the right path for myself - I bless and praise God for his presence here - would that I were worthy to be his companion".

After graduating, Joseph became Professor of Classics at King's College, at the astonishing age of 22 - what an academic career! We may be sure that he had the same Christian influence with his students as he had in his own student days.

After about only four years of teaching, he began to feel unwell and eventually went to the doctor, who confirmed his worst suspicions - he had consumption, the dreaded 'white plague', so common in those days, which seemed to afflict so many intellectual characters.

Joseph was now married and he and his young wife decided he must give up his college post and do the only thing known at that time - move to a warmer climate. He would not hear of going to the south of France, as many similar sufferers did, but as a compromise moved to Torquay, where he could earn a living and use his talents by doing private coaching. Eventually, as the disease took its grim course, he had to restrict his pupils to mornings, while in the afternoons he would rest and, if he felt able, compose and dictate verses to his loving wife.

So he continued until literally his last day when, completely exhausted after the second pupil, he died later the same day.

Gladstone was deeply grieved; he noted in his diary, "Heard to my deep sorrow of Anstice's death - his friends, his young widow, the world, can spare him ill". His sorrowing wife collected his hymns and had 52 of them printed as a memorial to him soon afterwards "to show the subjects which occupied his thought during the last few months of his life". So ended a life of only 28 years, which had radiated the spirit of his Master more than some many times longer.

The hymn "O Lord, how happy we should be if we could cast our care on Thee" (551 MHB) was written during this time of trial when disease was eating away his young life. See what simple and complete trust is expressed in these lines:

"O could we but relinquish all
Our earthly props, and simply fall
On Thine almighty arms."

"Leave all things to a Father's will,
And taste, before Him, lying still,
E'en in affliction, peace."

GEORGE RAWSON (1807 - 1889)

At a service I attended recently, two of the hymns were by George Rawson. This set me thinking; I looked through the hymns of his which are in most books, and it was clear why his hymns are chosen so often, for they speak in simple terms to the heart. So many hymns were written by rather outstanding people, often starting life with a brilliant academic career, some of them great preachers or reformers whose thoughts could be above our heads. It is refreshing, therefore, to find that some hymn writers were ordinary men and women like ourselves, yet with the gift of expressing devotional thought in verse.

George Rawson was such a man. After a good ordinary schooling, he trained as a solicitor in his home town of Leeds, meanwhile growing up in the Christian life in his local Congregational Church. He practised all his professional life in Leeds and was known as a regular but unobtrusive worshipper who took an interest in all sorts of good works, but who was so shy and retiring that he shunned the limelight like the plague.

He began writing hymns and devotional meditations quite secretly, but a friend who saw them persuaded him with difficulty to publish them locally, but only under the nom-de-plume of 'A Leeds Layman'. Eventually, to his embarrassment, the identity of the author of these much appreciated contributions became known.

Perhaps it was providential that about that time a project was afoot to publish a hymn book for the local Congregational Churches, and the reluctant Mr. Rawson was roped in to help in the preparation. So, at the age of 44, this too humble man saw some of his hymns published under his own name. They were received so well that, five years later, when the Baptists were compiling a new hymn book, he was invited to serve on the committee, and many of his hymns appeared in this book.

Still having to be pushed, George Rawson published eighty of his hymns at the age of 69 and a second book when he was 78!

I won't give you the numbers of his hymns in the Methodist Hymn Book - you can look them up in the index of authors. If you do this and read the hymns, I am sure that, whether it be a hymn of praise or a quiet meditation, each one will speak of a good, quiet man who lived close to his Lord.

DEAN HENRY ALFORD (1810 - 1871)

Henry Alford was the son of a London clergyman. From an early age he was drawn to the God whom his father served. Worship in his father's Church seemed the natural expression of his deepest, inner feelings, so when he came to years of discretion he decided to train for the Church. His career at Cambridge was one of distinction and, when ordained, he served a short curacy at Ampton, Suffolk, a lovely village with its Hall, its lake and its mediaeval Church, full of treasures. Soon he was to leave these idyllic surroundings to undertake a sterner job of work at Wymeswold in Leicestershire, where he found the Church - materially and spiritually - in a shocking state. He threw his energies into putting things right, materially by raising what was then the vast sum of £3,500 to restore the fabric, and spiritually by his vigorous evangelical preaching and constant visiting.

In spite of this busy life, bringing revival to a run-down Church and parish, he found time to make a start on something which was to be his great life's work, his famous Greek New Testament. He published many books, but it was this which established him as the outstanding Greek scholar of his age. Lord Palmerston, on seeing the first volume, was influenced to offer him the office of Dean of Canterbury. Here, released from pastoral duties, he completed the remaining three volumes of this monumental work. It took all his spare time for twenty years!

When I visited Canterbury Cathedral, I noticed in the porch a plaque listing the names and dates of past Deans. My eye ran down the list until I came to Henry Alford, with his period of service. I recalled my father telling me that, in his younger days, when searching for a faith to live by, he attended the Cathedral; it was during Alford's deanery and I recalled his comment on his preaching: "Good sermons; he fed us well with Greek roots; a bit dry, but very nourishing!" It does seem that his sermons became more scholarly and less forceful as he grew older. His time at Canterbury was noted for his brotherly co-operation with the Free Churches - something almost unheard of in his time.

Now to Dean Alford's hymns: if he had written nothing else, "Come, ye thankful people, come" (962 MHB) would have ensured his immortality. No harvest festival is complete without its full-blooded note of rejoicing, yet with the solemn reminder that harvest typifies a judgement which will separate the good from the bad. "Ten thousand times ten thousand" (828 MHB) was intended to be sung on saints' days, and it was sung at his own funeral, bringing a note of triumph to what must have been a sad occasion, for he was only sixty and still at the height of his powers.

His other well-known hymn "Forward! be our watchword" (619 MHB) was written by request for a processional at a Parochial Choirs Festival in the Cathedral. He submitted some verses to the precentor, Rev. J. G. Wood, who did not think them very suitable and tactfully suggested that the Dean should walk up the nave as if he was in procession and see if any new inspiration came. He did this and "Forward! be our watchword" was the result. This talented man also enclosed a tune to fit the words, with this note: "I have put it into its hat and boots - you can add the coat and trousers!" He had added the bass to the tune and left it at that! When the great day came, a thousand choristers from all over the diocese processed up the nave of that great Cathedral, singing this new hymn. The vast congregation agreed that "the effect was quite overwhelming".

DR. JOHN SAMUEL BEWLEY MONSELL (1811 - 1875)

One year when the season of Easter was nearly with us, I looked through the joyous hymns we hoped to be singing then. I realised that only one author, John Monsell, has more than one hymn in the 'Resurrection and Ascension' section of the Methodist Hymn Book.

John Monsell was a prolific writer of hymns, having published several collections totalling nearly three hundred hymns. He loved to write them to suit special occasions: for instance, "O worship the Lord in the beauty of holiness" (9 MHB) was intended as an Epiphany hymn (although popular for general use); while "Christ is the foundation" (981 MHB) was specially written for the stonelaying ceremony of a new church in Paddington.

Many of his general hymns have retained their popularity, such as "Rest of the weary" (101 MHB), "I hunger and I thirst" (462 MHB) and "Fight the good fight" (490 MHB). It is, however, his Easter hymns that I want to mention particularly. "Christ is risen, Hallelujah!" (206 MHB) is a rousing song of exuberant joy, especially when sung to the fine tune 'Morgenlied'; "Awake, glad soul, awake, awake" (214 MHB) is a little more restrained, but has the lovely idea of linking Christ's rising again with the renewal of life in spring; for round the empty grave . . .

"Where life is waking all around,
    Where love's sweet voices sing,
The first bright blossoms may be found
    Of an eternal spring."

The author adds a note that he wrote this amid the orange and olive groves of Italy, during a winter holiday spent there for his health's sake.

Dr. Monsell was in charge of several churches during his life and finally moved to St. Nicholas, Guildford. While he was there, the state of the building made it imperative that it should be rebuilt. He took a great interest in the work as it was going on, but one day he slipped and fell, injuring himself so badly that he died soon afterwards, aged 64. If you know the church, look a few yards from the east end and you will see a bronze plaque where he fell, inscribed to his memory.

Those who knew him said that his household was an ideal one, full of the *beauty* of holiness, and that his aim in writing his hymns was to combat the distant and reserved nature of praise so often offered to HIM who is the 'altogether lovely'.

Other hymns by Dr. Monsell are "Lord of the living harvest" (793 MHB) and "Earth below is teeming" (966 MHB).

WILLIAM MACLARDIE BUNTING (1805 - 1866)

Looking through these chapters, I find that the majority of the authors I have introduced have been Anglicans. The fact is that if we exclude the two great writers, Watts and Wesley (and the latter was a faithful Anglican to the end of his days!), we find how indebted we are to the Church of England clergy for the majority of popular hymns. This is largely due to the impetus given to potential authors by the publication of the first 'Hymns Ancient and Modern'.

But now I think we should turn from these men and think about some Methodist hymn writers. One of these, William Maclardie Bunting, was the eldest son of Dr. Jabez Bunting, the famous Methodist statesman of the second generation after Wesley. William was not attracted to the activities of his powerful father, but was a thoughtful boy. At the age of sixteen he was not a committed Christian, though went regularly to church and joined in family prayers. One day he was walking over the old London Bridge (of all unlikely places!) when a text he had recently heard - "Him that cometh unto me, I will in no wise cast out" - impressed itself on his mind so strongly that he gave himself to Christ there and then. This led to his immediate activity in the church and later to offering himself for the ministry, a position for which he was most fitted.

Those who were touched by his ministry testified that his preaching had an extraordinary depth of thought and tender poetic feeling. His ability to lead his hearers through penitence to God was felt by all. The secret of this power was that he examined himself most strictly and was always humble and penitent himself. If you read the hymn "Holy Spirit pity me" (296 MHB) you will see exactly what I mean. Something of his contemplative nature will be seen in "Blessed are the pure in heart" (571 MHB). His only other hymn in the Methodist Hymn Book, written when he was only eighteen, is "O God, how often hath Thine ear to me in willing mercy bowed" (750 MHB) - a covenant hymn - again showing, even in his youth, the ruthless self examination which later made him such an effective preacher.

Perhaps these hymns are not often sung, but the hymn book would be the poorer without them, for we must never forget that it is a manual of devotion as well as a book of sacred song. This type of hymn is especially suitable and helpful for personal use. Maybe we all would be more effective witnesses for Christ if we gave time to meditate on such gems of devotion. We should certainly be able to face the duties and challenges of daily life if, like young William Bunting, we kept in mind such promises as "Whoever comes to me I will never turn away".

DR. WILLIAM MORLEY PUNSHON (1824 - 1881)

Dr. Punshon was one of a type of Methodist preachers - perhaps fondly remembered by our parents - who were great orators and who found an enthusiastic response to their preaching and lecturing. He has left us two hymns, a morning one and an evening one, both very beautiful but probably unknown outside Methodism. "Sweet is the sunlight after rain" (662 MHB) is a hymn for Sunday morning, expressing gratitude for the day of rest - at a time when workers had a six-day week, often of 60 hours, yet were often glad to devote the whole of Sunday to Christian work; while "We rose today" (666 MHB) expresses the joy of evening worship, crowning a happy day's service.

William was the only son of a godly Methodist couple who lived in this way in Doncaster. When he left school he went to work in Hull in an uncle's business. While there his mother died and he felt the loss deeply. This seemed to make him realise that however much his parents' piety might have 'rubbed off' on to him, he could not honestly say he was a Christian. Fortunately he was close enough to his father to be able to write to him telling him of his distress, ending the letter with the words "O that I knew my sins forgiven". His father replied lovingly that "God would reveal Himself to one who truly sought Him". A few days later he was walking disconsolately by the docks when he met Rev. S. R. Hall, a young probationer who was a close friend and knew something of the struggle going on in William's mind. They walked and talked together and Mr. Hall urged him to "have faith in Jesus - now".

He accepted his friend's counsel and so began a life of most remarkable Christian service. Although only sixteen, he offered himself as a local preacher only a few weeks later; he was put 'on trial' and his exceptional gifts were soon recognised and at the age of twenty he entered Richmond College to train for the ministry.

His career in the ministry fully lived up to his early promise, his preaching being of the highest order and his organising ability leading to his being elected President in turn of the Canadian and British Conferences.

Dr. Punshon is possibly best remembered for his popular lectures for which he travelled incessantly, drawing huge crowds and devoting the fees to a fund which he launched to help towards the building of churches in growing holiday centres. You may know the Punshon Memorial Church in Bournemouth, not so named because he ministered there but because the original church was largely financed by this fund. (The present modern building replaces the old one which was burned down.)

A crowded life like this was eventually to take a serious toll of his strength and at the age of fifty he became ill and only lived another seven years. In his terminal illness he still hoped to get better and have strength to throw himself into his loved work once again, but his condition worsened. His doctor called one day and William asked for a straight answer, "Am I going?". "Yes," came the reply. He then affectionately said farewell to his wife, saying "We shall meet again in heaven soon". He lay back and said quite firmly, "Christ is to me a bright reality"; then with a smile he quietly repeated the precious name of his Lord: "Jesus - Jesus" - and was gone.

ALFRED, LORD TENNYSON (1809 - 1892)

Have you ever listened to the bells ringing out the old year and ringing in the new? As we listen to their message, we could not do better than cast our minds back to a New Year's Eve over a century ago, when the poet Tennyson listened to this same sound and was inspired to write the stirring lines "Ring out, wild bells" (905 MHB). The young Queen, Victoria, had come to the throne that year and a spirit of optimism was abroad which the poet captures, but he instils into it the Christian hope "Ring in the Christ that is to be". He feels the clangour of the bells driving out all that is evil - grief, disease, party strife, false pride in place and blood - to be replaced by love, peace and brotherhood.

Another of Tennyson's hymns "Crossing the Bar" (640 MHB) was written at the age of eighty, when after crossing over to his home on the Isle of Wight, the likeness of the journey to his passing to his eternal home suggested these verses. "It came in a moment," he declared, "and I knocked it off in ten minutes - the Pilot is that Divine and Unseen, who is always guiding us."

Alfred Tennyson was the son of the rector of Somersby, Lincolnshire, the Rev. George Tennyson, who taught his large family of twelve children and gave them the run of his extensive library. This family education sent Alfred to Trinity College, Cambridge, where his brilliance was soon recognised by his winning the Chancellor's Medal for English Poetry.

At Cambridge he formed a close friendship with another bright lad, Arthur Hallam, with whom he travelled on the Continent and who later became engaged to one of his sisters; but Arthur died suddenly at the age of twenty-two and his death was a cruel blow to Alfred, who poured out his grief in his poem 'In Memoriam'. His only other hymn in the Methodist Hymn Book, "Strong Son of God" (86 MHB) is part of this great poem of immortality.

Honours were showered on him from Cambridge and Oxford Universities. He was made Poet Laureate; Sir Robert Peel granted him a Civil List Pension of £200 at the age of thirty-four; and he was twice offered a baronetcy, but refused it. However, when at the express wish of the Queen he was offered a peerage, he felt he must accept it and so became Alfred, Lord Tennyson.

That he was a Christian poet there is no doubt, although he was not very orthodox in the doctrinal sense. He did not profess to be a hymn writer and it is doubtful whether he ever envisaged any of the poems I have mentioned being sung - with the possible exception of "Crossing the Bar"; in fact, he declared that "A good hymn is the most difficult thing in the world to write - you have to be both commonplace and poetical". So the author of 'Morte d'Arthur' and many other great poems found it difficult to write hymns!

Perhaps the best assessment of his character is Stopford Brooke's tribute: "He was among those who confess Jesus as the LIGHT OF THE WORLD - as their MASTER - as their LIFE."

REV. SIR HENRY WILLIAMS BAKER (1821 - 1877)

If you travel westwards through Leominster towards Hay and Brecon, you fork left on the A.4112 road and come to the village of

Monkland. The little church is on your left; if you have time to visit it you will find that the lych gate was erected to the memory of Rev. Sir Henry Williams Baker, who was vicar there for a quarter of last century; you will also find his grave nearby.

I have wondered how this man, a Londoner, the son of a wealthy Admiral from whom he inherited his title, came to bury himself in this small village for most of his life. Had he lived longer, for he was only fifty-six when he died, it seems he would still have been content to stay there. Perhaps the reason was that he devoted a good deal of time to writing, so a small and not too arduous parish would suit his needs. He never married - it seems that, like Newman and Faber, that was not for him.

He is remembered mainly for the hymns he left us, of which there are many in all hymn books. "Lord, thy word abideth" (308 MHB) and "The King of love my Shepherd is" (76 MHB) are perhaps the best known, but "O perfect life of love" (190 MHB), though not so well known, is thought by many to be his finest. His style is so beautiful and refined that no 'improvers' have dared to try and better his hymns!

He was a great hymnologist, doing a lot of good work compiling collections of hymns; he was also a composer in a small way and there are two of his tunes in the Methodist Hymn Book, set to "Art thou weary, art thou languid?" (320 MHB) and "My Father, for another night . ." (926 MHB); but his greatest work was as editor and chairman of the compilers of the first edition of 'Hymns Ancient and Modern'. It is difficult to imagine what Anglican worship was like before this book was published or what a revolution it made when it was introduced. Of Baker's own hymns, thirty-three were included.

It is interesting to note that the organist of Monkland Church, John Wilkes, a man thirty-six years older than his vicar, found a tune that appealed to him in a Moravian hymn book he had come across. He arranged it and submitted it to the vicar, who evidently thought it was a good tune, for he set it to his harvest hymn "Praise, O praise our God and King!" (19 MHB). It is now almost impossible to imagine it being sung to any other tune.

I like the title of one of Sir Henry Baker's books "Daily prayers for those who have to work hard", for it surely shows that, in spite of his wealth and position, he had great sympathy for the farm labourers and their families in his parish.

BISHOP WILLIAM WALSHAM HOW (1823 - 1897)

I expect many readers have travelled to North Wales along the A.5 (perhaps on holiday), passing through the village of Whittington in Shropshire. If so, like me, you may have paused to admire the massive towers of the castle on the left of the road; but perhaps (also like me!) you may have cast no more than a brief and contemptuous glance at the Parish Church on the opposite side. I have since realised that I should have gone inside - and if I pass that way again I shall certainly do so - for though hardly a place of beauty, it was here that William Walsham How, a native of the county, was rector for the long spell of twenty-eight years.

The church was built in 1804 to the design of an architect named Harrison, during the incumbency of a Mr. Davies. When William How became rector in 1851, at the age of twenty-eight, his opinion of the building was not very high either, for he wrote . . .

> "We will not censure Mr. Davies,
> Now, good man, he in his grave is,
> Nevertheless the church you gave us
> Ugly is beyond comparison,
> O you dreadful Mr. Harrison."

I think this shows his sense of fun which never left him. In later years he became Suffragen Bishop of London and later the first Bishop of the newly formed diocese of Wakefield; even then, when in the company of his grandchildren, he would throw off nonsense rhymes for their amusement. His popularity with children and young people in both his sees earned him the title which most gladdened his heart - 'The Children's Bishop'.

He did, however, also have a profound side, writing many learned books, including a commentary on the gospels (which I have and still use), while his hymns reveal his diverse gifts. Possibly "For all the saints" (832 MHB) is his most popular, but his love for children is reflected in "Behold a little Child" (164 MHB) and "It is a thing most wonderful" (854 MHB). A very different hymn "We give Thee but Thine own" (923 MHB) could be a description of his work in East London, where he strove with all his power to better the social as well as the spiritual condition of the people in that area.

"Summer suns are glowing" (673 MHB) gives a hint of his love for the country, a love which had to be denied when he felt deeply that God was calling him to use his gifts for the depressed people of East

London. This must have tested his obedience, but we have seen how it was rewarded. Actually he had already refused several tempting offers of preferment before he accepted this post.

Bishop How never retired, but died quite suddenly while on holiday in Ireland, aged 74. Such was the love and respect shown for him that Wakefield Cathedral was enlarged as a memorial to him. His body was brought back to Whittington and a memorial cross erected near his grave, while the church where he had ministered so long and which he thought 'ugly past all comparison' was beautified internally with woodwork carved to his memory.

His own son declared *"He was happy because he was good;* he rejoiced in the Lord always; no matter what the anxiety or the trouble, he was always ready to turn his face to the Sun and be gladdened by the Light"*. I have seen two photographs of Bishop How at different periods of life; on both he has a serene smile - not a superficial one, but one which reveals inner happiness.

JOHN ELLERTON (1826 - 1893)

What! yet another Anglican clergyman of the Victorian era? So many seemed above the average at school, brilliant at University, almost automatically took orders and had good appointments in the church - so why one more?

Well, it is impossible to exaggerate the importance of 'Hymns Ancient and Modern' and John Ellerton played a leading part in its production. With the movement towards hymn singing in the Churches gaining momentum, he used his poetic talent for writing new hymns. The quality of his work ensured him a place on the committee appointed to launch this book, and Henry Williams Baker, its editor, regarded him as one of its most important members, for he wrote not only hymns, but essays and books on the subject. Reading some of his comments, I feel that he did, over a century ago and with much more erudition, what I am trying to do today! He thought a new impetus for hymns was needed to suit the age "but it came to us from an unwelcome source - from the dissenters, eminently from the Methodists" - a back-handed compliment!

Unfortunately ill health interfered with these activities, in fact he had to resign his rectory to live for a year in Switzerland and Italy. On his return the kindly Bishop How found him the not too demanding living of White Roding (one of the many Rodings) in Essex, with its ancient Church with Roman bricks built into the nave walls.

His health improved enough for him to take an active part in the 1889 revision of 'Hymns Ancient and Modern'. Again his great experience made him most valuable. He was nominated as an Honorary Canon of St. Albans, but he was never installed, for ill health again laid him low, this time with severe paralysis from which he did not recover.

John Ellerton's contribution to hymns can be truly said to be immortal, although some of his work has been severely criticised, for he wrote some awful 'packing' to fill the new book. For example, he thought there should be a hymn for St. Bartholomew's Day, but he had a problem here, for we know next to nothing about this saint; still, he churned out some uninspired verse - a piece of chaff that was soon winnowed away with much more. In spite of this, a lot of his hymns were very fine, his strongest point being in hymns for special occasions; a glance at the index of authors will prove this. He was a lover of nature and he seems to have had a special love for the peace of evening in the country. This is borne out by the evening hymns he wrote: if he had written only one hymn "The day Thou gavest, Lord, is ended" (667 MHB), his fame would be secure for, in spite of one blemish, rhyming 'island' with 'silent', it is unique, with its broad vision of the worldwide Church praising God (perhaps linked with the optimism of the time when the Empire was expanding). In addition, he has given us "Saviour, again to Thy dear Name we raise" (691 MHB), among others. He wrote hymns for weddings and funerals which, in spite of their merits, have fallen out of favour. Who knows whether they will come back, like Victorian furniture? I think his best is the hymn for Sunday morning "This is the day of light" (660 MHB), with its reminder that the joy of Easter can be re-lived every Sunday . . .

"This is the first of days:
Send forth Thy quickening breath,
And wake dead souls to love and praise,
O Vanquisher of death!"

FRANCIS TURNER PALGRAVE (1824 - 1897)

How many readers can look back to their school days, as I do, and remember the poems we had to learn from Palgrave's 'Golden Treasury'? Whether such study gave us a taste for good poetry or just 'put us off' is a debatable point, but it is a good thing to take another look at that wonderful anthology, not unjustly considered the best of its kind. If you have a copy, why not take it down and dip into the gems of English poetry it contains?

Francis Turner Palgrave, the man who compiled this book with such good taste, was no mean poet himself and also wrote a few hymns. He thought this was the most difficult type of poem to write, because of the lofty themes one had to express.

He was the son of Sir F. Palgrave, author of many books and distinguished historian. He had a brilliant academic career, graduating with first class honours, was private secretary to the great Mr. Gladstone, whose liberal views he shared, and became the close friend of many poets, including Tennyson and Browning. Later he held a prominent post in the Department of Education, then became Professor of Poetry at Oxford University, yet was so diffident about writing hymns. He says, "My object is to try to write hymns which have more distinct matter for thought *and* feeling than many books offer - to be of use and comfort to readers". So let us look at the two in the Methodist Hymn Book.

Firstly, "O Thou not made with hands" (707 MHB). He gives this the title 'The Kingdom of God within'. Here he expressed the truth that God's Kingdom is not one of boasting grandeur and outward show, like earthly kingdoms, but . .

> "Where Christ's two or three
> In His name gathered are,"
> "Where faith bids fear depart,"
> "Where He is in the heart."

Then we have "Thou say'st: Take up thy cross" (158 MHB). This is a hesitating hymn which feels its way through difficulties and doubts to a firm faith in the last verse, with a definite commitment in the last line. I know some people have little use for a hymn like this, with its apparent wavering hold on the faith, but it is almost an autobiography of the man himself, for he seems to have inclined towards Unitarianism for a while, but later was deeply influenced by the Oxford Movement.

So this hymn may well help someone struggling through a time of doubt better than one that starts with too assured a tone.

Professor Palgrave's faith could be summed up in a couplet of his ...

"He who has framed and brought us hither
Holds in HIS hands the 'Whence' and 'Whither'."

WILLIAM CHATTERTON DIX (1837 - 1898)

In the city of Bristol, Mr. John Dix was a well known and respected surgeon who in his spare time enjoyed writing. He had been impressed with the short life and tragic death of the amazing boy-poet, Thomas Chatterton, so when his wife presented him with a little boy they gave him the names William Chatterton, and father settled down to write the life of the poet.

The parents were quite well-off, so William was given a good education, with the hope that he, too, would qualify as a doctor; but as often happens, the boy took his own line and joined an insurance company in the city. After several years' training, he took a job as manager of a marine insurance firm in far-away Glasgow. Like his father, he had a gift for writing and in his leisure would write poems.

Soon after joining the firm, William was taken seriously ill. When the doctors pronounced him out of danger he felt weak and ill and was very depressed. He had been trained to attend church and still did so when he left home, but somehow this illness drove him closer to God. He began to pray for the health and strength he so desperately needed to return to his job. He daily read the lessons as set in the Prayer Book and one day read the words of Jesus that seemed to fit his case, "Come unto Me, ye that are weary . . ." He asked for pen and paper, and although his hand was weak and trembling, he managed to write down the thoughts that came to him. The result was the hymn "Come unto Me, ye weary, and I will give you rest" (328 MHB).

"That was the turning point in that illness," he declared, and he was able to face a long, slow and frustrating convalescence, during which he wrote many of his immortal hymns. As he improved, the season of Christmas, then of Epiphany, came along, and when as usual he read the special lessons for that day, he took up his pen again and with firmer hand wrote "As with gladness men of old did the guiding star behold" (132 MHB). One more hymn which has become popular is the harvest hymn "To Thee, O Lord, our hearts we raise" (964 MHB). This was written a little later, for the Harvest services at his old Bristol Church, St. Raphael's. What a thrill for his parents to sing these words of their son who had been so ill, so far away, who still thought of his old Church with enough affection to write this specially for them!

Back in business, William had less time for writing, for his job was demanding, often very worrying. Glasgow was a busy port, with many ships coming and going daily. All needed insuring, passenger and cargo, sail and steam, for risks were greater then - no radar to penetrate that awful hazard, fog; no radio to contact anyone for help in times of danger (for Marconi was only just born); so there were often anxious days when ships were overdue. Sometimes one was lost, and then not only did William have to pay out a large sum, but he felt deeply the oppressive sense of tragedy that hung over the whole city.

One ship had set out for New Zealand loaded with emigrants; there were touching scenes as they parted from their loved ones, perhaps never to meet again - for it was a courageous act in those days to set out for this exciting new land on the other side of the world. William could not tell exactly when the ship would return, but days and weeks went by and anxiety mounted until everyone began to assume that the ship was lost. Then William recalled a little incident before she left port. The young Captain, a Christian man, came into William's office to finalise the policy for the voyage. He smiled as he read the wording where he signed his name, being described as 'Master (under God) for this voyage'. He said he was glad it said that, for he trusted God and felt he was in His hands, whatever happened.

William felt reassured and a few days later the ship was seen steaming up the estuary. The word spread and people rushed down to the docks to greet the ship, singing and dancing in a delirium of relief and joy . . . Then someone noticed William *kneeling* at the dockside, thanking God that He had honoured the trust that the Captain and he had put in Him, and many joined him in silent thanksgiving.

So we leave this good man whose work and faith were one - all to God's glory. Now an old man, a widower and his family grown up, and the longing for boyhood scenes returning, he went back to Clifton, where he lived the remaining years of his life with his married daughter.

William Dix's grave can be seen outside Cheddar's lovely Church - near the churchyard cross, if you ever pass that way.

Chapter 12

NINETEENTH CENTURY LADY AUTHORS

ANNE BRONTË (1820 - 1849)

It is strange that, while most of the men who have written our hymns were normal, well-educated men - many good Anglican clergy or nonconformist ministers - with women authors it seems different. They were mainly women of genius, sometimes eccentrics, often sufferers whose writings were the expression of their struggles with misfortune or ill-health.

Anne Brontë had something of all these qualities. The youngest of the famous and brilliant sisters, she was never strong and was always a shy and retiring girl.

Anne is not considered as great a novelist as her sisters, Charlotte and Emily, but 'Agnes Grey' and 'The Tenant of Wildfell Hall' have gained her an immortal place in the world of literature, while her poems are works of great beauty. Some of them speak tenderly of love, for she and her father's curate, young energetic William Weightman, were very fond of each other and she would have loved a home and children. William, however, was taken ill, died within a fortnight and was buried - all in her absence. It is easy to imagine the shock Anne felt when she returned home; and she never gave her heart to another.

Her upbringing was Anglican, her father being vicar of Haworth, but her mother died when she was quite young and the children were brought up by their mother's sister, Miss Branwell, who had forbidding Calvinist views. This had a disturbing effect on a sensitive child like Anne, and the fear of damnation was very real and terrible to her for a long while. Happily she was freed from this fear when she came to a simple faith in Jesus as her Saviour. Her experience is expressed in the hymn "Oppressed with sin and woe" (352 MHB), which she headed 'Confidence'. Will you read it and see how it tells of this act of faith?

During her childhood, Anne and Emily were great pals. When she grew up, Anne took a job as governess to the children of wealthy parents, but she was increasingly worried by the irresponsible behaviour of her brother Branwell. He couldn't keep a job and began drinking heavily, so she persuaded her employer to take him on as tutor to their sons, in order to keep an eye on him. While he was there he did keep more sober, yet he still gave her cause for anxiety. She prayed for him and pleaded earnestly with him, and he often expressed repentance but weakly went wrong again, until finally he was dismissed. Anne's hymn "Believe not those who say the upward path is smooth" (591 MHB) was written about this time and shows something of the burden her wayward brother was causing her to bear.

The year 1848 was one of tragedy for the Brontë family; Branwell died - a broken young man, a hopeless alcoholic - and later Emily died of consumption. Anne was unwell at the time and it was obvious that she also had the same dread disease. She died early the next year; - all within twelve months.

When the disease was diagnosed and she was told of the probability of an early death, Anne faced it with a wonderful Christian courage and calm; she went to her desk and wrote her most touching poem, part of which we have in the hymn "I hoped that with the brave and strong my portioned task might lie" (592 MHB). Charlotte says of this poem "the lines were written, the desk was closed and the pen laid aside - for ever". One does need to know these circumstances to understand this hymn - surely one which is only for personal use.

I should like to quote another verse of this poem which impressed me when I read it:-

> "I've begged to serve Thee - heart and soul
>   To sacrifice to Thee no niggard portion -
>   But the whole of my identity.
> Shall I with joy Thy blessings share
>   And not endure their loss,
>   Or hope the martyr's crown to wear
>   And cast away the cross?"

To quote Charlotte again, "her faith was sure and steadfast, on which she threw the weight of her human weakness and by which she was able to bear what was to be borne patiently, serenely, victoriously".

Summing up Anne's character, she says "longsuffering, self-denying, reflective and intelligent, she covered her feelings with a sort of nun-like veil, which was rarely lifted".

SARAH FLOWER ADAMS (1805 - 1848)

Many people tell me that the hymn "Nearer, my God, to Thee" (468 MHB) has come to mean much to them and would like to know more about the author.

Sarah Flower - for this was her maiden name - like many women of that time retained it as her second name on marriage. Her father, Benjamin Flower, an adventurous lad, went as a commercial traveller to France, got mixed up in the grim events of the French Revolution, and had to return to England. During this time he had adopted extreme radical views. He settled in Cambridge as a bookseller and proprietor/editor of the 'Cambridge Intelligencer', a local Liberal paper.

Do you remember James Montgomery getting into trouble publishing 'dangerous' views in his paper and being flung into prison for his trouble? Well, Mr. Flower was a contemporary of his and a similar sort of man. He was tried at the bar of the House of Lords and sentenced to six months in Newgate Prison. The little paper seems to have ceased publication, no doubt to the satisfaction of the authorities - all for denouncing the war with France!

While in prison, Benjamin was visited by a young lady sympathetic with his aims, who had also suffered some persecution. He fell in love with her and married her as soon as his sentence was over. An unusual romance, indeed! The couple settled down happily at Harlow, Essex, and had two little girls, Eliza and then the one who was to become a hymn writer, Sarah.

Unfortunately, tragedy in the form of tuberculosis, the 'white scourge' of those days, shattered the happiness of the little family, for Sarah was only five when her mother died, as the girls were to do later - but I am anticipating.

Benjamin managed bravely alone and gave the girls a good and surprisingly wide education, and took them regularly to a little Baptist chapel at Foster Street, a tiny hamlet a few miles out of the town. By the time he died, Sarah was twenty-four and had begun to devote her

117

time to writing, while Eliza was musically inclined and even set her sister's poems to music.

It was at this time Sarah's religious views underwent some modifications, for she joined the South Place Unitarian Chapel, Finsbury, and contributed to the book 'Hymns and Anthems' published by that chapel. "Nearer, my God, to Thee" first appeared in this book, set to a tune by Eliza. Since then the hymn has been sung to various tunes, but what happened to the original?

Sarah was described as a beautiful, tall, young women, full of wit and humour. It is not surprising that she won someone's heart - a young and successful engineer named William Bridges Adams, who was credited with the invention of the 'fishplates' to connect rails, allowing for expansion and contraction, so that trains could pass over safely in any temperature.

With her great love of good literature, Sarah became quite a success as a serious actress. The high point in her career was when she played Lady Macbeth at the age of thirty-two, but she found regular acting a great physical strain and finally had to give it up and return to her writing. This may have been the first sign of the disease which was to kill her, for after nursing Eliza until her death, she herself passed away - all within the period of a year - at the age of forty-three. All were buried in the same tomb in the burial ground at Foster Street.

Although Sarah had written several books and many hymns, "Nearer, my God, to Thee" is the only one to have survived in most hymn books. Based on Jacob's dream at Bethel, even with the reference to 'a cross' in the first verse pointing to an underlying Christian faith, it is a typically Unitarian hymn. Did Sarah believe in the One who said "No man comes to the Father but by Me" or was she content with Jacob's ladder between earth and heaven? We do not really know, but although many attempts have been made to add a specifically Christian dimension to this hymn, all have failed, for it is already a perfect expression of a *growing* reliance on God, into which we can read our own experience of the presence of the Lord Jesus Christ.

I ought not to end without saying that this great hymn has brought help to many who were 'up against it', but no example more dramatic than that of the 'unsinkable' Titanic, ripped open by an iceberg in 1912. About a third of that vast company on board had taken to the boats and the captain, seeing that few more could hope to be saved, ordered the ship's band to play this hymn (I wonder what tune?). The doomed passengers and crew joined in singing as the ship went lower, and survivors told of the indelible impression made by the singing, which went on until the final horror when the ship plunged below the icy waters and about 1,000 people were sucked down to their deaths.

It is not only in such overwhelming events that Sarah's words can be an inspiration, but in day to day living, whether in 'stony griefs' or 'on joyful wing', always aiming to be 'nearer, my God, to Thee'.

DORA GREENWELL (1821 - 1882)

It is strange that Dora Greenwell, that gentle poetess from the North, should have so impressed John Greenleaf Whittier, that tough American editor and reformer, that he wrote a preface to one of her books, praising her for "the light of Christian experience, the singular beauty of style and the steady march of argument" in her poems. Indeed, she was greatly admired by many literary figures of her day.

As a girl, Dora's life seemed set to be a sheltered one. Born in "Greenwell Ford", near Lanchester, Durham - the ancestral home since the time of Henry VIII - she grew up with her brothers, two of whom were training for the ministry of the Church of England. She might have expected this lovely house, with a small river flowing by, to be her permanent home, a place where she would be able to satisfy her great love of nature all her life - but this was not to be. By the time she was twenty-five she began to realise that her parents had lived far beyond their means, and the estate had been so badly managed, that it could no longer be kept up. Finally it was all sold up, but the assets were not even sufficient to buy another, smaller house.

By this time, Dora's elder brother, William, was ordained and had been inducted temporarily to the living of the picturesque village of Ovingham, in the adjoining county of Northumberland. There was a huge rectory, and he offered the family a home with him. So, with the future very unsure, they moved in.

Was it this unsettling and humiliating experience that made Dora look to her own faith? As she worshipped at her brother's ancient Church, with its hoary Saxon tower, she became a deeply committed Christian. She threw herself into the work of the parish, visiting and bringing help to the old and the sick, and in her spare time writing her poems with a new, Christian dimension.

119

It turned out to be only two years before William was made a minor Canon of Durham Cathedral, and the problem of accommodation arose again. Providentially, the younger brother, Alan, was by now Vicar of the newly created parish of Golbourne, Lancashire, and he was able to offer them rooms in his vicarage.

What a contrast! The move to Ovingham Rectory was to beautiful countryside, but now they were in ugly, industrial surroundings; but once again Dora engaged in parish work with all her strength, but here it was so different - crowds of young people were needing shepherding, and the sympathy and understanding which were her nature found their outlet in working for these.

Soon after this her father died and William found Dora and her mother a small house near him in Durham. At last she was to have a settled home, where she could devote more time to writing and caring for her ageing and increasingly difficult mother until she died eighteen years later.

Dora felt more free, following her mother's death, to do what she had been longing to do for some time - move to London to be nearer those who up till now had been pen friends, the other lady poets of her time:- Christina Rossetti, Jean Ingelow and Elizabeth Barrett Browning. So, at the age of fifty, and feeling financially more secure from the royalties on her books, she moved to a house in Westminster, where she could more easily enjoy the fellowship of these kindred souls. Her health began to give rise to anxiety after a few years, so she was eventually persuaded to move to Clifton, Bristol, to live with her brother who was now vicar there. She was a sick woman, and an accident hastened the end; she died there a year later at the age of sixty-one.

All Dora's poems are marked by great tenderness and sensitivity, many taking her observations of nature and spiritualising them. For example, in her poem 'The Sunflower' one might wonder what thoughts could be prompted by this large, coarse flower; but this is her reaction . . .

> "I lift my golden orb to His -
> Unsmitten when the roses die."

In her hymns, Dora is more direct. "And art Thou come with us to dwell?" (259 MHB) is from her 'Songs of Salvation' and represents a new vision, especially for her time, of the Advent of Christ; while "I am not skilled to understand what God hath willed, what God hath planned" (381 MHB) is surely one of the greatest and yet most intimate meditations on the Atoning work of Christ that we have.

I feel this latter hymn is the central point of this good woman's creed. It is a good hymn to sing, especially to A. E. Floyd's fitting tune 'Keston', and a good hymn to read and commit to memory, for inclusion in one's prayers if they show any signs of becoming merely formal.

> "I take God at His word and deed:
> Christ died to save me, this I read;
> And in my heart I find a need
>   Of Him to be my Saviour."

MRS. CECIL FRANCES ALEXANDER (1823 - 1895)

Major Humphries had seen much active service and it was with great relief that he retired to spend his time on his estate at Strabane, Ireland, and enjoy the company of his wife and children. His second daughter, Cecil Frances, was a specially promising girl, having developed a poetic talent at an early age. When she was twenty-three her 'Verses for Holy Seasons' were published. Being impressed by the Tractarians' emphasis on the Church's lectionary, she wrote these poems to fit the lessons throughout the year. Influential friends helped her to have several books published.

At the age of twenty-seven she married Rev. W. Alexander and became a model vicar's wife in the parishes in which he worked. With no nurses or social workers at that time, she gave herself unstintingly to the help of the poor and needy, and with no transport except her own two feet, she walked miles to relieve those in distress; how she was missed when they moved on to another parish! ·

When her own children came along, her good works were somewhat curtailed, but not stopped; but from then she felt her new sphere was, firstly, to train her own children in Christian ways. She now had evenings when the children were in bed, so was able to turn to writing again. Her hymns were nearly all written with children in mind - either her own or those in her Sunday School class. She believed in teaching the Creed systematically, and her best known hymns were written to explain the various articles. For example, "Once in royal David's city" (859 MHB) was based on "born of the Virgin Mary", while "There is a green hill" (180 MHB) illustrated ". . . was crucified, dead and buried". The opening of the creed, "I believe in God the Father Almighty, Maker of heaven and earth", inspired one of her happiest hymns "All things bright and beautiful" (851 MHB).

With all her good points, especially her love and understanding of children, Mrs. Alexander was very conscious of class distinctions and one verse of that last hymn was tactfully dropped a long time ago . . .

"The rich man in his castle, the poor man at his gate,
God made them high and lowly and ordered their estate."

Obviously this could not survive in our egalitarian society!

We must remember, however, that although Mrs. Alexander belonged to the 'upper class' and was a child of her time in thinking approvingly of the different social levels, she was a very sincere Christian who believed that any privilege she enjoyed was a gift from God, to be used, not for her own enjoyment, but for the good of others. This is an attitude we Christians should adopt towards those individuals - and nations - not so fortunate as ourselves.

See also "Jesus calls us" (157) and "I bind unto myself to-day" — her rendering of the ancient Irish "St Patrick's Breastplate" (392).

CATHERINE WINKWORTH (1829 - 1878)

It is a change, after reading the stormy lives of the authors of some of our hymns, to turn occasionally to these ladies who led a privileged, quiet and sheltered life and yet produced a list of immortal master-pieces. Do you think that is too strongly put? . . . Well, just look through the numbers of Catherine Winkworth's hymns in the index of your hymn book: "Now thank we all our God" (10 MHB); "Praise to the Lord, the Almighty, the King of creation" (64 MHB); the carol "All my heart this night rejoices" (121 MHB); and many others, some not as well known as these, but including that gem beyond price "Jesu, priceless treasure" (518 MHB).

You will also find from the index that all these hymns are translations - from one language, German. I have searched through all the hymnals I possess and I cannot find that Catherine ever wrote one *original* hymn, yet her translations are acknowledged to be among the best. Why was this?

Catherine was the daughter of a zealous evangelical clergyman, who was sufficiently well off to give her a good education. From the start she was a quick learner, excelling in literature and languages. Her father, noticing her great interest in German, gave her the opportunity - not the privilege of many girls at that time - to have an extended period of Continental travel to improve her grammar and pronunciation. Most of this time she chose to spend in Germany, and by worshipping in the churches there, she discovered a wealth of German hymns quite unknown to her which struck a sympathetic chord in her heart, exactly expressing her own religious convictions.

Thrilled with this whole new world that opened up to her, Catherine felt it would be wonderful if her friends at home could share in it, and in this way began her translations that we now know so well. She was the first to attempt this task since John Wesley had done, more than a century before. We have already seen how the Moravian hymns appealed to him, but it must be confessed that there was often a high proportion of John's thought and style in his work; Catherine, in contrast, laboured to transmit the original as closely as possible - in thought, style and even rhythm.

Between her travels Catherine lived quietly in her father's vicarage near Manchester, where she became very friendly with the Brontë sisters; then she lived in Malvern for a short spell; and finally settled in Bristol. She threw herself into many forms of Christian service wherever she was, and many were grateful for her loving acts when they were in trouble; but the sphere which most interested her was women's education. Having had such good chances herself, she felt deeply for her less fortunate sisters. The measure of her success was the endowing of two scholarships in her memory at the University of Bristol.

Catherine's great achievement, however, was the publication of the four volumes of her 'Lyra Germanica' and her 'Christian Singers of Germany'. Bishop Percival, whose beautiful memorial you may have seen in Hereford Cathedral, described the former as "one of the great devotional works of the nineteenth century."

Her life came to a sudden end as a result of a heart attack while enjoying her great love, foreign travel, at Monnetier in Savoy, at the early age of forty-nine. Her memory is perpetuated in Bristol University, and also by a plaque in the north transept of the nearby Cathedral; but, most of all, by her hymns which are in such large numbers in every hymn book.

CHRISTINA GEORGINA ROSSETTI (1830 - 1894)

Early in the nineteenth century an educated young man named Rossetti left his native Italy for political reasons and came to London to find a freer atmosphere in which to develop his talents. This he did, becoming Professor of Italian at King's College, London, then marrying a girl who was half Italian.

Two of their children were famous, their eldest son, Dante Gabriel, becoming leader of a group of artists and poets known as the 'Pre-Raphaelite Brotherhood'. Many critics class him as the leading poet of the Victorian era. When he was twelve years old, a sister was born, christened Christina Georgina.

While still quite young, Christina became a devout Christian and was confirmed in the Anglican Church. She too began to write poetry and although she never achieved the fame of her brother, many consider her the foremost lady poet of the time. Pictures of her in her 'teens show her as a beautiful, dark girl - Holman Hunt so admired her features that he employed her as a model for the face of Christ.

It is not surprising that she soon became engaged, to young James Collinson, but he became a Roman Catholic and although she loved him, she felt this division between them would make for unhappiness, so she broke off the engagement. There may have been another reason for this action, for about this time the poet W. B. Scott became friendly with the family. He was an attractive man and undoubtedly Christina fell for his charms. One cannot escape the fact that he 'led her on' before he admitted that he already had a wife (although their relationship was a curious, loveless one). Christina was deeply shocked, but even more so when she discovered that she was not the only woman on whom he bestowed his charms - in fact he boasted he could drive six horses without getting their reins tangled!

It is strange that she remained fond of him, in spite of the fact that she was repeatedly hurt by his callousness. She also met Mrs. Scott and they became firm friends.

It is significant that at this time she wrote many tender love poems, with rather pathetic expressions of unrequited affection. These happenings upset her greatly, and as a result her health had deteriorated by middle age, but it was in these later years that her faith saved her and the mystic love of Christ for the believer became her source of strength and joy, filling the aching void left in her heart by these unfortunate love affairs. Later still, she had another offer of marriage from a Mr. Caley. She declined, but he remained a loyal friend and helper all his life.

Although overshadowed by the genius of her brother, Christina became famous with the publication of 'Goblin Market' when she was thirty-two. Her sacred poetry comes, understandably, from the later years, when her reputation as a poet continued to grow.

The subject of Divine Love was her main theme and it does seem that the Christmas message was especially dear to her. Some of her Christmas poems have become popular carols: "In the bleak mid-winter" (137 MHB), "Love came down at Christmas" (138 MHB) and "The Shepherds had an Angel" (863 MHB) are well known and loved. Incidentally, Rev. Dr. F. Luke Wiseman must have been a great admirer of her poems, for he set the latter carol to music as well as two other of her hymns, including her greatest expression of her deep longing for Christ "None other Lamb" (94 MHB).

A strange character, perhaps, and not easy to understand - but, as one friend said, "her faith and love were the motive powers of her life". Another friend commented, "She never obtruded her piety, yet I felt I was in the presence of a holy woman".

JEAN INGELOW (1820 - 1897)

It is many years since I spent a holiday at Boston, Lincs, when I visited St. Botolph's Church and climbed the famous 'Stump' with its many steps - reputed to be as many as the days in the year! One of the things I missed was a memorial window to Jean Ingelow, depicting her as an elderly lady in her cap and shawl, with one of her books in her hands.

But then, that was long before 1933, the date of the publication of the present Methodist Hymn Book, and before Jean's hymn "And didst Thou love the race that loved not Thee?" (149 MHB) had hit me with incredible force when I joined with 2,000 young folk singing it in the Birmingham Central Hall. I suppose that was about 1930 and we were being introduced to a few gems from the coming new book (Recently we have been protesting against the exclusion of these words from the new one!)

But - back to Boston in 1820. William Ingelow had inherited his father's prosperous banking business, but times were getting bad; exports, on which Boston depended, had dropped alarmingly, and it was a rather worried young couple who were expecting their first baby. Business cares were swept away for a time with the arrival of a fine, healthy girl, and the new-found joy of parenthood. The proud parents took her to St. Botolph's, where she was baptised Jean after her mother.

Their joy was soon to be spoiled by further deterioration of the business, in spite of William's efforts. Recession - that dread word - was biting deeper, and by the time Jean was five, William was bankrupt. We do not know much about the following years except that William moved to Suffolk to work at another bank and, although not so well off, managed to educate his growing family well.

While still a girl, Jean showed talent as an author and poet, but she was too self-effacing to try to publish her work. She was persuaded, however, to offer contributions to 'Youth's Magazine' which were well received, so she was able to help out with the family's strained finances, which became worse when William's employers, in turn, were declared bankrupt.

During this time Jean had her own heartbreak. She had fallen in love with a young seaman, and it seemed they had a secret 'understanding' and hoped to marry when he came back from a long voyage - but he did not return and was finally reported lost at sea. We do not know how Jean faced this black time, but it seems even to have strengthened her faith. She certainly threw herself into her writing, to help her forget her grief. Some of her poems of this period have pathetic themes of young lovers being robbed of happiness by cruel tragedy.

Finally, she was persuaded to publish her first book - even then under a nom-de-plume, but Tennyson was shown a copy and was most impressed. It was not until she was forty-three that she published a book under her own name, and Tennyson, now Poet Laureate, declared, "You do the trick better than I do". He remained a close friend and source of encouragement to her, as did Christina Rossetti, John Ruskin and others.

When Tennyson died, these literary friends petitioned Queen Victoria for Jean to be appointed Poet Laureate in his place. It was acceptable for Victoria to be queen, but she would not countenance women in this literary position of honour! Being the sort of person she was, Jean might well have declined the offer had it been made, preferring to continue to serve her Lord in quiet ways.

In the words of another self-effacing poetess - Anna Waring:- "Content to fill a little space, if God be glorified". (Hymn 602).

FRANCES RIDLEY HAVERGAL (1836 - 1879)

Frances Ridley Havergal liked to be known by her full name, for the second name was after her godfather, Rev. W. H. Ridley, of whom she was very fond. She was born at Astley, Worcestershire, where her father, Rev. W. H. Havergal, was rector and where his body was brought back for burial. He was a rather outstanding man, who did a great work in searching out and publishing ancient and forgotten Church music. He was also a prolific composer of sacred music, and three of his hymn tunes are in the Methodist Hymn Book, two of them being set to his daughter's words.

Frances was constantly encouraged by her father to learn music and she was soon able to play the works of many classical composers without the music. She also began to compose, and her music attracted the attention of the great Ferdinand Hiller. We are fortunate in having two of her hymn tunes set, appropriately, to her own hymns: "I am trusting Thee, Lord Jesus" (521 MHB) and "Who is on the Lord's side" (820 MHB). This early promise, however, was not fulfilled, being crowded out by all her other activities.

Her parents began early to lead her in a life where prayer to God was as natural to her as confiding her needs in them. When Frances was five, her father moved to Worcester to become rector of St. Nicholas; and six years later her mother died - a blow from which she did not easily recover, for she declared years later that her influence still guided her.

After some years as a widower, Mr. Havergal contemplated marrying again, the lady of his choice being a Miss Cook, who lived at Okehampton. Frances spent a holiday with her, no doubt to see how she got along with her prospective stepmother. She must have been a wonderful woman, for as a result of their fellowship during that visit, Frances experienced her conversion.

Does anyone question whether a girl brought up as she was needed 'converting'? It is true that she did not seem to have wallowed in a 'slough of despond' as many a spiritual genius had done, but we must accept her own words on this event: "I committed my soul to the Saviour - earth and heaven seemed bright from that moment". This joy was typical of her; a school friend said "she was like a bird flashing into the room, her fair sunny curls falling to her shoulders, her bright eyes dancing and her fresh, sweet voice ringing . . ."

If her father had any doubts as to the wisdom of his proposed marriage, they were now removed and the wedding took place in less than three months.

As we look at Frances's later life we shall see something of the hymns she wrote and how they were related to stages in her spiritual development. For now, I suggest you read her two New Year hymns: "Another year is dawning" (954 MHB) and "Standing at the portal" (955 MHB), noting especially the line "Another year of progress" which was the key of her life, for the girlish joy and enthusiasm which marked the start of her Christian life must mature into something more adult and lasting.

So we find Frances as a young Christian, absolutely thrilled with the new relationship with her Master, yet with a longing to progress in the new life upon which she had entered. Her youthful ebullience passed into a more mature consecration of her gifts to Christ's service when she was about twenty-one. She began to realise her gifts as a poet, and she declared then and all through her life that she never had any stock of ideas: "My King suggests a thought," she said, "I look up and thank Him delightedly and go on with it! He keeps the gold and gives it me piece by piece - and no more."

About six years later came another 'step up'. It happened like this: she was staying in Germany and one day her friends, missing her, eventually found her gazing intently at a picture of Christ Crucified, crowned with thorns, with an inscription under it which she translated to mean "All this I have done for you, what are you doing for me?" Through this she felt a call to yet higher service, as a result of which she wrote the hymn "I gave my life for thee, what hast thou done for Me?" Compare this with the hymn as we have it, "Thy life was given for me" (391 MHB), and you will see it has been turned round so that the Christian is speaking to Jesus. She agreed to this alteration, but while admitting that this made it more suitable for general use, she still preferred her original version, as it recalled that vivid sense of *Christ* speaking to *her*. Even so, she did not think the verses worth publishing, but her father persuaded her to have them printed and wrote the tune 'Baca' to them - and his tune is still inseparable from her words.

We must now skip some years and we find Frances at a house party at Areley, where by her prayers and counselling she was able to lead several people to know Christ; she was so overwhelmed with joy that she could not sleep, so she employed the night writing "Take my life, and let it be consecrated, Lord, to Thee'' (400 MHB), feeling that she had been launched on another new voyage of usefulness.

The lesson this great woman's life teaches us is that, however far we have progressed in the Christian life, we have only just started, and there is scope for us all to 'grow in grace' and service to God and our fellows.

I often wonder what people like this looked like - do you? Did their faces portray their nature? Well, photographs were rare in those days, but I recently came across one of Frances, taken - I should think - when she was nearly forty. She could hardly be described pretty, for she had a broad forehead and a face that tapered down to a narrow chin; but the small mouth seemed ready to break into a disarming smile, and the keen, bright eyes seemed looking with hope and anticipation into the future. Yes, her face did show her character - an inner joy because of the nearness of her Master, and an expectation of still better things to come. Did she know the lines of her contemporary, Robert Browning? . . .

> "Grow old along with me!
> The best is yet to be,
> The last of life, for which the first was made;
> Our times are in His hand
> Who saith, "A whole I planned" . . ."

You may have noticed that most of the ladies discussed in this chapter did not marry, and perhaps you have wondered why. Some suffered the loss of their loved one, but others probably thought marriage was not for them. Frances Ridley Havergal was one of these. Someone once proposed to her and she confessed she was deeply moved that a love so pure and unselfish should be laid at her feet; yet she declined, although it nearly broke her heart to cause her lover such pain.

Was it because her spiritual love - the love of Jesus - was so deep that she could allow no rival? If you look up her hymns in the index of authors in your hymn book, and read them, you might feel this is the explanation.

If ever you happen to be in Worcester, look in St. Nicholas' Church, where you will find a memorial to Jane Havergal, the mother of Frances, who died in 1848; and also a brass, erected by his second wife and his children, to Rev. W. H. Havergal, who died in 1870.

Chapter 13

THE AMERICAN CONTRIBUTION

So far, no account has been taken of the hymnology of the United States of America, and we must therefore go back to the beginning of the nineteenth century, when the American conscience was being stirred by the great question of slavery.

Among the slaves themselves the Negro Spiritual had developed as an expression of the faith that enabled them to survive spiritually in a cruel situation. Without hope in this world, their songs concentrated largely on the hope of Heaven - like "Swing low, sweet chariot". But not all had this preoccupation, and a few, like the touching "Were you there when they crucified my Lord?", are being included in new hymnals and supplements.

This chapter will begin with notes on just a few of the influential white people who fought valiantly for the basic right of freedom for these oppressed people.

When at length emancipation was won, attention was turned to remedying the domestic social wrongs of society. Many Christians - and notably Unitarians - were concerned to preach the 'Social Gospel' and their hymns express their views.

Starting a little later, but overlapping this movement, was the quite different outbreak of revival associated with the Moody and Sankey Missions.

WILLIAM CULLEN BRYANT (1794 - 1878)

William Cullen Bryant is sometimes called America's first poet. It is true that some had written poetry before him in that vast country, but up till that time the job of colonising the New World was so big that there was little time to settle down to any of the arts; and Bryant was certainly the first to have his poetry published outside his own country. He was to be followed by greater men, such as Whittier, Wendell Holmes and Lowell, in a great literary period for America.

William Bryant was a privileged boy, the son of a doctor, who not only gave him a good education but supplemented it by his own teaching, thus giving him an auspicious start. He trained for the law and practised for ten years, writing a few poems in his spare time. These were well enough received to be published when he was twenty-three, so he became better known and was famous all over the States before he was thirty.

By this time he had lost interest in his work, for he had been bitten by the 'journalist bug', so he changed course and joined the staff of the New York Evening News, where he was to hold the post of editor for nearly fifty years.

William was brought up in the Presbyterian Church and attended Church regularly in spite of his busy life. Although not a deeply religious man, he knew the implications of his faith and was often disturbed by the social and moral evils which were all part of the news in his paper, such as poverty, slums, degrading sins and, most of all, the horrors of slavery. These all weighed on his mind; but he was an editor! . . . he could, and would, wage war through the columns of his paper! Thus he did all he could to awaken men's consciences and to press for reforms, throughout his long life.

He wrote only a few hymns, but one which has become well-known in recent years is "Look from Thy sphere of endless day" (790 MHB). This hymn seems to have an almost modern ring, even though written well over a century ago, and it must have reflected something of American life at that time. Here are the opening verses . . .

"Look from Thy sphere of endless day,
    O God of mercy and of might;
In pity look on those who stray
    Benighted in this land of light.

"In peopled vale, in lonely glen,
    In crowded mart, by stream or sea,
How many of the sons of men
    Hear not the message sent from Thee."

Was the "peopled vale" New York? The "crowded mart" his own small town in Massachusetts? The "lonely glen", the "stream", the "sea" well-known beauty spots where man did not match up to his environment? In all these situations he prays . . .

> "Send forth Thy heralds, Lord, to call
> The thoughtless young, the hardened old
> . . . . till all
> Be gathered to Thy peaceful fold."

When past middle age, William began to feel the strain of his exacting job, so he took long holidays, doing what he had longed to do - to travel, especially in Europe. Two events from these travels are worth noting.

He had long wanted to meet Elizabeth Barrett Browning (who spent her early years at Hope End, near Ledbury, Herefordshire) and the opportunity came while he was travelling with the famous author, Nathaniel Hawthorne and his family. The visit can hardly have been a success, for they were accompanied by Hawthorne's young son; Elizabeth also had a son, a rather weakly boy, for whom the young Hawthorne had nothing but contempt. Somehow the boys began to quarrel and might have come to blows if the parents had not parted them. We can imagine the embarrassment of the adults and with what apologies the visitors left. When alone, Hawthorne lectured his boy for nearly causing a scene - to which he replied that if he had been left to get on with it, he could have licked him easily, with one hand tied behind his back! In spite of this incident, Elizabeth was very impressed by the elderly Mr. Bryant "with his magnificent head and his snowy white beard".

The other visit was to Italy, with a friend who was a minister. Although William had been a believer all his life, the company of this good man showed him vistas of devotional life he had never realised and he experienced a wonderful deepening of his spiritual life. This is a glorious experience many Christians have in later life.

When he reached the age of seventy, there was a celebration, at which many literary and journalistic friends gathered to thank him for his lifetime of good works and to wish him well for the future (he had another fourteen years to go.) For this occasion, James Russell Lowell, author of 'Once to every man and nation" (898 MHB), wrote a tribute which contained these lines . . .

> " . . . he sang of faith in things unseen;
> Of freedome's birthright given to us in trust."

I should like to end with one of his poems, written when he was only twenty-one, entitled 'To a Waterfowl'. He is pondering the migration habits of some wild ducks he is watching, and he marvels - as we must have done - by what power these birds could possibly find their way over such vast distances. He exclaims . . .

"He who, from zone to zone
    Guides through the boundless sky thy certain flight,
In the long way that I must tread alone
    Will lead my steps aright."

In his long life this youthful conviction was vindicated.

JOHN GREENLEAF WHITTIER (1807 -1892) - Anti-Slavery Fighter.

Once again we are thinking of a man who had journalism in his blood - the great American poet, John Greenleaf Whittier.

Let me begin by quoting some words of his which help us to understand him: "I know nothing of music and do not claim to have written *one* hymn". As John was a Quaker, he would not be used to music of any sort in worship, in fact he probably did not approve of it. What he did write were poems intended to be read, but some of the verses of these poems breathe such an atmosphere of Christian devotion that they have been used in worship in almost every denomination.

John's father, a descendant of the pioneer settlers, was a struggling farmer and John's early life was one of hard work and poverty. When only sixteen, he had an article accepted by the local paper. The editor was so impressed that he persuaded his father to let him attend the local Academy to train as a teacher. He also worked in his spare time for a shoe factory, to help the family finances. After a few years' teaching he went into journalism for a Boston newspaper and quickly rose to be editor.

Slavery still existed in America and John increasingly felt the evil of the system and began to write against it. He found that a poem in his paper stuck in people's minds more than his reasoned and often trenchant leading articles. Other anti-slavery papers also bought his poems.

At the age of twenty-nine he was elected secretary of the American Anti-Slavery Society and later that year he became editor of an extreme anti-slavery paper, the 'Pennsylvania Freeman'. Thus began the most stormy part of his career, in which he was often set upon by mobs incited by anti-abolitionists. Owners or trustees of public halls were reluctant to let their premises to the Society for their meetings, sometimes because they opposed it, but usually because they feared damage to their property. But funds were pouring in and they decided to build their own 'Pennsylvania Hall' with the newspaper offices attached, which was opened with great rejoicings. Yet within a week a mob broke in to stop a meeting, completely vandalising doors, windows and furniture. In their fury they moved on into John's offices and began to set fire to them, urged on by business men who did not want to be deprived of their cheap slave labour. John watched this wanton destruction horrified for a few moments, then disguised himself in some old clothes and a wig and surged in with the mad crowd, gathering up his valuable papers, and then out again and back in, salvaging what he could, until beaten back by the smoke and flames, as his dream building became an inferno.

Notwithstanding blows like this, like many who have risked life and limb for a good cause, John lived to see the fruit of his labours and in his old age was an honoured hero of freedom.

I wonder if, like me, you have ever imagined this man leading the traditional placid poet's life, observing the beauties of nature, with plenty of leisure to write those beautiful verses which seem to well up from a soul at peace? Well, an editor's life is a tough one at any time, and when the paper was the 'Pennsylvania Freeman' it was open war!

Now we must look at this extraordinary man's poetry. I repeat that John Whittier was a poet, not a hymn writer, although compilers of hymnals have found selected verses from his religious poems most suitable for worship. If you have a copy of these poems, this chapter will mean more to you; but you will need at least a hymn book at your elbow. In the poems every verse is a gem in its own right, even though some are very controversial, as we shall see - but these are usually not in any hymnal!

Two of the most popular hymns "Immortal love, for ever full" (102 MHB) and "O Lord and Master of us all" (103 MHB) are selections from a long poem in praise of Jesus, entitled 'Our Master'. The Quaker dislike of 'forms and ceremonies' is shown in verse six of 103, but more strongly expressed in another verse of the poem . . .

> "Nor holy bread, nor blood of grape,
> The lineaments restore
> Of Him we know in outward shape
> And in the flesh no more."

Another very popular hymn "Dear Lord and Father of Mankind" (669 MHB) comes from 'The Brewing of Soma', a poem describing how the drink 'Soma' was made from an Indian herb found to have the power of producing hallucinations and ecstasies, and consequently worshipped as divine. The poet pityingly describes these heathen rites, with a sly thrust at Christians whose worship is mere escapism. He contrasts this, in the words we know so well, with worship which is a real fellowship with Christ, leading us to "Rise up and follow" Him. This hymn epitomises his ideal of worship as a Quaker would understand it, and it is strange it has won its way into the worship of almost all denominations - except the Quakers!

The poem "Worship", from which we get "O brother man, fold to thy heart thy brother" (911 MHB), takes a similar line. Firstly there is a picture of heathen worship, this time the ghastly rite of Moloch . . .

"With mothers offering, to the Fiend's embraces,
Bone of their bone, and blood of their own blood."
Then verses deriding ritual with solemn music, and "incense clouding up the twilight nave", followed by a scathing attack on Christians who practise slavery; finally, in sharp contrast, he says . . .

"To worship rightly is to love each other,
Each smile a hymn, each kindly deed a prayer."
Less well known are "All as God wills" (629 MHB), with its immortal lines . . .

" . . death seems but a covered way
Which opens into light."
and "O Love Divine! whose constant beam shines on the eyes that will not see" (674 MHB), which has been mangled to turn it into 'long metre'. However, the third verse still remains beautiful . . .

"Nor bounds nor clime nor creed Thou know'st,
Wide as our need Thy favours fall;
The white wings of the Holy Ghost
Stoop unseen o'er the heads of all."

Better known and much loved is "Who fathoms the Eternal Thought" (513 MHB). This is made up of verses from the poem "The Eternal Goodness" which is an argument against the rigid Calvinist creed, or any doctrine which in any way obscures or denies the undying goodness and love of God, as these lines show . . .

"I trace your lines of argument;
Your logic linked and strong . . ."

. . .

> "But still my human hands are weak
>   To hold your iron creeds."

Then follow his own positive beliefs, in the verses we know so well. Each verse has its message and magic for different people: some linger on verse two "Here in the maddening maze of things", while verse eight gets through to others "I know not where His islands lift . . ." and so on. The concluding verse of the poem, which is in some books (but not the MHB), is I think worth quoting . . .

> "And Thou, O Lord! by whom are seen
>   Thy creatures as they be,
> Forgive me if too close I lean
>   My human heart on Thee!"

Finally a little known, but beautiful hymn - little known because it is so personal - "When on my day of life the night is falling" (642 MHB). It is headed "At Last". Written when John was an old man, and at his request spoken at his bedside not long before he died, this is his last word - a sublime swan song. I think verse four is especially wonderful, the expression of a great man's humble faith . . .

> "Suffice it if - my good and ill unreckoned,
>   And both forgiven through Thy abounding grace -
> I find myself by hands familiar beckoned
>   Unto my fitting place."

HARRIET BEECHER STOWE (1812 - 1896)

"The woman who started a war" . . . that is what Harriet Beecher Stowe has been called. Is it an exaggeration? Perhaps so. But the fact remains this mother of seven children, whose writing had to be sandwiched between all the duties and frustrations of bringing up a large family, wrote one book which stood out from all her other work.

The book was 'Uncle Tom's Cabin', which opened her people's eyes to the evils of slavery, stabbed their consciences awake, and helped to trigger off the American Civil War. What Bryant and Whittier did in newspapers, Harriet Beecher Stowe did in a novel.

Here we have an outstanding personality. Harriet's father, Lyman Beecher, was a minister of the old school - proud of his descent from the Pilgrim Fathers and steeped in their traditions. Among his large family he had a famous son, Henry Ward Beecher, who has been

136

described as the greatest preacher since St. Paul. It is his gifted daughter, however, with whom we are now concerned, a precocious child who astonished her teachers by the profound essays she wrote, producing at the age of twelve one entitled 'Can the immortality of the soul be proved by nature?'

Harriet trained as a teacher and worked for some years at this profession.

She always looked back with affection to a Sunday when her father seemed to soften his severe Calvinist creed and preached earnestly on 'The Love of Christ'. When they returned home she flung her arms round her father, saying "I have given myself to Jesus today - *and* He has taken me!" Through tears of joy, old Lyman gently said "Then a new flower has blossomed in the Kingdom today".

Harriet was to find that this was not the end of her battles, but the beginning of a new one - of intellect, for the Love of Jesus she had found did not fit in with the forbidding doctrines of her Church and she had to think her way to a more moderate theology.

After a few years teaching, a young widower, Rev. Calvin Stowe, asked Harriet to marry him. He was attracted to her Christian character and her sincere questing spirit, for (in spite of his Christian name) he was a forward-looking thinker, with whom she found an immediate bond; so she accepted his proposal.

Their progress in Christian thinking led them to a horror of slavery, with its barbarity and the degradation of character that went with it, and so was born in Harriet's mind the idea of a novel based on the terrible facts she was continually learning. The book that resulted has eclipsed all her other work, although her hymns remain as evidence of the supreme motivation for writing - the indwelling God, to her a glorious reality.

There are two of her hymns in the Methodist Hymn Book: "Abide in Me and I in you" - the words of Jesus - were the basis of "That mystic Word of Thine, O sovereign Lord" (469 MHB). Perhaps the most impressive and beautiful part of this hymn is verse four, where Jesus dwelling in the soul is likened to "some rare perfume in a vase of clay".

The other hymn "Still, still with Thee, when purple morning breaketh" (474 MHB) was written, so she tells us, on a bright June day when busy with the household chores, and "I was so filled with a sense of the nearness of the Master, I took a pencil, sat by an open window and committed these words to paper almost as they are now." It traces the Divine presence with us, from morning till evening, and finally on the resurrection morning comes the glorious thought - "I am with Thee!"

Like her life, Harriet's hymns speak of the joy, peace and fulfilment of a life whose secret is the indwelling of the loving, Holy Spirit, and this was shown in the many firm friendships she developed. Many famous authors were among her pen friends and felt her friendship a great privilege. She visited Elizabeth Barrett Browning shortly before the latter's death; with some premonition of this, Elizabeth said, "This may be the last time I shall see you," to which Harriet replied, "Those who love Jesus *never* see each other for the last time."

More surprising was her friendship with George Eliot, an unbeliever. I find very touching some of her pleas to this rather wistful woman: "Christ is a living presence to me, the Inspirer and Strength of my life; and to read of those who struggle for goodness without knowing Him is as painful to me as to read of those who die of hunger when there is bread enough and to spare." In old age she wrote again: "For you too, dear, I believe in the Infinite Love, though perhaps through your tears you do not see Him."

REV. F. L. HOSMER (1840 - 1929) . . . and others

The American Civil War is over . . slavery is abolished . . the land settles down to re-build. Now we look at a group of American authors who have made a quite distinctive contribution to our hymnody, Frederick Lucian Hosmer being the youngest of these.

The best known of the others were SAMUEL JOHNSON (1822 - 1882) and SAMUEL LONGFELLOW (1819 - 1892) - youngest brother of the poet - whom I include because they all co-operated in writing and collecting hymns for publication; also, Mr. Hosmer admitted to modelling his style and the theological content of his hymns on these older brethren.

All three men were Unitarian ministers and, as such, rejected the doctrine of Christ's divinity, yet they accepted Him as the supreme example of human behaviour and were most emphatic about the social implications of His teaching.

Johnson's "City of God, how broad and far outspread thy walls sublime" (703 MHB), Longfellow's challenging "God's trumpet wakes the slumbering world" (401 MHB), and Hosmer's "Thy kingdom come - on bended knee the passing ages pray" (742 MHB) are all typical of the spirit of these men. They all express a facet of the gospel which we ignore at our peril - the 'Social' Gospel. We see that, however limited their view of Jesus might have been, they all preached and lived His ethical teaching zealously and used incidents in His life to drive their points home.

This is illustrated by a hymn (not in the Methodist Hymn Book) in which Frederick Hosmer uses Christ's Transfiguration to show that the joy of worship is useless unless expressed in the path of daily duty . . .

> "Not always on the mount may we
> Rapt in the heavenly vision be."

Similarly, while not accepting the Holy Spirit as the third person of the Holy Trinity, these Unitarian ministers firmly believed in the concept of the spirit of God as an influence for good, inspiring men to follow the teaching of Jesus in a positive way. To appreciate this, please get your hymn book and study the hymns already mentioned, and also read Johnson's "Life of ages, richly poured" (908 MHB), Longfellow's "Holy Spirit, truth Divine" (288 MHB) and Hosmer's "Go not, my soul, in search of Him" (281 MHB).

It is notable that the hymn book edited by these men was entitled 'Hymns of the Spirit'. It was published as an undenominational book, but it was Unitarian in thought, and in the preface its object was stated to be "to exclude all hymns which by their traditional phraseology or out-of-date thought forms would offend the sensibilities of a cultured liberal Christian". With all these good intentions this really meant no doctrinal and few scriptural hymns: Calvin out - and Wesley almost so - and no Oxford Movement!

Hosmer himself published several books and edited some hymnals after the deaths of his older friends. He also travelled widely, lecturing on hymnody. Although he wrote many hymns, only these few have survived, many being too nebulous in thought and doctrine to be acceptable in any denomination except his own; yet he occasionally rose above his official creed to be truly inspiring, as the following verse shows . . .

> "O gift of gifts! O grace of grace,
> That God should condescend
> To make thy heart His dwelling-place
> And be thy daily Friend!" (from 281 MHB).

THE MOODY - SANKEY MOVEMENT . . . FANNY CROSBY
(1820 - 1915) and others

We have looked at the Unitarian movement of social consciousness, but now we turn to another movement in America taking place at roughly the same time - yet the two could hardly have been more different. While the former men were rejecting, with commendable intellectual honesty, any dogma that they could not believe, a surge of new faith was sweeping the States in the form of the Moody and Sankey campaigns. The one was intellectual and social in outlook, while the other appealed to the will and to the emotions. In many ways they were antagonistic to one another in their time, and this tension is reflected in attitudes to the spate of hymns produced by this evangelistic movement.

A glance through various reference books reveals that these chorus hymns are sometimes completely ignored, sometimes contemptuously dismissed as "ephemeral ditties, historically of little account", or to quote another, "This type of hymn has undoubtedly helped the inner life of many people, though it is equally certain that it has hindered others."

Just as unreasonable is the attitude that asserts that the true Gospel is found only in this type of hymn and that neglects and despises the older treasures in our hymn books.

I feel the truth lies somewhere between these two extremes, for although many of the chorus hymns were written in a hurry and many are nauseatingly subjective, placing undue emphasis on one's personal salvation in the next world, and often with tunes tending to make a sensitive musician curl up (Vaughan Williams referred to a group of these tunes as 'a chamber of horrors!') - at the same time there are many, which can be sifted out from the enormous number of them, which have good doctrine, simply and beautifully expressed, with tunes that are persuasive and appealing, and which will be loved for generations to come.

It would be impossible to give details of all the writers and composers in a chapter like this, so I will look at a few typical ones. The foremost must surely have been Fanny Crosby - I give her maiden name, for this was what her husband preferred her to use as the author of her many hymns. (She is said to have written 7,000! - so it is not surprising if some were sub-standard.)

Little Frances was born near New York to a loving devout couple, who were worried from the start by their baby's eyes, which were inflamed; so they called in a doctor, who gave her treatment that caused the loss of her sight - never to return. In spite of this she grew up to be a healthy and bright girl, doing well at school. A new school for the blind had been opened in New York - the first in America - and when 14 years old she was sent there. Later, when grown up, she returned to this school as a teacher, and here she was to meet and marry another blind teacher, Mr. van Alstyne.

At school her love of poetry showed itself and she began to write poems herself. She was also taught to knit, and after a few initial mistakes she became so good at it that she never made another mistake. At the age of twenty-four she gathered up her youthful efforts and published them under the title 'The Blind Girl and other poems', These came to the notice of William Cullen Bryant (q.v.) and the kindly seventy year old poet encouraged her to carry on - which she did.

It is strange that, although she had a good upbringing and knew most of the Bible off by heart, at the age of thirty Frances could not sincerely call herself a Christian; but in the winter of that year she attended a series of evangelical services at the local Methodist Church, finally making a full surrender to Jesus Christ during the singing of a hymn by Isaac Watts, not well known today, that ended with the lines . . .

"Here, Lord, I give myself away -
'Tis all that I can do."

After such an act of consecration, Frances very naturally began to devote her poetic gifts to her new Master's service, but it was to be many years before she was to meet Ira D. Sankey, when a bond was immediately forged between them, and he began to set her words to his simple easy-to-learn tunes, so suitable for introduction at Moody's evangelistic meetings. Although these hymns are sometimes loosely called 'Sankey Hymns', he in fact wrote very few, his strong point being to set other people's words to music, which he did so easily that he could play his tunes impromptu, with just the words before him on the organ desk!

Frances never held any hard feelings for the doctor who had blundered so badly when she was a baby, in fact she often declared that even if the doctor had made a mistake, God had not - for although she had to live in physical darkness, she was not hindered by the distractions of sight, and so could better incite others to sing God's praise.

Her best known hymns are "To God be the glory" (313 MHB) and "Blessed assurance, Jesus is mine" (422 MHB); next, I think, I would place "I am Thine, O Lord; I have heard Thy voice" (746 MHB) and "O my Saviour, hear me" (453 MHB), both of which speak of progress in holiness following conversion - something in which she passionately believed. "Rescue the perishing, care for the dying" (338 MHB) has many perceptive lines on extending spiritual help to others, for example . . .

> "Down in the human heart, crushed by the tempter,
>> Feelings lie buried that grace can restore,
> Touched by a loving hand, wakened by kindness,
>> Chords that were broken will vibrate once more."

Next to Fanny Crosby, one of the outstanding characters of this group was PHILIPP BLISS (1838 - 1876) - a striking looking man, over six feet tall, handsome and bearded, with a deep mellow bass voice. He met D. L. Moody when he was an enthusiastic Christian, thirty years old, longing to use his gifts for the glory of God. The two joined forces and Philipp's fine voice was as moving as Moody's addresses.

Philipp Bliss was born in a remote forest area of North Pennysylvania. His parents were good folk, but desperately poor, and the boy had not even heard a piano or any other musical instrument when he was ten. Yet for years before that he had made instruments from hollow reeds and wire stretched over pieces of wood, and his parents were astonished at the boy's talent for playing on these crude instruments.

This natural instinct for music was used to the full in his co-operation with Moody, but much of it was of poor quality, often dashed off between meetings or scribbled on the train as he travelled from one campaign to another. Undoubtedly his best hymn, with his own tune 'Gethsemane' set to it, is "Man of Sorrows! what a name" (176 MHB) - and even that tune is usually 'polished' by editors of hymnals. Others are "Whosoever heareth! Shout, shout the sound" (317 MHB), "Hold the fort for I am coming" and "Jesus loves me" (these last two not included in the Methodist Hymn Book).

He was good at writing a hymn to draw a lesson from something topical. A case in point is "Let the lower lights be burning" (582 MHB), which was quickly written and based on a tragic disaster in Cleveland Harbour during a furious storm. Mr. Moody used the incident as an illustration and Philipp Bliss sang this solo, leading the great audience in the chorus, with telling effect. Whether this effect can be repeated a generation or more later, when the tragedy is no longer fresh in the mind, or not known about at all, is another matter.

This joyous activity was sadly short-lived, however. Philipp and his wife had visited the old home for Christmas and were returning by train, when there was a dreadful crash; the coach caught fire and he jumped clear, but his wife could not get out and in his efforts to save her he was overcome and perished in the flames. He was only thirty-eight, and one cannot help wondering if, had he been spared longer, he could have produced more mature and finished work.

There were many more . . . W. H. DOANE, W. B. BRADBURY and others, who spent their lives writing, composing, speaking and singing at these meetings - the list seems endless. But I will pass on to the last, and possibly the most accomplished, of this group, CHARLES HOMER GABRIEL (1856 - 1932). He is noted not only for the words and music he wrote, but also as a finisher and re-toucher of the less polished efforts of his brethren who had more zeal than taste!

His best known hymn is probably "In loving-kindness Jesus came (He lifted me)" (336 MHB). I can remember this hymn coming out, hot off the press! It is a beautiful hymn, full of doctrinal truth, and it made an immediate impact on all who heard it.

Like Philipp Bliss, Charles Gabriel had a hard start, farming on the wind-swept plains of Iowa; but when he was five, a prairie school was opened only a mile away from his home and here he got to know dulcimers, melodeons and other simple instruments. This gave him a good start and later in life he earned his living as a music teacher. Like Bliss, he could sing with dramatic power at evangelistic meetings, but in the tenor range. He also composed cantatas and operettas for schools and especially loved the Negro dialect, writing songs and monologues in it.

I hope I have given a glimpse of the many men and women who were associated with the Moody and Sankey missions at the end of last century, and the Torrey and Alexander missions in the present century, and of the hymns they wrote. God used them to help many into His Kingdom then . . . and we trust He will still.

Chapter 14

INTO THE TWENTIETH CENTURY

After our excursion to America, we return to England. We also begin to leave behind the Victorian age, with its veritable flood of new hymns, and enter a period of scarcity.

The authors in this chapter were not prolific hymn writers, but were more distinguished for other activities or other types of writing. Several were poets, but even these were all quite different. Robert Bridges was a Poet Laureate; Mrs. Chant and Silvester Horne were both Christian social reformers - and perhaps we might here include that colourful character, Studdert Kennedy. John Oxenham and Laurence Housman were better known for their other writing than for their hymns, while Rudyard Kipling was in a class of his own. Another poet who was in a yet different class was the Indian Christian, Narayan Tilak, whose one beautiful hymn "One who is all unfit to count as scholar in Thy school" is the first trickle of what is now a refreshing stream of hymns coming back to our land as a direct result of British Missionary enterprise.

The reduced output of hymns may be connected with the shaking of the old certainties in the present century, yet many Christians were driven back to the basics of the Christian Faith. Of these, some gave us hymns showing modification of doctrine, others challengingly defiant.

This, then, is a 'bridge' chapter, in which we look at these interesting and varied characters whose lives spanned two centuries.

ROBERT SEYMOUR BRIDGES (1844 - 1930)

Robert Bridges was educated at Eton College and Corpus Christi, Oxford, and trained to be a doctor, but after only eight years in practice he gave it up and retired to the village of Yattendon to devote his time to writing poetry.

He was a man of refined literary taste and style, yet he has never been widely read - perhaps he was too self-critical. Most poets have written lines which are so quotable that we can use them, often without realising their origin. I cannot think of any of Robert Bridges' that have had this quality, except perhaps that pathetic couplet that so perfectly expresses a fear of the future which must lie beneath the surface of many loving hearts:

> "When death to either shall come,
> I pray it be first to me."

This haunting beauty pervades much of his work, and in recognition of his qualities he was, at the age of sixty-nine, appointed Poet Laureate.

Robert Bridges had a quite different interest in his home village: he trained the Church Choir for many years and loved the job, but as might be expected, he was highly critical of many of the hymns that were sung. "Why," he asked, "should I have to sing in Church what insults my intelligence?" So he set himself to translate old hymns from German, Latin and Greek sources, to update old English hymns, and to write new ones - all of which he compiled to form the Yattendon Hymnal. This was quite an influential little book and to-day almost all hymnals contain some hymns from it.

Undoubtedly his translations are the best known, perhaps the most beautiful being "Ah, holy Jesu" (177 MHB), a deeply affecting meditation on Christ's sufferings, from the German of Johann Heermann, a Lutheran pastor who had more than his own fair share of suffering.

"O gladsome light" (936 MHB) has already been noted (Ch. 1) but his best known and most popular translation is without doubt "All my hope on God is founded" (70 MHB), a fine paraphrase - though a very free one - of a great hymn by another German pastor, the rebellious hymn-writer Johachim Neander. Incidentally, the powerful minor chorale often sung to these words was written (or arranged) by Neander himself and bears the opening words of his hymn "Meine Hoffnung."

LAURA ORMISTON CHANT (1848 - 1923)

If I am asked "Where do you get the facts about these hymn writers?" I think the answer is that one tries the easiest methods first: a biography of two or four hundred pages can be condensed into a few pages of interesting events; then there are reference books available, each giving something different about an author; then the odd reference in a book which has nothing to do with hymns or their authors.

The difficulties arise when an author seems to have escaped any biographer's attention. Such was the case of Mrs. Laura Ormiston Chant - one of the most difficult to fish up any information about, yet - I was convinced - one of the most interesting. I am writing more fully than usual, so that this remarkable life does not get forgotten.

My interest in Mrs. Chant began years ago, when her hymn "Light of the World" (636 MHB) was frequently sung. It appealed to me, and I wondered vaguely who this woman was.

Then in 1976, opening the 'Radio Times' I saw her picture against the background of the interior of a theatre, advertising a programme entitled 'The Night we Closed the Empire'. The picture showed a very attractive woman, well dressed in the fashion of Victorian times, aged perhaps nearly forty, with a firmness about the chin and determination about the mouth - even a defiant tilt of the head which could have been the terror of any who opposed her - yet with all this, a charming, disarming smile. The caption read 'October, 1894, and a triumph for Mrs. Ormiston Chant's Purity Party'. All very intriguing - obviously I was dealing with no ordinary woman.

For a long time I got no further, until in a guide book (of all unexpected places) I read "In the Quaker burial ground at Sibford Gower, Oxfordshire, lies a lady whose name was famous in her time - Mrs. Ormiston Chant . . . she suffered much to make the vulgar music halls cleaner and sweeter than they were."

My interest was really aroused now; was she an earlier Mary White-house? I decided to make a two-pronged attack on the problem: I would write to the B.B.C. to see if they could help (having unfortunately missed the radio programme in 1976); and then I would go to find Sibford Gower as soon as I had a chance. I don't know what I expected to find, but one is always hopeful, and burial grounds often speak volumes.

The B.B.C. enquiry took a long time - it seems difficult to trace a programme six years old! Eventually I was put in touch with the programme's researcher, Ian Liston, who kindly sent me a bundle of photostat copies of extracts from obscure books and contemporary newspaper cuttings, which were most helpful.

In the meantime I had been searching libraries, only to find that no biography of Mrs. Chant had ever been written, though I did eventually find a sketchy outline of her life in an old copy of 'Who's Who'. This revealed an even more interesting career than I had expected - visits to America and the Middle East, her marriage to an eminent surgeon, and the fact that she was the mother of four children, a son and three daughters. Surely it was probable that some descendants were alive who remembered her!

The chance came to go to Sibford Gower on a fine, warm day (so necessary for looking around graveyards - possibly overgrown!) We quickly found the Quaker Meeting House in a huge graveyard with hundreds of graves; obviously the burial place for a wide area. According to Quaker custom there were no elaborate or ostentatious memorials, just low, simple headstones, all alike. There are no class distinctions among the Friends, in life or death.

After a long search we found the grave we wanted, with the bare details of Mrs. Chant's name and the dates of her birth and death - all of which we already knew. We seemed to have come to a dead end, when we noticed nearby another stone in memory of Olive Ormiston Pursaill (née Chant). The dates seemed to suggest that she could be one of Laura's daughters, and the names Ormiston and Chant that there was some pride in being connected with the redoubtable Laura. Then the idea occurred to us, could any relatives still live in the district?

While we were discussing this, a man who was obviously curious about our activities and seemed connected with the Friends, asked if he could help us. We told him our story so far. He said he had only recently come to the district but knew someone who might help, but meanwhile "would we like to go into the Meeting House?" We said we would, very much, so he let us in, leaving us to drop the latch when we left; for a little while we sat and enjoyed the unique atmosphere of simplicity and peace that such a place imparts.

To cut this long story a bit shorter, our enquiries finally led us to Banbury, to Mrs. Marjory Lester, Olive Pursaill's daughter and Laura Chant's granddaughter. Laura's later life was spent mainly in their home, so into her public life I was able to weave a little girl's memories of a much loved but very determined grandmother.

Mrs. Lester confirmed my impression that the Sibford burial ground served a number of Quaker Meetings over a wide area, including the one at Banbury, where she still worships.

Our story of Laura Ormiston Chant really begins with the famous Isambard Kingdom Brunel, who was called in by the Great Western Railway to design a bridge to span the tidal estuary of the Wye at Chepstow - a project fraught with many difficulties. His fame had already been established by his revolutionary bridge over the Thames and his ambitious design for the Clifton Suspension Bridge - but that is another story. At Chepstow he designed a bridge incorporating quite new features which 130 years later still stands and carries trains across this chasm.

Brunel found a local contractor, Mr. E. Finch, and his right-hand engineer, Mr. F. W. Dibdin, who seemed an ideal pair to construct the new bridge, and so work began on one of his great successes. The pride which the chief participants felt in their work is shown by their names being inscribed on the ironwork for future generations to admire.

Mr. Dibdin, like many Victorians, was a craftsman who prided himself on hard work and believed in strict discipline in the home, and his large family had to 'toe the line'. If they did not, they were punished severely, the boys by father and the girls by mother. The sixth child, Laura, was full of energy - and mischief - and was a bit of a rebel; she consequently seemed to draw upon herself an undue proportion of beatings. She was brought up in the Unitarian Church, so Church and Sunday School were part of her training, and a welcome part, for there she found understanding that was lacking in her parents.

When she was four years old, Laura remembered a proud day for the family, for then the wonderful new bridge was opened, with father in the limelight, as the first train steamed triumphantly over the river.

As she grew older, and probably more difficult, punishments became more frequent; but she loved Charles, a rather weakly brother, who would comfort her when she was in trouble with her parents, restoring her to happiness; so imagine her sadness when he died and her only refuge in distress was taken away. She was seventeen and felt she could face the iron discipline no longer without her dearest pal, so she packed a few things and took the train to London - with a sigh of relief as the train rattled away to freedom.

She entered the London Hospital as a nurse, and by hard work and concentration on her studies she soon rose to be a sister.

Later, she was working with a clever young surgeon, Thomas Chant, who quickly became attracted to this girl with her dynamic personality. He fell in love with her and proposed to her. Feeling that his outlook and hers were alike, she accepted, for here was a Christian man who believed in serving his God and his fellow men through his profession. They agreed, however, that their love would have to be a secret, for hospital rules would not allow an engaged couple to work together there.

Laura soon found a job as a governess to a nice couple with two little girls and here she found herself accepted as one of the family and was ideally happy - so happy that her marriage to Thomas took place from their home, her parents being antagonistic.

Now she was the wife of an eminent surgeon with a fashionable practice in Gower Street, which brought in a large income, but Thomas also had a clinic in a really poor part of London, where he treated patients who could usually only repay him with gratitude. Laura loved him dearly because of this, for it exactly matched her own desire to help the helpless.

To go back a few years, Laura had attended various Churches after leaving home, but had become attracted especially to the Baptist and Methodist Churches in slum areas, where the gospel was expressed in social work as well as in the spiritual message. Having seen the evils of drink in her hospital work, she admired their efforts through Bands of Hope and other youth activities to combat this evil and she joined with them, often speaking at their meetings - finding that she had a talent for speaking, especially to young people. She also found new ideas welling up in her mind and she wrote and produced sketches and action songs for the children.

After her marriage she continued these activities with Tom's blessing, but when the babies began to arrive she naturally had to curtail her work; but Tom was now quite well off and able to employ a nursemaid, so releasing her for more good work.

Laura was thirty-seven years old when her youngest child Olive was born. The birth was a difficult one and Laura was ill for a long time, but at last her old strength built up and she became active again.

An illuminating sidelight on Laura's character is shown by the fact that, although the family ostracised her for 'running away from home', yet when one of her sisters died, it was to her that they turned for help with the orphaned children, so she had two nieces and a nephew added to the family.

She now developed her writing of sketches, recitations and action songs, and with her self-contained concert party of seven, and herself at the piano, she toured the East End of London giving shows at Church Halls and bringing brightness to sad and drab lives.

These numbers for children became so popular that Curwens, the music publishers, accepted them and they were widely used in schools, bringing in royalties which were to come in useful later.

Later on, Mrs. Dibdin, Laura's mother, became ill, and in spite of the bitterness she had shown to her 'erring' daughter, Laura and her faithful Tom nursed her lovingly until she died.

Laura's life until this time was happy and full; but she was now to become engaged in bitter controversy. In her nursing days she enjoyed, as relaxation from her demanding job, a visit to the Theatre, Opera or Ballet - even sometimes to the Music Hall for a good laugh; and although now a wife, mother and foster-mother, she still loved some entertainment occasionally.

While enjoying this little relief, she was saddened by the crude and shocking turns that were sometimes put on, especially at the Empire, Leicester Square. Discussing this with some friends, she found that others, like herself, thought some action should be taken for the sake of young people, who they felt were being contaminated. Preliminary enquiries were made and representations made to the manager of the offending Hall, but with little result.

Imagine Laura's horror when she found that the girls ostensibly employed as chorus girls were in fact organised as prostitutes by the management. So began what came to be known as the 'Purity Party' to fight these abuses. Let a few extracts from the 'Daily Telegraph' of 11th October, 1894, tell the story . . .

"THE EMPIRE, LEICESTER SQUARE"

"In 1892 another Select Committee was appointed to investigate the current state of the Theatrical Licensing Acts. The Committee was mainly concerned with activities on the stage, but . . . prostitution and the Theatre had always been closely linked; at Music Halls the link was even more obvious. Leicester Square had become the centre of the trade in the 'nineties and the Empire . . found that its promenade was a major attraction."

(A plan of the hall is then shown, with its notorious promenade - larger in area than the seating and surrounding it on three sides. It was here that soliciting took place.)

The 'Telegraph' continues . . .

"Unfortunately two less-than-worldly Americans were solicited and stormed out to inform an English acquaintance of the outrage. Their acquaintance was that formidable campaigner against vice, Mrs. Ormiston Chant, who took the opportunity to oppose the renewal of the Empire's licence."

It would take a long time to tell of the hearings that followed and the way Laura battled on daily against opposition, insults and the clever intrigues of her opponents. It was admitted that the box-office takings did not cover the Hall's expenses, and if it were not for the promenade's attraction, it would have to close.

Laura had the 'honour' of being bitterly opposed by a young Army Officer from Sandhurst, with ambitions for a Parliamentary career, who occasionally visited the Empire. He attacked her as a 'busybody intent on interfering with the people's liberty!' - his name, Winston Churchill! Others accused her of plotting to throw useful people out of work; cab drivers and others ganged up against her.

She and her friends even picketed the queues at the Empire for support and earned themselves the banner headlines in next morning's papers "Prudes on the prowl in Leicester Square". This is only one example of the abuse she had to suffer from all quarters: Music Halls replied by staging songs ridiculing her - I heard one on the radio the other day, saying something like "Don't do what Mrs. Chant wouldn't do!" An effigy of her was burnt at the stake; her house was damaged; and a police guard had to be mounted for several months to protect her and her family.

In the end, decent public opinion prevailed and the Empire was forced to clean up; but Laura was a sensitive woman and all this caused her much mental and emotional strain. Two things kept her going: the conviction that she was doing God's will, saving young people from exploitation by unscrupulous profiteers; and the knowledge that she had the support of her loving, understanding Tom, to whom she would return at the end of a harassing day.

The reference to American acquaintances may seem surprising, but the fact was that Laura's fame as a speaker for social reform had spread to the United States, where she had already made several lecture tours; in fact, she had to rush off across the Atlantic as soon as victory was won, for another course of lectures. This disappearance from the English scene was maliciously interpreted as cowardice, for fear of reprisals!

Now followed two slightly less hectic years - yet a heroine like Laura could hardly be left alone: requests to speak at meetings and preach at churches all over the country poured in, and her amazing eloquence could sway vast audiences, yet she would as willingly address a small women's meeting - if it could be fitted in!

Then in 1896 another great cause demanded her attention. In politics Laura was a Liberal and thought highly, as many did, of the 'Grand Old Man' Mr. Gladstone; but he was now growing old and had retired from active politics, when horrifying reports of Turkish atrocities against the Armenians filtered through to England. These helpless people had risen against the Turkish officials because of their oppression and cruelty, and the rising had been savagely crushed by the most atrocious massacre imaginable. It is estimated that 80,000 Armenian Christians were brutally murdered in three years. The resentment for these atrocities still smoulders! Decent public opinion was appalled and Mr. Gladstone wrote repeated letters urging that action should be taken, single-handed if necessary, against "The Assassin of Europe."

To Britain's everlasting shame, nothing was done - on the grounds of political expediency! Laura's heart was touched by the thought of the dreadful suffering that lay behind the bald statistics, and although she could not deal with the Turks nor move the Government, there was something she could and would do.

She rallied a team of workers, begged for money, and led these brave women - social workers and nurses - travelling there to nurse the sick and injured, shelter the homeless, feed the starving and relieve suffering in every way possible. She stayed long enough to see effective relief being rendered, then travelled back to continue her advocacy of the good work. One suspects that a good deal of the financial burden was borne by the ever loyal Tom.

Again when fighting broke out on the Greek frontier, Laura leapt to action once more, sailing with a similar team to the battlefronts involved. Here they worked on a larger scale, moving their quarters as the fighting progressed. So effective was this work that the Greek Government felt she should receive some recognition for her services, so she had the honour of receiving the Red Cross, presented by Queen Victoria on behalf of the King and Queen of Greece, together with a small pension, for her heroic work.

A full account of all her exploits in this field would fill a book, yet little is recorded about these years, as the newspapers took little notice of them. Unfortunately, such positive work does not make news like her more sensational activities connected with the Empire, Leicester Square.

While on these expeditions, Laura took numerous photographs - a thing unusual for an amateur at that time. Many of these she had developed into slides, with which she would enliven future lectures.

What a woman! Was there anything she could not do, or would not attempt, especially if it was going to benefit her fellow creatures? How did she fit it all into one life?

At the age of sixty-five, Laura seemed fit to battle on for at least another ten years, but then the blow fell - Tom died. Until that day, few had any idea how much she leaned on him; she was now a broken woman. Had she ever stopped to think how she could face life without him! It was not simply his moral support, important as that was, but the supply of money was abruptly cut off. Neither of them had been provident, spending their money liberally, usually on doing good to others; now she was suddenly in very reduced circumstances.

Then came the shock of the war in 1914. The children were all married by now; the youngest, Olive, with whom she seemed especially close, had married Robert Pursaill, an East End boy who had been befriended by Quakers who ran an Adult School. He had joined the Society and had been set up in life by these godly men. He registered as a conscientious objector and the tribunal accepted his claim, so he was drafted into the Friends' Ambulance Unit. Laura set up house with Olive and her new baby, Marjory (my informant). They moved about somewhat and gradually Laura's strength and valiant spirit returned. They took a large house in London, near a munitions factory, and let lodgings to the workers.

Then the air raids began and of course the factory was a prime target. Air raids then were nothing compared with those in the second world war, but they were new and terrifying and totally unprepared for. When there were serious explosions near by, Laura's friends testified that this indomitable woman, now nearly seventy, was there making tea and coffee to give to the injured, the homeless and those who were carrying on rescue work.

As those dark years dragged on, it became clear to these two brave women that the boarding house was losing money, so that when peace came and Robert was demobilised, he came home to find his wife and mother-in-law almost destitute. However, he soon got a job in Banbury as manager of a bakery and confectionery business, so they moved there and set up a permanent home. It was an uphill struggle for the Pursaills, but Laura used her skills at needlework to help the young couple's finances.

From time to time Laura would go for extended stays to the homes of her other children; for instance, in 1921 she was living with another daughter and her husband on their farm at Pinvin (near Pershore, Worcestershire); but her 'home' was at Banbury. Here she was happy with Olive, little Marjory and her hard-working Quaker son-in-law Robert. She attended the Quaker meetings with them and grew to love the peace and tranquillity of their outlook in her old age; and it was at her request that she was buried at Sibford.

In the last months of her life she began to complain of a painful swelling under her arm that made it difficult for her to write and sew. Having been a nurse, she must have known what was coming on, yet she refused an operation until breast cancer was diagnosed. She was then operated on, rather against her will, but it was too late. Her granddaughter remembers her lying in bed one day and speaking of the beautiful singing of the larks outside; then she lay quiet for a minute, when suddenly she sat up, held out her arms as if to someone at the foot of the bed and said "Tom! Tom!" and fell back on her pillow and was gone. So her valiant spirit sped to be with her beloved Tom in God's presence.

We have seen how Laura's talents were in demand as a speaker and preacher in churches of many denominations; she was especially welcome at the Manchester Methodist Mission, where the minister, the Rev. S. F. Collier, was a great friend. One day he requested her to write a hymn for his people to sing "with a Hallelujah ring in it". "Light of the World" (636 MHB) was the result.

This hymn, once sung frequently, now seems unjustly neglected; is it not time to revive it? It is evidently based on Newman's better known hymn "Lead, kindly Light", but it has a much more positive note about it. It is a thrilling hymn to sing and it is this extraordinary woman's testimony to her faith in Christ who is the LIGHT OF THE WORLD . . .

"In days long past we missed our homeward way;
        We could not see;
Blind were our eyes, our feet were bound to stray:
        How blind to Thee!

154

But Thou didst pity, Lord, our gloomy plight;
And Thou didst touch our eyes, and give them sight.

"Now hallelujahs rise along the road
    Our glad feet tread;
Thy love hath shared our sorrow's heavy load,
    There's light o'erhead:
Glory to Thee whose love hath led us on,
Glory for all the great things Thou hast done."

I came across this beautiful tribute to Laura recently . . . "She was no longer young, except in heart - throughout her long and gracious life it was beating for the love of mankind."

CHARLES SILVESTER HORNE (1865 - 1914)

After the extended life of Laura Chant, we turn to another social reformer and hymn writer - a man who may be remembered by some older people. My own father knew and admired him greatly, so to increase my small knowledge of Charles Silvester Horne, I went to the beautiful little town of Church Stretton and made a few enquiries. These took me to the peaceful burial ground not far from the Church, in the shadow of the great bulk of the Long Mynd. There I found his grave, giving the facts of his death, followed by the text "Greater love hath no man than this, that a man lay down his life for his friends".

This has caused some speculation as to whether he died in some heroic act, but on no less an authority than his daughter, Mrs. Bridget Bull, this simply means that he died at the early age of forty-nine, worn out by his incessant toil for the poor in London's slums, through the agency of both the Church and Parliament.

As I left the churchyard, I held the gate open for a neatly-dressed little old lady, approaching with a bunch of flowers. She smiled, and after the usual remarks about the weather, she said, "I'm putting some flowers on my husband's grave, it's his birthday today, you see . . he would have been 81 . ." She broke off, her eyes filling with tears, but she quickly controlled herself and changed the subject.

She was obviously curious why I should be poking about among the graves, so I told her I had just found Silvester Horne's grave, still cared for, with a glowing border of tagetes. "Ah," she said, "I never knew him; I only came here to live in 1920 and he died before that, but

I knew Mrs. Horne, who lived a long time after that, in the house over there." She indicated the direction, making it clear that the house had a glorious view of the mountains.

"Of course," she continued, "he was the father of Kenneth Horne." I smiled a wry smile; I had already heard this twice that day! Strange that this burning prophet of social righteousness, whose zeal inspired thousands in the early years of this century, should now be known as the obscure father of a famous comedian!

Silvester's father, although trained for the Congregational ministry, turned to journalism, feeling he was more suited to spreading the Christian message in this way. He became editor of the local paper at Newport, Salop, and it was here that his son grew up and was educated - and it was to Shropshire that he returned when his health began to fail.

Trained in the worship of the Newport Congregational Church and Sunday School, he too felt the call to the ministry, taking his M.A. at Glasgow University, and then entering the newly-opened Mansfield College, Oxford, to study theology under Dr. Fairbairn. At the age of twenty-four he was ordained and became minister of a large church in Kensington, where he stayed fourteen years.

Then came the big move - he was appointed minister of the vast Whitefield's Tabernacle, a job which, as well as plunging him into work among London's poor, demanded three sermons each Sunday - morning worship, an afternoon service with special emphasis on young people, and an evening service where men predominated. Crowds thronged the building, drawn by his forthright preaching, backed up by his dedication to the social implications of his faith.

With his abilities, duties increased; his gift of leadership led to his election as Chairman of the Congregational Union, and his capabilities with men meant that he was pressed to be President of the Brotherhood Movement; he was in demand for lectures, here, there and everywhere, always returning to his beloved Whitefields for each Sunday. His life had become so full that he had forgotten what spare time was!

These constant demands on his time were taking a serious toll of his strength, when he did something which seemed absolute madness to all who knew him. In his concern for the poor in the slums of London he became increasingly aware that in this field the law must often be changed to bring the social justice he preached so sincerely, so he offered himself as Liberal candidate for Ipswich and was elected as an

M.P. in 1909. He was already doing two men's work, but somehow he pursued his new job with vigour, still retaining his pastorate at Whitefields, but reducing some of his travelling to lectures and sermons during the week.

After two years all this work began to make him show signs of strain and he had to consult doctors several times. He was told in blunt terms that he must give up something. It was at this time, he bought the house in Church Stretton as a retreat where he could relax and hope to 're-charge his batteries'. Much as he loved his work at the Tabernacle, he felt he must resign; providentially a suitable replacement was now available - William Charter Piggott (see Hymn 657 MHB) - so he entered into a brief period of semi-retirement (so-called!). Although he still loved to preach from his old pulpit occasionally, everyone seemed to think he was now a man of leisure and pressing invitations poured in for him to write, preach and lecture.

He did accept the commission from the London Missionary Society to write a biography of David Livingstone, a man he had always admired. This brought him in touch with another admirer of Livingstone, the up and coming young Scots musician Hamish McCunn (composer of the 'Land of Mountain and Flood') and they co-operated in writing a cantata on the life of Livingstone (has anyone seen a copy of this?).

Another invitation he accepted was to give a series of lectures at Yale University. His doctor strongly advised him against it, but Silvester assured him that the lectures would not be a great strain and the sea voyage would do him good; so he was reluctantly allowed to go.

He delivered the lectures with all his old verve, but on the return journey he and his wife were standing on deck watching their approach to Toronto, when he suddenly fell dead at her feet.

Sadly she accompanied the body home and he was laid to rest where he had often loved to relax.

When a memorial was suggested, funds flowed in from all over Britain and beyond, and a comprehensive community centre was built in Church Stretton, still known as the Silvester Horne Institute.

What sort of hymns has this great and good man left us? As we would expect, they are forthright and challenging. "Sing we the King" (116 MHB) shows his passion for social righteousness, not based on sentiment or even political reform, but squarely on the truth of the saving power of God through Jesus Christ. "For the might of Thine arm we bless Thee" (715 MHB) proclaims the continuing Church as the surest bulwark against the evils of the world.

Silvester Horne was typical of the upsurge of the 'Nonconformist Conscience' around the turn of the century - a movement which was expressed in Methodism by the erection and staffing of the 'Central Missions' in big cities, in the passionate belief in the salvation of mankind, both spiritual and material (in that order).

Thinking of Silvester Horne's dedicated life, the words of another social worker come to mind . . .

"The coming age invokes our aid, the voice of old inspires;
Shall we, thy sons and daughters, be less worthy than our sires?"

(Ernest Dodgshun - 897 MHB)

REV. G. A. STUDDERT-KENNEDY (1883 - 1929)

"Awake, awake to love and work, the lark is in the sky" (588 MHB) is a cheerful morning hymn we sometimes sing - a hymn that reflects the outlook and character of the author, Rev. G. A. Studdert-Kennedy. Perhaps, too, you have enjoyed his books: 'Rough Rhymes', 'Food for the Fed-up', etc.

How many readers remember this remarkable man? He came to Worcester in 1914 as Vicar of St. Paul's, then one of the worst slum areas in the city. All of the dreadful little houses have now been demolished, but I remember a few, empty and forlorn, showing the awful conditions of his parish in those days. He set to work to relieve hardship and suffering with all his power, constantly giving away clothing and other necessities which he really needed for himself; he even once carted a bed from the vicarage for a sick woman he found sleeping on the floor.

Soon, however, war broke out and he went to France as a Chaplain to the Forces. With utter unselfishness he gave himself to the service of the men, under the incredibly horrifying conditions of that sector of the war. In spite of suffering from asthma, he was with them in the worst battles, carrying his haversack from which he distributed copies of the Gospels and packets of cigarettes - earning himself the nickname 'Woodbine Willie'. As he did this he tried to tell them of God's love - under conditions which he realised all too acutely, flatly denied it. For his heroic services he was awarded the Military Cross.

After the war he joined the newly-formed Industrial Christian Fellowship and was appointed a travelling speaker in their campaigns in all the great cities. His earlier experiences caused him to make social justice and peace his two great themes, preaching them with such force that vast audiences came to hear him wherever he went. In spite of increasing ill-health, he continued this exhausting work until he died, worn out, at the age of forty-six.

How truly he lived up to his own words . . .

> "To give, and give, and give again,
> What God hath given thee;
> To spend thy self nor count the cost,
> To serve right gloriously . . . ."

How ashamed he must make us feel of our half-heartedness, our lack of zeal and love for our fellows!

JOHN OXENHAM (1852 - 1941)

We continue this chapter with that curious, humble man who was known as William Arthur Dunkerly among his friends at the Congregational Church where his father was a faithful, life-long worker, and where he was later to serve as deacon and Bible Class leader.

William entered his father's business and travelled abroad a good deal on his behalf; but he began to write poems and became interested in publishing, in which he co-operated with Jerome K. Jerome. He was so shy of people knowing of these activities that he adopted the nom-de-plume of 'John Oxenham'. If you know Kingsley's 'Westward Ho!' you will know that this was the name of the leader of the ill-fated expedition on which the hero, Amyas Leigh, intended to go, and whose daughter he eventually married, after his incredible adventures and hardships had left him maimed and blind.

So William Dunkerly kept up this harmless deception for many years, known to many as just another good Church worker, and to far more as the popular author, John Oxenham.

During his last illness he lost consciousness and had a strange vision of the after life. When he 'came round' he told his daughter about this, and they thought it should be preserved in writing, so with his little remaining strength and with her help - for much of it was dictated - the little book 'Out of the Body' was completed before he died, a testimony of his faith in an eternal life with his Master.

He is best known as a hymn writer by "In Christ there is no East or West" which has found its way into most modern supplements, including the 'Hymns and Songs' supplement to the Methodist Hymn Book (No. 34). This is a forward-looking hymn, expressing the great new fact of our time - the World-wide Church.

LAURENCE HOUSMAN (1865 - 1959)

Laurence Housman seems to be one of those unfortunate people who, though very gifted, was doomed to be obscured by a more famous brother, A. E. Housman - so much so, that while there are at least six biographies of Alfred, including one by Laurence himself, no-one seems to have written up Laurence's life. This has made research more difficult, but much more rewarding. Again, I am writing more fully than usual, because the facts are not so well known. It seems unfair, too, that so little notice has been taken of Laurence, for although he and his brother were both eccentrics, he emerges as the more normal and far more likeable of the two.

Laurence Housman is represented in the Methodist Hymn Book by only one hymn, the Christmas carol "The Maker of the sun and moon" (136 MHB), although he has as many as fifteen in some books. Some are translations of ancient Latin hymns, while others, like this one (which is from his Nativity play 'Bethlehem') are extracts from the many Biblical plays he wrote. Someone once called him the most censored playwright of his time, which seems strange to us, for the main trouble was that he loved to dramatise Biblical characters, which was apparently not approved then. He also ran into trouble with some plays depicting Royalty - even with their faults - which were promptly banned! His total output of plays was enormous, and although few are known to-day, early this century he was living very comfortably on his many successful productions. In a successful season, his Victorian plays being produced in New York brought in £500 a week!

Alfred and Laurence were the eldest and the sixth children of the large family of a Bromsgrove solicitor, who lived at Fockbury, a few miles out of the town. He had moved to this country house because he wanted to live the life of a country gentleman, but he found this far beyond his means, so rather than retreat to his town house, he foolishly took up mortgages on his properties, using up his capital to such an extent that, when his affairs were settled up after his death, his family found they were financially ruined. I mention this because the shock of discovering all this when they thought they were fairly well off had a terrible effect on all the children.

Their mother was a pious woman with strong 'High Church' leanings. The boys were very fond of her and suffered another deep disturbance when she died. Neither of them married and, although they had followed their beloved mother's faith, they both began to question it after her death. Alfred remained an agnostic all his life, but Laurence was later attracted to the Roman Catholic Church, which explains his love of the old Latin hymns; but he found he could not accept some of the dogmas involved and, after some wanderings, found his spiritual home with the Quakers.

To return to Laurence's youth . . . he left Bromsgrove School with an impressive list of prizes for art, drama, poetry and many other subjects, and went on to the College of Art to gain further prizes. This study was cut short by the hard fact of having to earn a living because of his father's irresponsibility, and he got a job as illustrator for magazines, for his line drawings were much in demand. You may find examples of these in the beautifully bound Victorian books of poems that were the fashion then - notably the works of Christina Rossetti and Shelley. He became well-known enough to obtain the post of Art Critic of the 'Manchester Guardian' and it was this work which gave him the incentive to take up writing more fully.

If Laurence suffered from his father's financial incompetence, his eldest sister, Clemence, was affected much more, for on her had fallen the task of trying to straighten up the shaky family finances. Laurence shared this unenviable job with her when he had time, and this seemed to make a bond between these two, so that when the family finally broke up, they settled down together in London.

Clemence was a clever young lady who helped with the finances by wood engraving for books and magazines. She also tried her hand at writing, but after some initial success she had a number of failures, and she resigned herself to the fact that her talents were not quite good enough for this very competitive world, so she devoted herself to housekeeping for her busy and successful brother. One of his most successful books at this early stage was 'An English Woman's Love Letters' - a book that had everyone guessing who was the author!

It is a curious fact that Laurence was a well-known writer long before anyone had heard of his much older brother Alfred, who had devoted his life to academic pursuits as Professor at Latin at London and Cambridge. It was not until he was thirty-seven that he wrote the poem that was to make him famous - 'The Shropshire Lad'. It was typical of Laurence, who already had a long list of London successes for his plays, that he wrote to his brother when this was published, congratulating him heartily by saying, "This is worth more than all I have written." His generous spirit is seen in his 'Little Plays of St. Francis' where there is an epilogue in which he (the author) is depicted on his death bed, when a nurse comes in and says, "You have written quite a lot of books, someone told me." To which the author replies, "In my life - more than I ought - my brother used to say I wrote faster than he could read! *He* wrote two books of poems - better than all mine put together!"

This understanding between the two brothers was a long lasting relationship, although Alfred did strain it occasionally. This happened particularly at the time Laurence was regaining his Christian faith, which he expressed in a book of devotional poems with the lovely title 'Spikenard' - a fragrant offering to anoint the feet of Jesus. Alfred wrote him a congratulatory letter - or that was his intention - but it was full of facetious comments which Laurence took to be sneers at the Christian tone of the poems. He was deeply hurt; he had not expected him to agree with him, but he had hoped he would understand his Christian outlook and not ridicule him. Perhaps Laurence was suffering from an inferiority complex and was a bit touchy, but still the frivolous remarks left a wound that took many years to heal, and he was unhappy until it did.

When Mrs. Pankhurst began her movement for Women's Suffrage, she found in Clemence Housman an enthusiastic supporter. Laurence was in full sympathy with their aims and lent as much background help as he could, designing and painting banners and posters used in the crusade. Then the war came in 1914 and women were in demand in factories, in fact doing many men's jobs that they had never tackled before, and the way was open for the victory of the Movement in 1918. It was the war that changed Laurence's religious views again, for he noted with admiration the Quakers' uncompromising stand for peace. He and his sister worked with a couple, Roger and Sarah Clark, who were already deeply involved, and the friendship and co-operation with these people became so close that in 1920 he persuaded his sister to sell up their home and move to Street, in Somerset, where the Clarks were active members of the local Quaker community. He recorded this move in a little poem which ends . . .

"Request your undertaker
To lay out half an acre
(The cost a hundred pound) -
Good measure, meted out, and running over
Into a field of elms, cows, rooks and clover,
Where, fronting south, near by, in pleasant hands
The little watch-tower of gazebo stands
And sees beneath its walls of close-trimmed fruits,
Roger, the quiet Quaker, on his wheel,
Steering an even keel,
Off to his daily work of making boots."

The last lines refer, of course, to his dearest friend Roger Clark, who cycled to work, although he was director of the famous footwear firm of C. & J. Clark - and it is to the archives department of this great company that I owe much information on Laurence's later life.

It is good to know that the present head of the firm is Roger's grandson and that the Quaker tradition is still strong in both management and workforce - in fact Street is largely the Clarks' creation, rather as Cadbury's and other Quaker businessmen have founded their ideal communities around their factories.

So Laurence and Clemence's dream home 'Longmeadow' was built "fronting south" and within sight of the Clarks' home, with whom they had almost daily contact.

Here Laurence settled down happily to write some of his best works, and to complete his cycle of plays on the life of St. Francis of Assisi and his Victorian plays.

When that famous pacifist, Rev. Dick Sheppard, started his Peace Pledge Movement in 1936, Laurence joined him, speaking at his meetings with other well-known pacifists like Donald Soper and George Lansbury. He worked with him until war broke out again in 1939, when that well-intentioned movement collapsed for lack of support, as many who had supported its ideals found themselves forced into total war, even if they disagreed with it. The correspondence between these two sincere men on this glorious failure was published in 1939 under the title 'What can we believe?'. There was no admission of defeat, and the following year saw the publication of one of Laurence's most influential books 'The Preparation of Peace'.

Laurence had often declared that he intended to die at the age of sixty-seven - he didn't think he would be much use after that - so when he was sixty-nine he published a book which he fully intended to be his last, entitled 'The unexpected years' - those years he had not expected to see, and which to his delight he found to be useful. In fact he lived to the age of ninety-four! He was a hale and hearty old man of eighty-seven when he published his last full-length book, a book of short stories.

Even in his old age he was by no means idle: as well as being a brilliant playwright, he was also a good actor, loving to take part in productions of his own religious plays at nearby Glastonbury and giving lecture-recitals all over England with great zest. I have already referred to his 'Epilogue' to the 'Little Plays of St. Francis'; in the revival of those plays at Glastonbury he played himself - the author - in the 'deathbed' scene, making an impression on all who saw it that was quite unforgettable.

These plays are a reminder of Laurence's part in the very successful Glastonbury Festival, an enterprise in which many famous men were involved. It was here that Rutland Boughton produced his best-known opera 'The Immortal Hour' as well as lesser known works. Unfortunately the Second World War cut it short and although efforts were made to revive it, the peak of enthusiasm had passed and many of the wealthy sponsors had died, or were growing old - as were Roger Clark and Laurence himself; sadly, therefore, it petered out. Yet who knows if yet another group of gifted men might revive it?

Laurence was still physically fit and alert at the age of ninety, but from then on he began to decline. He had always been a handsome and neatly dressed little man, with an Imperial beard and a mass of hair, well groomed and with bright, penetrating eyes; but in the last two years he began to 'let himself go'. He ceased to write: his inspiration had dried up, and the old inferiority complex - possibly from the growing fame of his brother - tended to increase, revealing itself in a defensive aggressiveness.

Long before this, Roger Clark's influence had drawn him constantly to the Quaker meetings until he joined them in membership. He would often contribute to the meetings, sometimes reciting one of Blake's mystical poems, of which he was particularly fond. In these last years his remarks in the meetings became less helpful and more controversial, and even the patient Roger eventually says, "Laurence is spoilt by being too full of himself - his besetting fault." I suppose when you have done so many things and done them well, it must be difficult not to degenerate into a bore! But even at this last difficult stage, the love and understanding of the Friends was his main support.

Here, then, we have the story of a full and varied life: a happy childhood in the Worcestershire countryside; an anxious and difficult adolescence and young manhood, dogged by serious financial problems; a period of spiritual 'no-man's land'; financial success through sheer hard work; the dawning of new faith; immersion in good causes which he felt were God's will for him, in spite of the apparent failure of his efforts for peace in 1939; an unexpectedly prolonged life of usefulness; and a happy old age, in the peace of a loving Quaker community.

RUDYARD KIPLING (1865 - 1936)

It may come as a surprise to find Rudyard Kipling classed as a hymn writer. It is true he seems more a patriot and imperialist than a practising Christian, but he had a strong basic belief in God and His providence, as shown in his patriotic poems which have come to be included in many hymn books. These and his other writings reflect a colourful and adventurous life, in which he travelled almost the whole world.

His parents were as remarkable, though not as famous as he was. His father, John Lockwood Kipling, was a Methodist minister's son of great artistic ability. He was due to start a job in Bombay and went with his family on a picnic to Lake Rudyard in Staffordshire, where they met another minister and his family, from Bewdley - Rev. George Macdonald, son of the President of the Conference, with his bevy of attractive daughters.

It is worth a slight digression to look at these girls, for every one became either wife or mother to a famous man. Two married great artists, Sir Edward Burne-Jones and Sir Edward Poynter; a third was Stanley Baldwin's mother; and Alice, the fourth, was the one who stole the heart of young John Kipling on the memorable day of the picnic. The sailing was postponed to enable them to marry, and then they both sailed for the mysterious East. Here was born their son, whom they named Rudyard, after the beauty spot where they first met and fell in love.

When old enough to go to school, Rudyard was sent to England, but he always seemed to hanker for the land of his birth, so when his schooling was over, he did not stop in England to go to University, but returned to India, to earn his living as a reporter. He had written poems and stories at school, and now he wrote both articles and poems for insertion in his paper, mostly on current affairs, and with that pungent flavour that was to become typical of the man. These were something new, and were eagerly sought after by periodicals and just as eagerly devoured by readers.

As soon as he could afford to do so, he travelled widely, marrying an American lady, but eventually settled, at the age of twenty-seven, at Rottingdean, near his uncle and aunt - parents of his cousin, Stanley Baldwin.

It was here that he wrote his famous 'Recessional', "Lest we forget" (889 MHB). He had been watching the bonfires along the coast, and on the downs inland, to celebrate Queen Victoria's Diamond Jubilee in 1897. The 'Times' had pressed him to contribute a poem for this occasion, but he could not write to order and so did not come up with anything suitable; but as the fires began to die down, these lines came into his mind, and he quickly wrote them down in a notebook . . .

> "On dune and headland sinks the fire;
> Lo, all our pomp of yesterday
> Is one with Nineveh and Tyre!"

When he returned to his study he threw these scribbled lines into the waste paper basket, but a friend found them and insisted that they should be published. The great day had gone, but he agreed to revise the poem and send it off - it was in the 'Times' next morning.

The verses hold many allusions like the one above, which are not easy to follow, but the overall message is that the British Empire, in which he sincerely believed, would last - but only as long as our leaders were content to submit to the guidance of Almighty God. Exception has been taken to the rather contemptuous lines . . .

> "Such boasting as the Gentiles use,
> Or lesser breeds without the law . ."

- but he was quick to point out that this was a composite quotation from St. Paul, who was probably referring (more charitably) to the Roman Empire as not having God's law. This highlights the fact that Kipling was well versed in Scripture, into which he could infuse his own brand of satire.

The fine patriotic poem "Land of our Birth, we pledge to thee . ." (899 MHB) was written much later. He headed it 'The Children's Song'. It is a noble call to youth to take their part in the service of others and of their country - which needs to be heeded by to-day's youth as much as yesterday's. Note particularly the lines . . .

> "Teach us to look, in all our ends,
> On Thee for Judge, and not our friends."

and the oft-quoted couplet . . .

> "Teach us delight in simple things,
> And mirth that has no bitter springs."

In middle life Rudyard Kipling became quite wealthy and was able to buy the large house 'Batemans' - happily now a Kipling Museum, in the care of the National Trust.

When war broke out, he became depressed and pessimistic, for the submerged fears of his 'Recessional' were being realised; this depression was deepened when his only son was killed early in the war, but in time his faith triumphed over both these griefs. In post-war years relations with his cousin Stanley Baldwin became strained. Rudyard was an extreme, old-fashioned Tory, and he found Baldwin's Conservative Party's policies much too liberal for his liking; this led to frequent and sometimes acrimonious arguments, which were not conducive to the usual happy fellowship in the family. (I should like to know what Kipling thought of my father, Mr. S. Hancock, who twice opposed Stanley Baldwin, as a Liberal candidate for the - then - Bewdley Division of Worcestershire!) Fortunately these misunderstandings did not last long.

Now we must try to define this unusual man's faith - not an easy task, for he was naturally very reticent about such deep things. The best course for me to take is to quote a few things he wrote, for he could write of spiritual matters better than he could speak. I have not so far mentioned Edith Macdonald, the only sister who did not marry, who became the one in whom he could confide more easily than anyone else; when she was very old, he wrote her these lines of comfort: "Dear Aunt Edie, He who put us into this life does not abandon His work for any reason, or default, at the end of it." Also, in one of his poems his basic humility shows through . . .

> "If there be any good in what I wrought,
> Thy hand compelled it, Master, Thine;
> Where I have failed to meet Thy thought,
> I know, through Thee, the blame was mine."

In spite of his Methodist background, a generation earlier, he seemed unable to subscribe to the formulas of any Church. He became an Anglican, but one feels, with reservations. Perhaps his views are best summed up in his own words: "I suppose every man has to work out his creed according to his own wavelength, and the hope is that the Great Receiving Station is tuned to take all wavelengths."

NARAYAN VAMAN TILAK (1862 - 1919)

We conclude this chapter with a brief look beyond our shores at a remarkable Indian teacher, who became a Christian and wrote a number of hymns.

One of the hymns of Narayan Vaman Tilak, "One who is all unfit to count as scholar in Thy school", (159 MHB), is deservedly very popular, being a beautifully spiritual expression of Christian humility in the light of Christ's sacrifice for mankind on the Cross. It is the only example there is of an Indian hymn in the 1933 Methodist Hymn Book, although the 'Hymns and Songs' supplement has a larger scope. The translation is by Dr. N. Macnicol, a Free Church Missionary in India, and it was first published in England by the S.P.C.K.

Tilak was the son of an Indian Government Official. He trained as a teacher and was by religion a Hindu - very devout and proud of Hindu traditions. At the age of thirty-two, he was on a long train journey when he got into conversation with a missionary who had been reading his New Testament as he travelled. When Tilak remarked that his companion must have a love of books, the missionary asked if he too was a book lover. Tilak replied that he loved books, especially the Hindu Holy Books, and that in fact he was on his way to a new appointment as a librarian.

"Then you are a Hindu?" asked the missionary.

Tilak nodded: "Yes, I was even a hermit for a year, then I helped with a new edition of the Hindu Scriptures." He went on to confide in this stranger something of his family troubles and his still unsatisfied longing to experience the reality of God speaking to him.

This gave the missionary his opening: "God has spoken to us through this book," he said, holding up his New Testament; "He has spoken to us through Jesus Christ."

"Oh, He is a foreign God, I understand," he replied.

"Look," said the missionary, "I must leave you now, here is my station. Take this and read it - you will find God is speaking to you."

So saying, and without giving his name, he gave Tilak a New Testament as they parted. The words of Jesus made such an instant impact on him that, in his own words, "I could not tear myself away from those burning words of love, tenderness and truth: here, in the Sermon on the Mount, is the answer to the most abstruse and profound problems of Hindu philosophy."

He believed that, if India could be shown Christ in all His beauty, she would acknowledge Him as the supreme Guru and lay her richest treasures at His feet.

From that time he dedicated his life to this end, working as a teacher, preacher, hymn writer and social worker, until his death in 1919.

His chosen profession, turned to Christian ends, is reflected in the opening lines of the hymn quoted above. It is moving and encouraging that the missionary effort from the West should receive a 'feed-back' in fine hymns like this. The hymn in question is one that will repay study and meditation - for this is what an Indian author would have us do.

So the witness of an unknown missionary bore fruit in the life of a great Christian. I wonder if we helped to send him?

Chapter 15

THE TWENTIETH CENTURY

It was difficult to know just where to end the previous chapter and begin this one, but Dr. Percy Dearmer's life seems a good place to make a break, especially as Dearmer was in many ways ahead of his time. Canon George Briggs and Dean Cyril Alington follow a little later, both spending the influential part of their lives in the present century. These are a small group of typical Anglican divines who have given us hymns which are timeless, and whose academic careers were all brilliant.

Yet each one was an important influence in his own right. Perhaps their lives do not make such exciting reading as those saints of old like St. Francis Xavier, Richard Baxter or Bishop Ken, who lived in times of civil strife, religious intolerance and difficult travel, yet their lives have the solid virtues of men who were re-stating the gospel faithfully in a period of apparent decline.

Dr. PERCY DEARMER (1867 - 1938)

Percy Dearmer was the son of Thomas Dearmer, a well-known artist in his time. Inheriting his father's love of art and something of his talent, Percy was called to serve God in the Church, and after graduating at Christ Church, Oxford, he became vicar of St. Mary, Primrose Hill. Concurrently with this appointment, he was also Professor of Ecclesiastical Art at King's College, London. He was also elected chairman of the League of Arts.

All seemed settled for a busy academic and church life when the Great War upset his - and many others' - plans. He was sent as Chaplain to the British units in Serbia. His wife, on hearing this news, volunteered as a hospital orderly for the Red Cross in the same area. Another crippling blow was to fall, for within a few weeks she went down with the deadly typhus fever and died, after courageously serving those from whom she contracted the disease. There followed a sad and testing time for Percy Dearmer, as he continued to try to help others while his own faith was being tried so severely. A good friend, Mary Knowles, was a comfort to him at this time; friendship deepened into love and they were married during the war.

With the coming of peace, the Dearmers settled down to parish work until 1931, when Percy was appointed Canon of Westminster Abbey, an office which involved no pastoral work, thus giving him more time to devote his peculiar talents to other things.

We have looked at his work for Christian Art - he also wrote some theological works, and his work for social justice was outstanding. We have already seen how the conscience of Christians had long been concerned with the scandal of the inequalities between the 'haves' and the 'have-nots', and from the time of Kingsley and Maurice, courageous voices were raised against this evil - courageous because some were Anglicans and their Church was mainly supported by the 'haves'. This is not the place to go into this subject in detail; suffice it to say that Percy Dearmer, with Henry Scott Holland (see 883 MHB) and others, founded the Christian Social Union and for many years was secretary - a post which understandably involved him in some controversy.

His theological views were hotly attacked, too. He had become a modernist and, like others before him, he questioned among other things the doctrine of eternal punishment as being incompatible with the love of God. To him the whole idea was a product of the sadistic mediaeval mind - derived from the Jewish figure of the Valley of Hinnom, the everlasting bonfire outside Jerusalem where garbage was destroyed. To know his views on this subject one should read his book 'The Legend of Hell'.

It is, however, with Percy Dearmer's work as a hymnologist that we are mainly concerned. The English Hymnal was published in 1906 and he was both a member of the board and a contributor to this book. Many of his hymns were translations of ancient Latin office hymns, but a few were original compositions, including "Father, who on man dost shower gifts of plenty from Thy dower" (894 MHB) - a fine prayer for the right use of God's gifts and for the grace of temperance. As we have seen, this was something in which he passionately believed.

His adaptation of Bunyan's "Who would true valour see" has already been noted (page 34).

Dearmer also edited the Oxford Book of Carols - a project which involved him in years of research; but his great chance came when a new hymn book was suggested, mainly for use in schools, and he was appointed as editor. The result was 'Songs of Praise'. This was a job after his own heart, but here again he was controversial: he threw out masses of Victorian hymns and tunes, and even Wesley and Watts did not fare very well - in fact he succumbed to the temptation of all compilers and included more of his own hymns than Charles Wesley's!

It is perhaps significant that one of his musical collaborators in 'Songs of Praise' was Martin Shaw, a man whose musical taste fitted in with Dr. Dearmer's literary taste. Shaw was organist at Primrose Hill while Dearmer was vicar. Both wanted freedom from the dead hand of Germanic influence and the revival of an English tradition. Martin Shaw even burnt a copy of Beethoven's sonatas as a symbolic act of stating his aims! While one understands his enthusiasms, this seems just arrogance! Nor did Victorian music escape his destructive zeal, either.

I remember approaching an organist friend for the loan of some copies of a very respected Victorian work, only to be told "Yes, it used to be sung in our church when I was a choirboy, but my predecessor hated that style of thing and the whole lot was destroyed!" Obviously a disciple of Martin Shaw!

Martin and his equally talented brother Geoffrey have more than their fair share of tunes in 'Songs of Praise' - yet we owe a debt to these men for clearing out a good deal of rubbish. Happily, less extreme opinions are now more widely held.

So we finish with Percy Dearmer's positive contribution to our hymnody. I could quote many examples, but I would choose "O Holy Spirit, God, all loveliness is Thine" (279 MHB). He felt that existing hymns on the Holy Spirit overlooked some aspects of this doctrine that might appeal to young people. There are certainly many choice thoughts in these verses, for example "The sunshine Thou of God" and "Thou art the stream of love", while "The light that gleams beyond our dreams is something Thou hast thought" can open up new worlds of thought . . . the old, old story - told in a new way.

CANON GEORGE WALLACE BRIGGS (1875 - 1959)

We now turn to a much more orthodox character, Canon George W. Briggs.

Although his university career was interrupted by ill-health, he was eventually ordained in 1899, and after serving as a curate, he became a Naval Chaplain for several years. He held several livings until he accepted a Crown appointment as Canon Residentiary of Worcester Cathedral in 1934, and was promoted to Vice Dean in 1944.

Canon Briggs was noted for his interest in young people, serving on Diocesan Boards of Education and as editor, with Ralph Vaughan Williams, Martin Shaw and Percy Dearmer, of the series 'Services and Hymns for Schools'. He also co-operated with Eric Milner-White in the production of that wonderful little book 'Daily Prayer', which has brought together the prayers of Christians from very ancient times until the present day.

His hymn "Our Father, by whose servants Our House was built of old" (979 MHB) deserves to be used more for Anniversaries and Patronal Festivals, but more typical of the man is that simple child's hymn "God, my Father, loving me" (840 MHB), which shows him as a mature educated man who can still write effectively for youth.

Two more of his hymns deserve special mention: "Christ is the world's true Light" looks forward grandly to the time when men shall "to ploughshare beat the sword, to pruning-hook the spear"; while "God, who hast given us power to sound depths hitherto unknown" is a very modern challenge to use the discoveries of science for the good of mankind. (These are included in the 'Hymns and Songs' supplement to the Methodist Hymn Book - numbers 9 and 25 - and in other supplements).

DR. CYRIL ALINGTON (1872 - 1955)

We shall now be looking at an inspiring Easter hymn "Good Christian men, rejoice and sing!" (No. 29, 'Hymns and Songs' Supplement to the Methodist Hym Book.) by C. A. Alington, which has swept into popularity with most denominations.

Once again, the problem of writing a short biography of such a recent writer arose, and again I am taking the liberty of recounting my researches into this man's life and work. By chance I discovered that

Dr. Alington had retired to Treago, in Herefordshire, and that his daughter, Lady Mynors, still lived there and would, no doubt, be willing to give me the information I wanted. She had married into one of Herefordshire's oldest families, the Mynors, and Treago was their ancestral home. At the time of Dr. Alington's retirement, she and her husband, Sir Roger Mynors, were not living there, but in a 'tied' house attached to his job, so Dr. Alington and his wife were installed and lived out their declining years there very happily.

The de Mynors came over at the Norman Conquest, and although it is not known how soon they settled at Treago, the building has parts which are seven centuries old, so they can claim continuous ownership for at least that long - something of a record!

In the parish Church of St. Weonard there are memorials to the Mynors family commencing 1521, through the centuries, confirming this; also in the chancel is an oak plaque recording that Dr. Alington worshipped there from 1951 until 1955.

I found Lady Mynors willing and eager to tell me about her father, of whom she was very proud, and she suggested an unhurried visit to meet her husband and have a good talk.

So it was that, on a bright morning with a touch of frost in the air, we arrived at Treago. I had passed it before and had called it 'Treago Castle', but Sir Roger corrected me: "Technically it is not a castle, it was never part of the King's strategic line of defence on the Welsh border; it is just a fortified house - anyhow, we don't want to make ourselves sound grander than we are," he added modestly.

In spite of this, it looked like a castle as we drove up to it, yet its position bore out Sir Roger's view, for it is situated, not on an eminence like most castles, but in the secluded valley of the Garren Brook where raiding parties could easily pass it by. Only once is it recorded that it was attacked, by a party of Welsh out for a foray in 1512, and they were repulsed without too much trouble.

This morning there were no archers stationed at the menacing cross-loops in the round corner towers to drive off unwelcome visitors, but a warm welcome from Lady Mynors. She and her husband showed us around the evidences of building alterations through the ages, and age-old furniture, embroideries and woodwork. We saw the room where Dr. Alington would sit and write, and the private chapel where he would retire to pray and where, if he was not fit enough to attend the parish Church, he would celebrate Communion himself.

Finally, we settled down to talk about Dr. Alington; old photograph albums were brought out and various mementos of his life were shown us - and copious notes taken.

After lunch our conversation wandered from Dr. Alington and hymns, to all sorts of topics. Somehow the subject of the New English Bible came up and I asked Sir Roger his opinion of it. He hesitated and smiled - then replied, "Well, my opinion is bound to be biased; you see, I played a small part in it." So it gradually came out that this unassuming man was a scholar in his own right and was on the 'literary panel' that finalised the wording of this great work. When I registered surprise, he added "In fact, we met in different places, and the Book of Job was done here, at Treago." He paid a glowing tribute to two quiet, humble men whose influence on all the committees was incredibly strong - Bishop A. P. T. Williams and Professor C. H. Dodd. See the preface to the New English Bible (Old Testament).

Yet another surprise was in store; as we were leaving and I thanked them both for their kindness, I casually remarked that I hoped to visit Professor Caird soon, when he cut in "What - *George* Caird?" "Yes," I replied, "the same; why, do you know him?" "I should think I do; why, he and I co-operated on the Apocrypha for the N.E.B. - do give him my kind regards when you go there." So here - unexpectedly - is a link with the next chapter, when we pass to authors who are still alive and active among us.

It is now many years since I read a book entitled 'Elementary Christianity' by C. A. Alington. I remember thinking it was about the best summary of Christian doctrine I had come across. Then, when I found that the author was Headmaster of Eton College, I was glad that the basics of the faith were presented to these young people in so clear and forceful a manner.

Some years later, at a Sunday School Anniversary, a stirring hymn in leaflet form was introduced. It was quite new to me and it was by the same man. I instantly recognised the same style. The hymn "Good Christian men, rejoice and sing" - sometimes altered to "Good Christians all . . ." (29 'Hymns and Songs') is a song of assurance and joy for Easter, but would make an inspiring start for any Sunday morning worship.

Cyril Alington was a clergyman's son, educated at Marlborough and All Souls, Oxford. After graduating he declared, "I had always wanted to be a schoolmaster, and I was by this time sufficiently confident of my faith to impart it to my pupils" - so at the age of twenty-three he was appointed to a sixth-form teaching post at the school where he had been educated - Marlborough. While teaching here, he felt the call to be ordained, and after three years' teaching he returned to All Souls for a further year for theology.

After his ordination he found a teaching post vacant at Eton College, where it was felt that greater emphasis should be placed on religious teaching and this bright young clergyman was just right for the job. Here began a love for this College that remained all his life.

It soon became evident that he had a gift for leadership which was calling him to yet higher things, and so it was that, at the astonishingly early age of twenty-eight, he became Headmaster of the famous Shrewsbury School. After eight successful years there the headmastership of Eton became vacant. He applied and to his great joy was appointed. This seemed the culmination of all his ambitions - he had reached the top of the tree!

At Eton he had some really great colleagues. Dr. 'Monty' James, the great antiquarian, was Provost; and the organist and music director was Dr. Henry G. Ley. It was during this partnership that Dr. Alington's most popular hymn "Good Christian men" was written. He wrote many more hymns, but none has achieved the fame of this one and not a little of its success was due to the stirring old German melody that Dr. Ley adapted for it. It must have been a thrilling experience to hear it sung in the place of its birth - Eton College Chapel.

After seventeen years at his beloved Eton, in 1933, he felt he should make way for a younger man. Then followed a period of conflicting emotions, but finally a call to be Dean of Durham settled the question and here he stayed until the great age of seventy-nine.

Up till now his ministry had been mainly to the young, but now he was to work with all ages - and how he worked! He broke new ground when he welcomed the Methodists to hold their 'Big Day' in the Cathedral - he found these annual events an inspiring example of Christian unity.

Another way of breaking down barriers was the holding of the great Miners' Gala services, when the vast Cathedral was too small to hold the numbers who wanted to attend.

One of his activities - almost a relaxing hobby - was the restoration of the wonderful oak carvings which were made for the Cathedral under Bishop Cosin (He was the man who gave us the best translation of the tenth century Latin hymn "Veni, Creator Spiritus" (779 MHB)). I haven't mentioned him before - but then you cannot include everybody in a book of this size!

These carvings had been removed in a Victorian 'restoration' and Dr. Alington found bits of them in all sorts of odd places. He had hours of fun tracing missing pieces and the final satisfaction of seeing this fine work back where it had originally been.

He admitted to being a musical ignoramus, yet he found the flawless music of the Cathedral choir a constant inspiration, but when it came to hymns, he confessed to enjoying the hymns which the professional musicians detest!

A dark cloud spoilt his long stay in Durham - the death of one of his sons, killed in action in 1943; even then he consoled himself by writing a poem about the sad loss.

The love and respect in which he was held was shown by the fact that he was made a Freeman of the City of Durham in 1949. I have seen a photograph of this happy occasion, with the Dean standing head and shoulders above the civic dignitaries in their grand robes (for he was a very tall man), and with that twinkling smile which seems a feature of all pictures of him, even when surrounded by his friends Archbishops William Temple and Cosmo Lang and Bishops Gore and Henson - all looking suitably serious and dignified, except the Dean who towered above them all!

His sense of humour is something by which he is remembered by all who knew him, especially by his daughter, Lady Mynors, to whose recollections I owe the picture I have tried to give of this wonderful man.

Lady Mynors very kindly lent me his last book 'A Dean's Apology', which was written at Treago. I have mentioned his earlier book 'Elementary Christianity', but what a contrast this was! The first was a book of doctrine, serious of intent, but this was an octogenarian's reminiscences of a long, full and distinguished life, yet told with total humility and with his infectious humour always breaking through. It was easy to imagine him, sitting in his armchair (as he did in his latter years) writing these memoirs in the snug little room I was shown, with his wife by his side, unable to suppress the occasional smile or even chuckle as he remembered the funny things of years ago.

In his younger days Dr. Alington had been chaplain to Bishop Gore, himself author of many popular religious books - he was the first Bishop of Birmingham when that diocese was carved out of the huge old Worcester diocese. Dr. Alington's friendship with Charles Gore remained very close to the end of his life and left him with many precious - and amusing - memories which still made him smile fifty years later.

He recounts with great relish how they were travelling in Italy and were quite misdirected by some locals in the village of Rocca di Papa, causing them to lose their way and waste a lot of time. When at last they got on to the right road, they amused themselves by composing limericks about this hitch. He quotes one (presumably by Gore):

"The people of Rocca di Papa
Have morals to shock a card-sharper:
  So filthy their mien,
  They could scarcely get clean
If they washed in Abana or Pharpar."

He was himself a master of witty sallies. Someone was discussing with him Pope Pius IX and his setting out the doctrine of the Immaculate Conception, when he replied that he was sure that many Catholics must wish that the Pope would let sleeping *dogmas* lie!

He seems to have found a lot of humour in printers' errors: he recounts how Archbishop Lang was very upset when, after writing a Jacobite song ending with the words "Come back to us, Charlie, the King of us a'," it came back from the printers as "Come back to us, Charlie, the King of U.S.A."!

Another of his own hymns, on the resurrection of the dead, ended with the words: "Grant us to sleep, and wake at last with Thee". To his surprise, these words on the proof-sheet read "Grant us to sleep, and wake at last with Three". His comment was typical: "If such a triple resurrection were in fact to be allowed, my tripartite ghost could hover happily round the playing fields of Marlborough, Shrewsbury and Eton." He then apologises for not being able to fit Durham into this scheme, for he had a deep affection for the many friends he had made there, and their love remained a source of encouragement to him.

I have not yet said much about his books. He began with 'A Schoolmaster's Apology', written while he was teaching at Marlborough, and his last had the complementary title of 'A Dean's Apology', but between these he wrote about forty books, from some on light - even humorous - subjects, to profound theological studies - a truly amazingly versatile output for such a busy man.

So what is your overall impression of this remarkable man? I see him as a young man with many gifts of intellect, willing to consecrate them to the Lord Jesus Christ, whom he had been brought up to love and reverence and whom he served with glad obedience . . . A long and fruitful life gratefully remembered by the many pupils who were in his care . . . and the City of Durham where he spent his maturer years - as he felt - a humble successor to St. Cuthbert and Bede.

The Dean retired in 1951 to spend his last days happily in the peace and quiet of remote Treago, still busy writing his last few books, which are such a delight to read.

TREAGO OCT 1981   C.P.H.

TREAGO, ST WEONARDS, HEREFORDSHIRE

Chapter 16

EPILOGUE — TO-DAY AND TOMORROW

The hymns and authors mentioned in this final chapter are only to be found in modern books, many of them supplements to older hymn books. The numbers in brackets refer to a typical supplement 'Hymns and Songs' (the 1969 Supplement to the Methodist Hymn Book). We are passing on to modern authors, most of whom are happily still with us, and to a period of great quickening in hymn writing, after the lull of the early part of the twentieth century.

Forty or fifty years ago it might have been thought that the fount of hymns was drying up, but now the sheer number of hymns - and hymn books - being produced is simply staggering. Inevitably the sifting process, which in the past has separated the wheat from the chaff of poor writing - or just outdated sentiments - will go on; so any assessment I make must represent my own opinion, as I try to look into the future and assess what will endure.

DR. G. B. CAIRD

When I was introduced to the hymn "Not far beyond the sea" (49 H. & S.), for instance, I thought I recognised a winner. Its appeal was immediate, yet there seemed something durable about it; also, these two qualities seldom go together, so why did I think they did here?

On looking more closely at these verses, I saw the reason: from beginning to end they were firmly based on the Bible, so the well-loved phrases 'rang a bell' in one's mind straight away and, Scripture being imperishable, this hymn was built to last. Charles Wesley's best hymns can be analysed line by line and will be found to be based on a string of texts from all books of the Bible. This hymn by *DR. GEORGE CAIRD* is fairly wide-ranging too - Psalms, Matthew, Romans, Corinthians, Ephesians, Philippians, etc. (I am disappointed that '100 Hymns for To-day' omits the masterly second verse).

I am only giving very brief notes about some of the many contemporary writers, but just a few longer ones on some who I hope are typical.

When I had the opportunity of meeting Dr. George Caird, it was a rare experience. Instead of researching into the life and character of someone long dead, and having to rely on and accept the verdict of biographers or, in a few rare cases, that of a near relative, I was now talking to a living author, by his cosy study fire in Queen's College, Oxford, where he holds the chair of Dean Ireland's Professor of Exegesis of Holy Scripture.

I put the question to him: "Did he feel he was in a way a successor of Charles Wesley, in view of the structure of his most popular hymn?" "In one way I'm not," he replied, "For I've written only a few hymns, yet in another way I am, for I believe, to be good, a hymn must be scriptural; but you know, it wasn't Wesley who inspired this hymn, but S. J. Stone, with his hymn "The Church's one foundation" (701 MHB) that gave me the idea of echoes of Scripture being sounded through a modern hymn - his hymn is full of scriptural allusions from start to finish. The only difference is that Stone's hymn is about the Church, mine is about the Bible. I was in Canada when the idea came to me."

"You say you have only written a few hymns. I know three - how many more are there?" I asked. He laughed: "That is all I have written," he said, "So you know them all! They keep me too busy lecturing and writing to do much at it."

"Ah, yes, how many books have you written?" I asked him. "Oh, I don't know - it all depends what you call a book." He took me over to a small bookcase with fifty or more books in it. "These are mine," he said; "I keep them separate from the rest. They vary from this large book, to paperbacks and to things like these" - he picked up some small theological theses of thirty to fifty pages, and religious books for schools.

I was curious to know if he had written on anything but theology. "No, not really," he said. "My whole life has been devoted to the Universities, although I have a few books which you could call peripheral, like these" - and he handed me two paperbacks. "This one was the result of a visit to South Africa, to confer with the Dutch Reformed Church." Then he showed me the second, larger book, with a photograph showing him shaking hands with Pope John XXIII on the cover; it was entitled 'Our dialogue with Rome'. "You see, I was sent as an observer to the Second Vatican Council," he said.

Subsequently, he also held office as Moderator of the General Assembly of the United Reformed Church.

I happened to say that some of my friends seemed surprised that I was going to see a hymn writer who was still very active. "Whatever do they think I'm like?" he laughed. "That's the trouble when you've written a few hymns, everybody knows your age! - but you know, hymn writers come a lot younger: Fred Kaan, for instance, with his simple, direct style; and Brian Wren, who was one of my pupils - I don't know how many hymns he's written - he's a name to watch." †

We then turned to the subject of translating the New English Bible. I knew, from Sir Roger Mynors, that he had been involved in this. "Yes," he said, "Roger was on the literary panel; they vetted our English after we had finished the translation, then it came back to us to check that any alterations they had made didn't give wrong meanings." (See the Preface to the New English Bible - with the Old Testament.)

"Unfortunately," he continued, "I was in Canada when most of the Bible was done, but the Apocrypha was mainly mine. It was quite a problem, really, for this was the first time it had been translated properly. When the Authorised Version was made, the Apocrypha was left until last and was badly skimped. Now we have a better translation than there has ever been."

I glanced at my watch: Professor Caird had kindly promised to give me forty-five minutes. He had already spared me nearly forty minutes of his valuable time and I would like to have stayed longer - so many things I could have asked him; but this interview was fitted in between lectures, so not wanting to impose on good nature, I rose to go. He shook hands heartily - the hand that had grasped the Pope's! I went away feeling that I had been in the presence of a really great man - a present-day saint, so accomplished, yet so humble.

Graduating at Cambridge, George Caird had passed on to Mansfield

---

† Both these authors are well represented in the new Methodist Hymn Book - "Hymns and Psalms."

Dr. George B. Caird

College to train for the (then) Congregational ministry; and after a short pastorate at Highgate Congregational Church, it was recognised that he was destined for higher things. As one of his friends told me, "He is a profound thinker, with a gift for communicating with ordinary men and women." So apart from his term as Moderator, his whole life has been devoted to training young men for the ministry.

Sought after by colleges and universities everywhere, he has been Professor of Old Testament at the University of Edmonton, Alberta; and of New Testament at Montreal; later he was Principal of his old college, Mansfield College, until 1977, when he took up his present position at Queen's College.

A busy man, lecturing and writing on weekdays and preaching on Sundays, he doesn't have much time to relax, but he loves to listen to good music when he can; or if the weather is fine, he goes out on to the downs round his home near Wantage, bird watching - his favourite hobby. I would guess he finds God is as near him in the wide open spaces as in the study, lecture room or pulpit.

As I walked back down 'the High', I passed the University Church of Great St. Mary, and there was the Rev. George B. Caird's name among the distinguished preachers in that famous Church for that month.

The much-loved Headmaster of Malvern College for many years, *H. C. A. GAUNT,* has given us many good hymns, mainly in the Anglican supplements. He is well known for his book about the vicissitudes of the College when its buildings were suddenly requisitioned during the Second World War for research into the mysterious new secret weapon, radar - 'A School in Wartime' he called it. After a distinguished academic career he felt the call to leave this behind and be ordained, and is now Canon of Winchester Cathedral.

DONALD HUGHES, another headmaster, although unfortunately not now with us, having died at the age of fifty-seven, has contributed many good hymns, to be found in most new books. His harvest hymn "O Father, whose creating hand brings harvest from the fruitful land" (55 H. & S.) is possibly his best known.

DR. ERIK ROUTLEY is perhaps our greatest modern hymnologist, being the author of many fine books on the subject. He has also written a number of good hymns, of which "All who love and serve your city" (3 H & S) is a good example.

REV. F. PRATT GREEN's "Christ is the world's Light" (8 H & S) is deservedly popular among his many new hymns.

Dr. Fred Kaan

And so the list could go on; but I will conclude this group with a look at one of the most prolific of our present-day authors, *REV. FRED KAAN,* that gifted Dutchman whom I have already mentioned. He has made himself at home in this country and is currently Moderator of the West Midlands Province of the United Reformed Church. He describes the present renewed output of hymns as "This Hymn Explosion" and he summarises the emphasis of all this new work as twofold: the humanity of Jesus; and concern for our fellow human beings; - thus, he says, filling a gap in our theology.

"Was there one?" I asked myself, thinking I could quote a dozen older hymns that expressed both these facets of Christian truth; but I will not argue the point! I have seen Fred in full flow of enthusiasm and it was obvious that this most prolific hymn writer was full of ideas for more hymns to follow such fine ones as "We turn to you, O God of every nation" (73 H & S), entitled 'The Family of Nations'; and his Communion hymn "Now let us from this table rise" (50 H & S). Someone did ask him "Why don't you modern writers write hymns like "Immortal, invisible, God only wise" (34 MHB). I don't know quite why that particular hymn was chosen, but Fred's short answer was "because *that* has already been done!"

While these modern authors are giving us new insights into our faith, they use traditional metres, which can be set to a variety of tunes; but there is a host of hymns of other types, usually with the tune composed for the words, some in the 'folk' tradition, some like modern versions of the Sankey type hymn, and yet others springing from the Charismatic Movement - and many more. There are not only new types of hymns, but a bewildering number of new hymn books, all of which seem to be selling well. 'Hymn explosion' certainly describes it! Being still in it, it is even more difficult for us to tell what will last and what is just ephemeral.

PATRICK APPLEFORD has given us "Lord Jesus Christ" (86 H & S) - both words and music - which has swept into popularity and seems likely to stay. *SYDNEY CARTER* has produced some remarkable compositions - again complete with both words and music. Personally, "The Lord of the Dance" (82 H & S) does not impress me - it seems he is striving for originality for its own sake - but "Every star shall sing a carol" (77 H & S) is a remarkable conception of God's redemption throughout the universe; while "Judas and Mary" (91 H & S) is a good example of the modern technique of taking a passage of Scripture and interpreting it in modern terms.

Yet another remarkable modern development is the inflow of hymns from what used to be called the 'mission field', now more correctly the 'Church Overseas'. We have seen how Tilak led the way with a hymn which has won all hearts; and many Negro Spirituals are being found suitable in our worship; "Let us break bread together" (84 H & S) and "Were you there when they crucified my Lord?" (93 H & S) are just two examples. In addition the West Indies have given us such treasures as the Calypso setting of "Our Father" (89 H & S), while from the Urdu we have both words and music of "Jesus the Lord said, 'I am the Bread" (83 H & S), a most effective hymn on the titles our Lord gave himself. "Golden breaks the dawn" (28 H & S) is a composite hymn, the tune from China and the first verse a translation of a verse by the Chinese Christian, *PROFESSOR T. C. CHAO*, added to which *DR. DANIEL T. NILES* has added his paraphrase of 'Our Father' to make a complete and appealing hymn. †

Daniel Niles is author of a number of hymns, many of which are finding their way into new hymn books. He was a remarkable man - only sixty-two years old when he died, or we might have heard still more of him. He became a Christian when young, and after progressing well at Mission School in Ceylon (as it was then), he entered the University of Ceylon to study law and so follow his father's profession. He then did a remarkable thing: he chose to stay in the Hindu Students' Hostel, rather than the Christian one, feeling that he could influence those who did not know about Jesus Christ by living with them. The Warden, a devout Hindu, was so impressed with the sincerity of this young Christian student that he persuaded him to abandon the law and study for the Christian ministry. How strange and illuminating that God's call should come in this way!

Daniel served in Methodist Circuits in his home land for some years, then as Principal of Jaffna Central College, and finally as Chairman of the North Ceylon District. His exceptional brilliance of mind, coupled with a deep devotion to the Lord Jesus Christ, destined him for even greater things, and he moved out to become a leader of the World Church before he was forty.

It would take too long to trace all that his clear-sighted statesmanship enabled him to achieve at the World Conferences at Amsterdam, Geneva and Upsala, but the remarkable thing is that although he could have been swamped by administrative duties, he never lost his fervent

† In "Hymns and Psalms" this first verse is omitted, so the hymn is entirely Dr. Niles' paraphrase.

spirit of evangelism or his scholarly work as an interpreter of Scripture. A long list of theological and devotional books bears witness to this, and many were selected as 'World Christian Books', so wide was their appeal. All over the world there are many men and women who owe to this good man's books and preaching their faith in Jesus Christ.

It is hardly necessary to add that the power of such a fruitful life sprang from the habit of constant communion with his Lord.

So I end my very sketchy review of to-day's scene in the world of hymns . . . but what of the future?

The new "Hymns & Psalms" is now published and over 400,000 are already ordered! We are looking forward to these various streams of new hymnody mingling happily with the best of the old.

The question might be asked, therefore, "Why produce this 'Companion' when the 1933 book is due to 'bow out' so soon?" Well, firstly, the new hymn book will only replace the present one as existing stocks wear out (and as funds become available!); and secondly, when it has done so, the 1933 book will remain historically as one of the best and most comprehensive collections of all time, and certainly one of the longest lived - 50 years!

One final question . . . with all this new material coming in, is there going to be a demand for it? I think we can confidently answer "Yes". I have mentioned the sales of new hymn books, which shows that hymn singing is still going to be an essential part of worship. The B.B.C. publishes from time to time figures, based on listener research, of the numbers tuning in to programmes like 'Sunday Half-hour' (Radio 2) and 'Songs of Praise' (B.B.C.1). These are truly amazing: 'Sunday Half-hour' alone commands a world audience of 60 million! - and still increasing. It is sometimes urged that these large audiences are middle-aged to elderly, but with the new-style hymns capturing the imagination of youth, I just cannot believe it!

So I repeat the question "How many of these new works will last, like some of the 'Old Favourites'?" In many instances the authors and composers frankly do not expect them to - only to serve the present age; but some will last and only the next generation can decide which they will be.

I wonder if, in fifty years time, when a new hymn book is contemplated, the compilers will be urged to retain Pat Appleford's "Lord Jesus Christ" because it is such a favourite with the old folks? ? ?

ALPHABETICAL INDEX OF FIRST LINES OF
HYMNS MENTIONED

	Page	No. in Methodist Hymn Book or Hymns & Songs	No. in 'Hymns & Psalms'
Earth below is teeming	104	966	—
Ere God had built the mountains	65	60	32
Ere I sleep, for every favour	58	947	638
Every star shall sing a carol	184	H&S77	—
Faith of our fathers, living still	90	402	—
Father, if justly still we claim	29	284	299
Father, I know that all my life	126	602	—
Father, who on man dost shower	171	894	341
Father of mercies, in Thy word	62	302	—
Fight the good fight with all thy might	103	490	710
Firmly I believe and truly	88	H&S17	—
For all the saints who from their labours rest	109	832	814
For the might of Thine arm we bless Thee	157	715	435
For those we love within the veil	157	657	—
Forward! be our watchword	102	619	—
From Greenland's icy mountains	78	801	—
From Thee all skill and science flow	95	921	389
Give heed, my heart, lift up thine eyes (From Heaven above)	10	126	100*
Glorious things of Thee are spoken	64	706	817
Glory to Thee, my God, this night	37	943	642
Go not, my soul, in search of Him	139	281	—
God is ascended up on high	29	220	—
God is love; His mercy brightens	82	53	—
God moves in a mysterious way	65	503	65
God my Father, loving me	173	840	—

	Page	No. in Methodist Hymn Book or Hymns & Songs	No. in 'Hymns & Psalms'
God of our fathers, known of old	166	889	—
God's trumpet wakes the slumbering world	138-9	401	—
God, who hast given us power to sound	173	H&S25	345*
Golden breaks the dawn (Father God in Heaven)	185	H&S28	518*
Good Christian men, rejoice	87	143	104*
Good Christian men, rejoice and sing!	173	H&S29	191*
Guide me, O Thou great Jehovah	67	615	437
Hail, gladdening Light, of His pure glory poured	1:86	937	644
Hail to the Lord's Anointed	75	245	125
Hark, my soul! it is the Lord	65	432	521
Hark the glad sound! the Saviour comes	48	82	82
Hark! the herald-angels sing	69	117	106
He dies! the Friend of Sinners dies	69	195	—
He that is down needs fear no fall	34	514	676
He wants not friends that hath Thy love	31	714	495
Heal us, Immanuel; hear our prayer	65	155	390
Hold the fort, for I am coming	142	—	—
Holy, holy, holy, Lord God Almighty	78	36	7
Holy Spirit, pity me	104	296	—
Holy Spirit, truth Divine	139	288	289
How shall I sing that majesty	39	78	8
How sweet the name of Jesus sounds	64	99	257
I am not skilled to understand	120-1	381	221
I am Thine, O Lord; I have heard Thy voice	142	746	—
I am trusting Thee, Lord Jesus	127	521	—
I bind unto myself to-day	7:122	392	695
I danced in the morning	184	H&S82	—

	Page	No. in Methodist Hymn Book or Hymns & Songs	No. in 'Hymns & Psalms'
I hoped that with the brave and strong	116	592	—
I hunger and I thirst	103	462	730
I met the good Shepherd	91	174	—
Immortal, invisible, God only wise	184	34	9
Immortal Love, for ever full	134	102	392
In Christ there is no East or West	160	H&S34	758
In loving-kindness Jesus came	143	336	—
In memory of the Saviour's love	76	762	—
In the bleak mid-winter	125	137	107
In the Cross of Christ I glory	82	183	167
Infinite God, to Thee we raise	3	33	—
It is a thing most wonderful	109	854	224
Jesus calls us!	122	157	141
Jesus, my Lord, how rich Thy grace	48	H&S36	147
Jesus the Lord said: 'I am the Bread'	185	H&S83	137
Jesu, Lover of my soul	54-5	110	528
Jesu, priceless treasure	122	518	259
Jesus shall reign where'er the sun	46	272	239
Jesus, still lead on	13	624	—
Jesu! The very thought is sweet	87	106	—
Jesu, the very thought of Thee	91-2	108	265
Jesu, Thy blood and righteousness	13:51	370	225
Jesu, Thy boundless love to me	12:51	430	696
Jesus, where'er Thy people meet	65	675	549
Judge eternal, throned in splendour	171	883	409
Just as I am, without one plea	79-80	353	697
King of glory, King of peace	23	23	499

	Page	No. in Methodist Hymn Book or Hymns & Songs	No. in 'Hymns & Psalms'
Land of our Birth, we pledge to Thee	166	899	—
Lead, kindly Light, amid the encircling gloom	88	612	67
Lead us, heavenly Father, lead us	68	611	68
Let all the world in every corner sing	23	5	10
Let us break bread together	185	H&S84	615
Let us with a gladsome mind	26	18	27
Life of ages, richly poured	139	908	—
Light of the world, faint were our weary feet	146:154	636	—
Lo, God is here! Let us adore	51	683	531
Look from Thy sphere of endless day	131	790	—
Lord, it belongs not to my care	31	647	679
Lord Jesus Christ, you have come to us	184:186	H&S86	617
Lord Jesus, think on me	5	239	533
Lord of our life, and God of our salvation	84	729	—
Lord of the living harvest	104	793	—
Lord, Thy word abideth	108	308	476
Love came down at Christmas	125	138	105
Man of Sorrows! What a name	142	176	228
My Father, for another night	108	926	—
My God, and is Thy table spread?	48	H&S46	—
My God, how wonderful Thou art	90	73	51
My God, I love Thee - not because	14	446	171
My heart and voice I raise	72	115	268
My soul, praise the Lord	20	45	—
My soul, there is a country	33	466	—
My spirit longs for Thee	47	467	—

	Page	No. in Methodist Hymn Book or Hymns & Songs	No. in 'Hymns & Psalms'
Nearer, my God, to Thee	117-9	468	451
None other Lamb, none other Name	125	94	271
Not always on the mount may we	139	—	—
Not far beyond the sea nor high	180	H&S49	477
Now all the woods are sleeping	12	946	647*
Now I have found the ground wherein	51	375	684
Now let us from this table rise	184	H&S50	619
Now thank we all our God	11:122	10	566
Now the day is over	92	944	—
O brother man, fold to thy heart thy brother	135	911	—
O come, all ye faithful	91	118	110
O come, O come, Immanuel	87	257	85
O'er the gloomy hills of darkness	67	—	—
O Father, whose creating hand	183	H&S55	349
O for a closer walk with God	65	461	—
O gladsome light, O grace	1:145	936	—
O God, how often hath Thine ear	104	750	—
O God, my God, my all Thou art	51	471	—
O God, my strength and fortitude	19	24	—
O God of Bethel, by whose hand	48	607	442
O God, our help in ages past	46	878	358
O happy band of pilgrims	87	618	—
O happy day that fixed my choice	48	744	702
O Holy Spirit, God	172	279	—
O Jesus, King most wonderful	92	107	269
O Lord and Master of us all	134	103	717
O Lord, enlarge our scanty thought	13:51	449	568
O Lord, how happy should we be	100	551	—

	Page	No. in Methodist Hymn Book or Hymns & Songs	No. in 'Hymns & Psalms'
O Love Divine! whose constant beam	135	674	—
O my Saviour, hear me	142	453	—
O perfect life of love	108	190	—
O sacred Head once wounded	12	202	176*
O splendour of God's glory bright	3	932	461
O strength and stay	3	—	—
O Thou not made with hands	112	707	656
O timely happy, timely wise (New every morning)	86	927	636*
O worship the King	20:80	8	28
O worship the Lord in the beauty of holiness	103	9	505
Of the Father's love begotten	4:87	83	79
On all the earth Thy Spirit shower	29	301	321
Once in royal David's city	121	859	114
Once to every man and nation	132	898	—
One there is above all others	65	100	149
One who is all unfit to count	144:168	159	539
Onward! Christian soldiers	92-3	822	718
Oppressed with sin and woe	115	352	—
Our Father, by whose servants	173	979	—
Our Father, who art in heaven	185	H&S89	—
Out of the depths I cry to Thee	9	359	429
Praise, my soul, the King of heaven	97-8	12	13
Praise, O praise our God and King	26:108	19	359
Praise the Lord! Ye heavens, adore Him	68	13	15
Praise to the Holiest in the height	88	74	231
Praise to the Lord, the Almighty	122	64	16
Prayer is the soul's sincere desire	75	533	557

	Page	No. in Methodist Hymn Book or Hymns & Songs	No. in 'Hymns & Psalms'
Rescue the perishing, care for the dying	142	338	—
Rest of the weary	103	101	—
Ring out, wild bells, to the wild sky	106	905	—
Rise, my soul	58	—	—
Safe home, safe home in port	87	977	—
Said Judas to Mary, 'Now what will you do?'	184	H&S91	—
Saviour, again to Thy dear name we raise	111	691	643
Saviour, when in dust to Thee	81	726	—
See, amid the winter's snow	91	124	117
Sing we the King who is coming to reign	157	116	244
Sometimes a light surprises	65	527	571
Souls of men, why will ye scatter	90	318	230*
Sow in the morn thy seed	75	599	—
Stand up and bless the Lord	75	685	513
Standing at the portal	128	955	—
Still, still with Thee, when purple morning breaketh	137	474	—
Strong Son of God, immortal Love	107	86	—
Summer suns are glowing	109	673	361
Sun of my soul, Thou Saviour dear	86	942	646
Sunset and evening star	106	640	—
Sweet is the sunlight after rain	105	662	—
Sweet is the work, my God, my King	46	665	514
Take my life, and let it be	128-9	400	705
Te Deum Laudamus	3	2 (Ancient Hymns & Canticles)	883*

	Page	No. in Methodist Hymn Book or Hymns & Songs	No. in 'Hymns & Psalms'
Ten thousand times ten thousand	102	828	—
That mystic Word of Thine, O sovereign Lord	137	469	—
The Church's one foundation	85:181	701	515
The day is past and over	87	951	—
The day of resurrection!	7:87	208	208
The day Thou gavest, Lord, is ended	111	667	648
The foe behind, the deep before	87	218	—
The God of Abraham praise	57	21	452
The King of love my Shepherd is	108	76	69
The Lord will come, and not be slow	26	813	245
The Maker of the sun and moon	160	136	—
The royal banners forward go	7:87	184	179*
The Saviour, when to heaven He rose	48	H&S69	211
The shepherds had an angel	125	863	—
The Son of God goes forth to war	78	816	—
The spacious firmament on high	44	44	339
The Spirit breathes upon the word	65	307	—
The voice that breathed o'er Eden	86	775	—
There is a book, who runs may read	86	43	340
There is a green hill far away	70:122	180	178
This is the day of light	111	660	—
This, this is the God we adore	56	69	277
Thou great Redeemer, dying Lamb	58	104	—
Thou hidden love of God, whose height	51	433	544
Thou say'st: Take up thy cross	112	158	—
Through all the changing scenes of life	42	427	73
Thy kingdom come - on bended knee	139	742	—

	Page	No. in Methodist Hymn Book or Hymns & Songs	No. in 'Hymns & Psalms'
Thy life was given for me	128	391	—
To God be the glory	142	313	463
To the Name of our salvation	87	93	80
To Thee, O Lord, our hearts we raise	114	964	362
We give Thee but Thine own	109	923	—
Were you there when they crucified my Lord?	130:185	H&S93	181
We rose to-day with anthems sweet	105	666	—
We turn to you, O God of every nation	184	H&S73	412
What service shall we render Thee	158	897	—
What shall we offer our good Lord	51	784	807
When all Thy mercies, O my God	44	413	573
When God of old came down from heaven	86	276	—
When I survey the wondrous Cross	46	182	180
When morning gilds the skies	91	113	276
When on my day of life the night is falling	136	642	—
When rising from the bed of death	44	—	—
When wilt Thou save the people	73	909	—
While shepherds watched their flocks by night	42	129	120
Who fathoms the eternal thought	135	513	432
Who is on the Lord's side	127	820	722
Who would true valour see	34:172	620	688
Whosoever heareth! Shout, shout the sound	142	317	—
Workman of God! O lose not heart	90	489	—
Ye holy angels bright	31	26	20
Ye humble souls that seek the Lord	47	217	—

INDEX OF AUTHORS